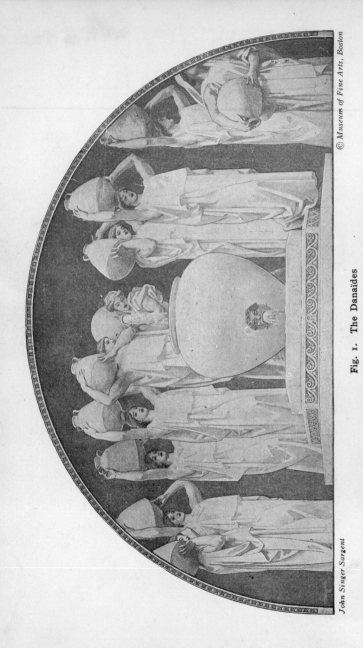

John Singer Sargent

Fig. 1. The Danaïdes

As a punishment for killing their husbands on the wedding night, these sisters were compelled in Hades to pour water continually into sieves or, as in this illustration, into a jar which had an opening at the bottom. For the story, see page 163.

CLASSICAL MYTHS
THAT LIVE TODAY

BY

FRANCES E. SABIN

DIRECTOR OF THE SERVICE BUREAU FOR CLASSICAL TEACHERS
MAINTAINED BY THE AMERICAN CLASSICAL LEAGUE
AT TEACHERS COLLEGE, COLUMBIA UNIVERSITY
FORMERLY ASSISTANT PROFESSOR OF LATIN
UNIVERSITY OF WISCONSIN

RALPH VAN DEMAN MAGOFFIN

PROFESSOR AND HEAD, DEPARTMENT OF CLASSICS
NEW YORK UNIVERSITY

Classical Editor

SILVER, BURDETT AND COMPANY

NEW YORK   NEWARK   BOSTON   CHICAGO   SAN FRANCISCO

EDITOR'S PREFACE

THE purpose of this book is to bring to its readers the best of those Greek and Roman myths that for nearly twenty-seven hundred years have influenced and embellished the literature, the art, and even the daily speech of the civilized world. With their mingling of fact and fancy, of realities and ideals, these myths represent the aspirations of man throughout the centuries for a knowledge of the mysterious and the unseen.

A new statement of the educational potentialities inherent in these deathless tales of ancient days has long been needed. In CLASSICAL MYTHS THAT LIVE TODAY Miss Sabin has produced a book that deals intelligently with scholarly problems connected with the myths, a book which tells the stories in a simpler and more concise form than is the case with most text-books dealing with mythology, and one which makes such connections with modern life as to challenge the interest of everyone. The volume is the result of many years of experience with both students and teachers. A glance at its contents and arrangement will disclose how skilfully the author has adapted the book to the needs, the capacities, and the interests of young people.

This is a book of the widest application, but perhaps of all the educational fields in which its use is likely to prove productive, English will come first. Certainly there are few English classics the understanding of which will not be vastly aided by the reading of CLASSICAL MYTHS THAT LIVE TODAY.

RALPH VAN DEMAN MAGOFFIN

NEW YORK UNIVERSITY

v

AUTHOR'S PREFACE

THIS book may be used to advantage in any year of the high school, either as a textbook or for purposes of reference. Teachers who wish to use it as a textbook will find the review questions helpful for all pupils, and the suggestions for optional work stimulating for those who have the ability and the desire to read beyond the limits set for the class as a whole. Inasmuch as the time allowed in the average school for the study of mythology is short, the stories have been more or less condensed. The most important topics, moreover, have been starred in the table of contents so that in case of necessity certain chapters may be omitted. For the convenience of those who cannot read the book consecutively, the accent of proper names has been indicated the first time the word occurs in each chapter, unless, of course, the pronunciation is already known to the pupil.

Obviously the educational values resulting from the study of any subject will be in proportion to the time spent upon it. Now that the cultural background of Latin and Greek in the secondary schools has been recognized by the Report of the Latin Investigation, not only as a legitimate but as a most important ultimate objective of the study of the classics, an objective which teachers of English and ancient history have always taken for granted, it is to be hoped that principals and school officials in general will see their way to organizing a course in mythology which shall be considered as a permanent part of the curriculum, and for which an adequate amount of time will be provided. For such a course, this book in its entirety will be found suitable.

One of the unfortunate aspects of our present system of education, and one which has been sharply and widely criticized, especially in the case of academic subjects which have long been a part of the curriculum, is the tendency to make little connection between the contents of the textbook and life. To guide both teacher and pupil in making this connection, a section entitled "In the World of Today" has been added to every important chapter, and certain projects for individual or group investigation have been suggested in the Appendix (pages xx–xxvi). Teachers to whom such laboratory work does not appeal may disregard the suggestions and confine themselves to the reading of the stories. It has been the experience of the author, however, that there is no better way of establishing a basis of lasting interest in any subject than to provide pupils with ample opportunities for observation and independent study.

In attempting to present the subject of classical mythology to young people, the writer is not unaware of the danger involved. Not only are the myths countless in number, but in many cases there are several versions of the same myth. The question as to which myths and which versions to select has not been an easy one. For the most part, however, the writer has followed well-worn paths, inasmuch as the book is written solely in the interests of young people who as yet have had neither time nor opportunity to become intimately acquainted with the classical myths in any form. Under such circumstances, it seems highly desirable that whatever the pupil may undertake later in the way of scientific study of mythology, he should first make himself familiar with those versions of the myths which have been current for centuries and which still exist in the popular mind.

For permission to print various poems, the author is indebted to the following publishers : The Atlantic Monthly Company for "Remembrance" by Hortense Flexner; Brentano's for "Homeric Retrospect" from *The Sea and the Dunes and Other Poems* by

Harry Kemp; Houghton Mifflin Company for lines from *A Second Century of Charades* by William Bellamy; *Life* for a poem; Longmans, Green and Company for the extract from Conington's verse translation of the *Aeneid;* The Macmillan Company for extracts from *Ulysses* by Stephen Phillips; Norman, Remington Company for "A Song of Syrinx" by Patrick Chalmers; *Punch* for "Pan Pipes"; Charles Scribner's Sons for a poem by Henry van Dyke; Sidgwick and Jackson, for "Ares, God of War" by Lieutenant Herbert Asquith; and the Yale University Press for an extract from "The Argo's Chantey" by William Rose Benét.

To individuals and to various firms who have generously allowed the publishers to reproduce certain pictures, the author extends her thanks. Especially does she appreciate the kindness of Will H. Low, who has put at her disposal his beautiful drawings from Keats's *Lamia*, which have contributed so largely to the attractiveness of the book.

To those professional friends whose sympathy, advice, and active coöperation have made the book possible, the author is deeply grateful. Her debt is especially large in the case of the following persons:

Katherine Goetzinger, Columbia University; Eugene S. McCartney, University of Michigan; William Sherwood Fox, Western University, London, Canada; George D. Hadzsits, University of Pennsylvania; Margaret Englar, Baltimore; Mary L. Breene, Pittsburgh, Pa.; Mason D. Gray, Rochester, New York; A. W. Smalley, Chicago; Roland G. Kent, University of Pennsylvania (for special help in the pronunciation of proper names); and to Ralph Van Deman Magoffin, classical editor, whose encouragement and assistance have been an unfailing source of inspiration.

FRANCES E. SABIN

THE SERVICE BUREAU FOR CLASSICAL TEACHERS
TEACHERS COLLEGE, COLUMBIA UNIVERSITY

CONTENTS

NOTE: The more important chapters have been starred.

LIST OF ILLUSTRATIONS

SOME PRELIMINARY QUESTIONS AND THEIR ANSWERS

(For the teacher and the more mature pupil.)

Q. What is a myth?

A. " Myths are stories of the acts of superhuman beings, often improbable to us, but believed to be true by those who related them." [1]

Q. What is meant by " classical mythology "?

A. Classical mythology is a collection of myths about gods, semi-divine beings, and heroes possessed of superhuman powers, which were handed down to the Greeks and Romans by word of mouth for a long period of time, and put into written form by poets who, moreover, did not hesitate to make changes in the stories whenever it suited their purposes to do so.

Q. Is there any basis of fact in these myths, or are they pure fancy?

A. In general the myths are pure fancy. They represent for the most part the attempt of a highly imaginative race to account for the world of nature and for the facts of life as experienced by man, in an age when scientific study was practically unknown. The conceptions which the myths embody are the result of feeling and a strong poetical sense rather than of knowledge. However, a close study of the myths in the light of what we know about the physical world, the history and the civilization of the times in which the stories originated, and about human nature, which is much the same in all ages,

---

[1] Fairbanks, *Mythology of Greece and Rome*, p. 1.

enables us to catch an occasional glimpse of a fact which may have given rise to a certain myth, although scholars are far from agreeing as to the proper interpretation in the majority of cases. It is reasonable to think, for example, that the seeming passage of the sun across the sky each day appears in a dramatized form in the story of Apollo (or Helios), who every morning mounted his shining chariot in the east and drove his divine steeds through the heavens. It has been suggested, also, that the lightning may account for the tale that Vulcan, the god of fire, was hurled to the earth by an angry father, or for the story that it was from heaven that the Titan Prometheus obtained the fire which he presented as a gift to men. Some think, moreover, that the many tales of monsters sent by Neptune, god of the sea, to ravage the land or destroy some person are only a personification of the violence of the storms which sweep over the ocean, bringing death and destruction with them.

A very interesting explanation of a myth which is not concerned with natural phenomena, but rather with what may have been a historical fact, is found in a book called *Crete, the Forerunner of Greece*, written by Charles Henry Hawes and Harriet Boyd Hawes.[1] In discussing the story of King Minos of Crete, who each year exacted as tribute from the Athenians seven young men and seven young maidens and threw them to a monster (called the Minotaur) to be devoured, the authors say, " If, after the defeat of the Boers by England in the South African War, certain Boers should have been sent to England and there put to death, it might have been said in the language of mythology that they had been devoured by the British Lion." It is barely possible that several of the tales in this book may be explained in a similar way.

[1] Harper and Brothers, N. Y.

Sometimes economic conditions seem to explain certain myths. On page 122 the story of a princess from Lydia, a part of Asia Minor, is related. We are told that this maiden challenged Minerva, goddess of spinning and weaving and a patron of Athens, to a contest at the loom. One may fancy that commercial rivalry between Athens and the East is at the basis of this tale.

A myth may have as its origin some characteristic or quality of man or some experience of life, which is personified in the story. And certainly one cannot read far in any text in classical mythology without seeing that the virtues and the weaknesses of human nature are mirrored in these tales of the gods, who, as the Greeks felt,[1] in spite of the fact that they were larger and possessed of superhuman powers, closely resembled men.

The theories suggested above as a basis for the interpretation of the myths on rational grounds are only a few of those which have been proposed by scholars. But inasmuch as there are seldom, if ever, sufficient data at hand to warrant anything definite in the way of a conclusion, it is perhaps wiser for those who are not specialists in the subject to regard the myths as purely fanciful — the product of a race highly endowed with imagination and an artistic sense, which made them see beauty even in things which we regard as ugly and somewhat gross, and, in common with all primitive peoples, inclined to express their thoughts in the form of stories. Certainly an extended discussion of exactly why certain myths should have arisen is beyond the province of this book.

---

[1] The intelligent reader of this book will not need to be told that such expressions as "according to the Greeks," and "as the Greeks thought," are not to be connected with the thoughtful Greek of historical times, but rather with the primitive Greeks who lived long before Homer.

Q. Did the Greeks in the historical period accept without question the myths as they were handed down by tradition?

A. While the myths were accepted by the mass of the Greeks without criticism, the more thoughtful person, who was inclined to reflect upon what he saw or read, did not share the faith of the people. He regarded the myths as interesting legends but worked out for himself a system of belief which, in the case of at least a few of the leading thinkers, approaches the idea that many of us hold, namely, that there is but a single god, who is supreme, eternal, and altogether righteous, differing radically in character from the Jupiter of the myths. In accounting for the world of nature, moreover, the intellectually-minded man made use of reason and of all the help that the philosophic systems of his day could give him, and while his conclusions regarding the working of natural laws were not scientific from the modern point of view, they were far in advance of the ideas presented in the myths. But though his keener insight made it impossible for him to accept the myths literally, he did not wish to discard them entirely, but chose rather to look upon them as a priceless inheritance from the early days of his race.

Q. Should the fact that the myths contained in this book are only " stories " rather than historical accounts, and that they do not represent the belief of the thoughtful Greek of later times, mar the reader's pleasure or make him feel that he is wasting his time in studying them?

A. Certainly not. Some of the most beautiful and worth-while things in life cannot be catalogued under the heading of fact. They are felt and understood, and play a dominant part in the development of our finer selves. For example, we should be rash indeed to discard all poetry — and in a way we must look upon these myths as poetical expression — or music, or art, because as a rule they are apart from what we call " fact."

Moreover, on the side of intelligence alone and with a view to practical value only, we cannot afford to be ignorant of material which for almost 2700 years has permeated the literature and art of the Western World of which we are today a part.   Greece passed the legacy of the myths to Rome, and Rome left it to her heirs, Italy, France, Spain, and Portugal, whose languages are still called " Romance," from the Latin adjective " Romanus."   As the centuries passed, these nations shared their inheritance with other countries of Europe.   France, for example, through the Norman Conquest in 1066 A.D., gave to England priceless gifts in the forms of language, literature, and art — a part of that culture which she had received from the Romans centuries before. England has continued to spread this classical inheritance throughout the English-speaking world.   And thus we who live in the United States have come to share in the legacy of Greece and Rome.

The extent to which we have incorporated classical mythology in our civilization is far greater than the average person suspects.   One can rarely read a book, magazine, or newspaper without meeting allusions to these stories, an understanding of which is vital to the comprehension of the passage.   Without adequate acquaintance with them he can neither enjoy art galleries nor see the reason for certain paintings which appear upon the walls of such public buildings as the Congressional Library at Washington, many of our state capitols, and countless opera houses and theaters.   Moreover, unless he knows something of these myths, he cannot fully appreciate the decorative designs on the outside of many buildings as he walks along the streets of any large city, or in all cases understand the statuary which he sees in elaborate gardens or parks and in other open-air places. A knowledge of classical mythology also adds a picturesque touch to many scientific terms and to names of flowers, trees, animals, and places, many of which go back to the myths for their origin. Evidence for these statements will be found in the second part of each chapter in this book and in the various pictures.

It will be obvious to the thoughtful reader that the examples cited above are merely indicative of countless others. For to mention more than a limited number of such connections with the modern world would be impossible within the limits of the average textbook. Such an attempt, moreover, would defeat one of the main purposes of this volume, for it would make any research on the part of the student unnecessary, and therefore rob him of the pleasure and profit that attend one's own discoveries.

Q. Did the Romans play as large a part as the Greeks in the creation of these myths? And, if not, why are the Latinized forms of the proper names used in this book rather than the Greek?

A. The Romans had almost no mythology of their own. They were too practical and too lacking in imaginative power to create the kind of myth that the Greeks associated with the gods. Accordingly, they did not as a rule regard their divinities, who presided over almost every act of life, as " persons," but were inclined to think of them as powers without bodily form. However, long before Rome completed the conquest of Greece in 146 B.C., she was gradually absorbing Greek ideas and finally took over almost entirely the Greek myths, identifying them wherever possible with native gods, and in other cases adding deities as new members of her religious system.

Naturally the Romans used the Latin names for divinities which they identified with the Greek, and it is this form which has come down to us through the pages of the Roman writers. Since these authors are read in our schools and colleges much more widely than are the Greek, it has been thought best in this book to refer to the characters mentioned in the stories under the names which will be the more familiar to the reader, although the Greek forms are also given in most cases.   The author realizes that there are serious objections to this procedure, inasmuch as the Roman god was rarely exactly the same as the Greek divinity with which it became identified, and in some cases was widely different.   In the interests of uniformity, however, it has seemed wise in the case of the present volume to disregard this inconsistency, inasmuch as the book is obviously designed for readers who will not wish to be taken too far afield in the discussion of questions which are still to some extent matters of controversy among scholars.

THE
DIVINITIES

Fig. 2. From within the temple of Apollo at Corinth

THE GODS IN GENERAL [1]

I. THE BIRTH OF THE GODS

THE Greeks thought that U'ra nus (Heaven) and Gae'a (Earth) were the first rulers of the universe, and the parents of the Cy clo'pes, the Gi'ants, and the Ti'tans. The Cyclopes symbolized the thunder and lightning; the Giants, the violence of the sea; and the Titans represented the uncontrolled forces of nature as a whole. It was from two of the Titans, Cro'nus [2] and Rhe'a, that the six children, later known as the gods, were born: Ves'ta, Ce'res, Ju'no, Nep'tune, Plu'to, and Ju'pi ter. These are the names by which the Romans knew them. The Greeks, however, called these divinities Hes'tia, De me'ter, He'ra, Po sei'don, Ha'des, and Zeus.

The story of the birth of the gods is indeed curious. The myths say that Cronus was a most unnatural parent, for he swallowed the first five children as soon as they were born, and doubtless would have done the same thing in the case of the sixth, had not Rhea saved its life by substituting in place of the infant a stone wrapped in the child's clothes. This strange procedure on the

---

[1] The mature pupil will find interesting material on the subjects mentioned in this chapter in Seymour's *Life in the Homeric Age*, chap. xiv, pp. 392–420, 445–455 (Macmillan).

[2] Identified by the Romans with a god called Sat'urn.

part of Cronus was due to a report that his son would some day
deprive him of the royal power — a disaster which Cronus was
determined to prevent. And how could it possibly occur, he
reasoned, if there were no offspring? Obviously in such a case
his throne would be safe.

But the ruler's plans were quite upset by the fact that the infant
Jupiter had escaped; for when the boy grew up, he made Cronus
drink a strong potion and thus disgorge the five children whom he
had swallowed.

2. HOW THE GODS BECAME SUPREME

No sooner had Jupiter brought his brothers and sisters back to
life than he at once organized a war against Cronus. A fortress
was built on Mt. O lym'pus in Thes'sa ly, and from this center
Jupiter launched his attacks. The struggle lasted ten years and
was all the more terrible because Cronus had summoned to his
aid the powerful Titans, while Jupiter had gained the assistance
of the Cyclopes and the hundred-handed Giants. Thessaly was
the battlefield of this strange war, the fury of which could be
judged, as the Greeks said, by the enormous rocks and bowlders
which lay scattered here and there over the plains, and which
could only have been hurled by the arms of warriors possessed of
superhuman strength.

But victory finally came to the gods. The Titans were punished by being confined in Tar'ta rus, a region deep down in the
earth, and a government was set up for directing the affairs of the
universe. Jupiter was to be the supreme ruler of both gods and
men, and in addition was to be charged with special responsibility
for the sky; Neptune had for his realm the sea and the waters
of the earth in general; and Pluto had dominion over the Lower
World, known as the land of the dead.

3. THE GODS AS THEY APPEAR IN THE MYTHS

In Thessaly there is a mountain named Olympus, the snowy
peaks of which tower high into the sky.   On the summits of this
The home of   mountain, so the Greeks thought, were the shining
the gods   palaces of the gods.   To be sure they never saw them,
but they explained this by saying that the encircling clouds shut
off the wonderful vision from the eyes of mortals.   Whether each
god had his own dwelling place on some one of the various peaks,
or whether there was one palace in which all the divinities lived,
was a matter of speculation, although the Greeks inclined to the
former view.   But in any case, they felt sure that the abodes of
the gods were not far from the great and splendid palace of Jupiter, which was even higher than the clouds (in fact, up in the
realms of pure ether), for the king's council hall was the common
meeting place.   Here the gods assembled to discuss matters of
state and talk over their affairs in general.   Here, too, they
sought relaxation at the banquet, and through music and enter-
tainments of various kinds passed many a pleasant hour.

In general the gods resembled mortals in appearance although
they were much larger and stronger.   Ho'mer says that when
What did the   Mars fell to the ground, as he did on one occasion
gods look   when he was overthrown in battle, he covered almost
like?   two acres.   Once, too, when Neptune was hurt, he
roared so loudly that it sounded as though nine or ten thousand
men were shouting.   Only an enormous being could have made
so great a noise.

The Greeks imagined the gods as living much the same kind of
life as did their own nobles.   The latter, of course, did not labor,
Manner of   but spent their time hunting, feasting, and looking
living   after their dependents.   In similar ways the gods
enjoyed themselves on Olympus, finding their chief interest, how-

ever, in the affairs of mortals, in which they often played an active part. Only one of them seems to have had any profession or steady occupation, and that was Vul'can.

They required food and drink, although this did not consist of bread and wine but of a delicious substance called " ambrosia " and a liquid known as " nectar." While the fragrance of the sacrifices (often some animal roasted upon the altar) was pleasing to them, they never cooked or prepared any food for themselves. When they went down to earth to mingle with mortals, however, they seem to have partaken very heartily of whatever was placed upon the table.

The gods wore clothing very similar to that of mortals. When they entered the palace at Olympus they removed their sandals, as men did, calling for them when they left. And when they went forth to battle they had armor and the usual equipment of warriors preparing to fight.

At night they went to sleep just as any mortal did. Moreover, they were sometimes so troubled and anxious over some affair that they lay awake for a part of the night. Jupiter, for example, often found it impossible to put aside his cares when he went to his couch.

In short, these divine beings, except for their immortality, which made it impossible for them to die, and for certain super-human powers which they possessed, were very much like men. They were born, grew up, married, and experienced the usual joys and sorrows of life.

The gods were really organized under a monarchy, with Jupiter as their king. He was the supreme ruler and was mightier than Social any of them, but, although his will was law, not even organization he could set aside the decrees of the Fates. The meetings in the great council hall of his palace, however, must have resembled those in which some powerful Greek prince called

the members of his clan together for consultation and instruction.
And as one reads Homer he often has the feeling that Jupiter on
such an occasion is presiding only over a great household, so much
at liberty do the gods feel to talk freely with their leader, even
though they are careful not to forget the respect which is due to
him.

One would naturally think that a god would be above such
human weaknesses as anger, revenge, selfishness, cruelty, and

Very human
in their
feelings

arrogance, and would be inspired only with the feelings which we like to associate with a perfect being.
But as we read the stories of Greek mythology we
find that this is not the case, and that, on the other hand, these
gods were very much like people in that they possessed both
good and bad qualities. In general, however, they were kindly
and upheld the virtues which the Greeks of the highest type
admired, namely, bravery, wisdom, self-control, and justice,
also esteeming highly patriotism, friendship, and hospitality.
Moreover, they sympathized with family affection and grieved at
men's sorrows. They were frequently angry and revengeful,
however, pursuing mortals for many years with relentless hate.
They were jealous of other divinities and, under certain circumstances, of mortals as well. Petty quarrels were common on
Olympus, and Homer's poems contain accounts of certain episodes
which show plainly that the gods were often quite lacking in
dignity. The following story illustrates how very human one of
these divinities was.

Vulcan, god of fire, who acted as builder and smith for the
dwellers on Olympus, was working at his forge one day, when he
heard that the lovely The'tis, a sea-nymph, was coming to consult him about making some armor for her son A chil'les. " I
must stop and clean up a bit," said the god to himself. " I don't
want her to see me looking like this." Accordingly he laid away

his tools and cleaned up the shop, washed his face and hands, and put on a clean tunic, just as any man would think of doing on such an occasion.

Similar passages in which the various qualities of the gods, both good and bad, are illustrated, appear in the pages of this book.

The gods could control the forces of nature to a greater or less extent in carrying out their plans. We often read, for example, **Extent of their powers** of divinities sending a breeze to waft ships on their way, or of others wrapping themselves or some mortal in a cloud of mist for purposes of concealment. They could change their forms at will (Jupiter often appeared as an eagle) or could transform men, making them assume the shapes of animals or trees or some other objects in nature. They had the power, also, of directing the minds of men through such agencies as dreams, the words of soothsayers and of the priests who presided over the oracles, and through various signs and portents.

With such privileges as these it might seem that the gods could have done just about as they pleased. But there were two limitations to their powers — the decrees of the Fates and the interference of other gods. Some of the strong-willed divinities tried to override these barriers in attaining a desired end. But they found that while they might delay the fulfillment of the Fates' will, they could never thwart it ultimately, and that it was impossible to triumph in every case over other gods quite as determined as themselves.

In return for their protecting care, the gods demanded that all rites and ceremonies in connection with their worship should **What the gods expected from men** be carefully observed. They were not so much concerned with the kind of life a man led as they were with the fulfillment of his religious obligations. He must be " god-fearing " in the sense that he leave nothing undone in the way of offering sacrifice, or in the strict performance of other duties attendant upon their worship. Nor was the priest in the temple charged with the task of instructing men how to live aright; his duty was to see that the ceremonies which religious tradition had associated with his special shrine were properly carried out.

The ordinary man did not reason much about the gods, but accepted the ideas about them which had been handed down.

How men regarded the gods

He had no difficulty in believing that they were divine beings — how otherwise could the sun rise and pass across the sky? Or how could the lightning flash or the thunder roll without some agency stronger than man? What made the grain grow from the ground? To countless questions of this kind he found only one answer — superhuman powers were at work.

These powers which men felt all about them in the world of nature did not take the form, as they do with us, of natural laws working in a uniform way, but were looked upon rather as "persons." It was really I′ris, Juno's messenger, who came down from the sky and left the rainbow in her wake. It was actually A pol′lo, the sun-god, who each day mounted his chariot in order to give light to men. It was the lovely Cyn′thi a herself (one of Di a′na′s names) who appeared at night as the silver moon. Every tree and every stream was the haunt of semi-divine maidens known as nymphs. At any moment, too, one might hear Pan's pipes on some sunny hillside or meet a shaggy satyr in the forest path.

It may seem strange to us that the Greeks could think about nature in so personal and intimate a way. But we should remember that as a race they were highly endowed with the power of imagination and could very easily express their thoughts in the form of stories; also, that they were artists, and therefore loved to fashion beautiful statues embodying their ideas of the gods. The latter fact especially helped the average person to visualize the divinities as actual beings whom he could come to know.

Moreover, these gods became the companions of men, real friends in time of need and, in the case of wrong-doing, stern avengers. While they were seldom visible (rarely appearing to mortals), the Greeks never doubted that the divinities were very near and interested in everything that they did. When a child was sick, the mother begged Apollo's help in healing it, and when it recovered, sought the god's shrine in gratitude. The sailor, saved from a shipwreck, thought his escape due to Neptune's kindly protection and gladly hung up a gift in one of the temples of this god of the sea. The housewife knew that Vesta, goddess of the hearth, was never far away from her, and the smith who had finished a particularly fine piece of work felt that he owed his success to Vulcan's inspiration. In other words, the Greeks brought their gods down into their daily life and by so doing added dignity to its most commonplace details.

APOLLO

THE world would be a very uncomfortable place, and indeed quite uninhabitable, if there were no sun. The Greeks understood this very well and therefore held in the greatest reverence the god who gave light and heat to the earth. They called him by various names, He'li os in the earlier days, and later A pol'lo, or sometimes Phoe'bus Apollo. When they saw the first faint coloring of rose and gold in the eastern sky at the break of day, they said, "The sun-god has mounted his chariot and is starting out on his daily course across the sky." When they saw the fiery ball which we call the sun sinking in the west and perceived that the shades of evening were approaching, they thought that the god and his steeds were disappearing into the ocean only to pass under the earth, which they supposed to be flat, and so to return to their station in the east.

A sun-god

Since the sun is necessary for health, it is easy to understand why the Greeks associated healing powers with Apollo. They did not regard him as the god of medicine, however, preferring rather to give this title to his son Aes cu la'pi us (As cle'pi us), whose skill as a physician was so great that he was able even to restore the dead to life. In fact, Plu'to, the god of the Lower World, complained to Ju'pi ter, the king of the gods, that the population of his realm was being notably reduced by the marvelous cures which Aesculapius was able to bring about. It seemed to Jupiter that in justice to his brother Pluto, such a state of affairs should not

A god with healing powers and the father of Aesculapius

9

be allowed to continue. Therefore he killed Aesculapius with a thunderbolt. In revenge, Apollo sought out the Cy clo′pes who had forged Jupiter's weapon and shot them with his deadly arrows. Obviously such an act even on the part of a god could not go unpunished. Apollo was forced to serve a mortal for a certain number of months, performing for King Ad me′tus in Thes′sa ly the duties of a shepherd.

Uffizi Gallery, Florence   Photograph by Alinari
Fig. 3. Aesculapius

Apollo represented for the Greeks the highest type of manly beauty. They saw in him their ideal of physical perfection, and in the education of their youth sought to emulate him by putting great emphasis upon the training of the body. Such sports as running, boxing, wrestling, and throwing the spear and the discus were not only encouraged,

A patron of athletes

but were regarded as essential to the development of a young man of the highest type. Therefore Apollo became the patron of athletes, and it was to him that the Greek youth prayed for success in his contests in the gymnasium and on the track.

But it was not only because of Apollo's power to contribute to the physical well-being of mortals that the Greeks worshiped him. They esteemed him quite as highly as the giver of intellectual gifts and the inspirer of song. He was the divinity who presided over poetry and music, and the lyre was regarded as his special property, although its rude beginnings were associated also with the god Mer′cu ry.

The god of poetry and music

From the Raguenet drawings

Fig. 4. This is not a decorative design chosen at random for a school of medicine at Paris; on the contrary, everything in it has a special meaning. The head is that of Hygeia, goddess of health; the serpents are symbolic of Aesculapius, god of medicine; the laurel branches are associated with Apollo, the god of healing; and the horn of plenty stands for prosperity and well-being.

People have always wished to know what is going to happen to them and the Greeks were no exception in this respect. Therefore, in Apollo's supposed power to disclose the future they found still another reason for honoring him. For centuries men continued to seek help from his oracle at Del′phi, where the god was supposed to speak to mortals through the lips of a priestess called Pyth′i a.

The inspiration for oracles, soothsayers, and prophets

The answers to the questions, to be sure, were seldom clear, and it was often quite possible to interpret them in several ways. Once, for example, Croe′sus, a rich king of A′sia Mi′nor, before going to war with the ruler of Per′sia, asked the oracle what would be the result. The reply was that if he crossed a certain river he would destroy a great empire. Because this response seemed to promise good fortune, Croesus crossed the river. Here he met the Persian king and suffered a serious defeat. It was therefore his own empire that was destroyed rather than that of his enemy; no one, however, could say that the oracle had spoken falsely.

But in spite of the unsatisfactory nature of the ambiguous replies of the oracle, so great was the faith of the people that they sought it again and again, and brought money and treasures of various kinds as a return for the service rendered. Apollo's shrine therefore became extremely wealthy, and its priests very early assumed a place of great importance in the politics of the times.

An incident that happened just before Apollo founded the oracle at Delphi explains the name of his priestess and the reason why the god himself was sometimes called the " Pyth'i an."

Apollo was once passing through the region near Delphi — although it was before this city was built — when he heard that

Why Apollo was called " Pythian " a monster in the form of an enormous serpent was making the country so unsafe that men hardly dared to go abroad. Apollo sought out the gloomy cave in which this terrible creature lived, and succeeded in slaying it with his arrows. This victory over Py'tho — for so the monster was called — brought great fame to the god, and soon the adjective " Pythian " became connected with his name. At least it was not long after this fight that the god established his oracle at Delphi.

It was in this region that one of the most important of the Greek national festivals took place; namely, the Pythian Games, held every four years in honor of Apollo, and surpassed in fame only by the Olympian Games in honor of Jupiter. The prize was a wreath of laurel leaves. While athletic contests were not neglected on these occasions, they were regarded as of less importance than those connected with music. Minstrels from all parts of the Greek world vied with one another in celebrating in song the victory of the god over the serpent Pytho, and the musical compositions that resulted became widely known.

In view of the fact that Apollo played so large a part in the welfare of men, it is easy to see why his worship should have been so widespread, and why so many stories should have been connected with his name. One of these legends is concerned with his birthplace.

Juno, wife of Jupiter, could be very disagreeable and even cruel at times, especially when her jealousy was aroused, as it was once in the case of a goddess named La to'na (Le'to). To punish the latter for having met with favor in the eyes of Jupiter, the queen pursued her for many months, driving her from one country to another and never allowing her to rest. But at last some of the gods were so moved by Latona's sufferings that they decided to help her find a land where she could remain in peace. The only spot they could think of was a small island afterwards called De'los, which, curiously enough, had been floating about for many years in the Ae ge'an Sea. Here Latona remained, and here her children, Apollo and his twin sister Di a'na, were born.

A strange tale about Apollo's birthplace

It is said that Jupiter was ever afterward so fond of the island that he fastened it by adamantine chains to the bottom of the sea (or, as Ver'gil says, to other islands), and so made it stationary, as it is today.

Another well-known story about Apollo and Latona is concerned with the way in which the latter avenged what seemed to her an insult. Ni'o be was the wife of the king of Thebes, a city in central Greece, and had very good reasons, as she thought, for her pride. In the first place,

The punishment of Niobe

she was very beautiful. Secondly, she was of high birth, one of her grandfathers being the great At'las, and the other, Jupiter himself. Moreover, her husband, Am phi'on, was not only a man of power and wealth, but he ranked as one of the great musicians of the world, second only to Or'pheus. In addition

William Henry Rinehart   *Courtesy of the Metropolitan Museum, New York*

Fig. 5. Latona with the infants Diana and Apollo

to all these reasons for congratulation, she was the mother of seven sons and seven daughters, a family of which any woman might well be proud.

It irritated the queen to see the The'bans thronging to the temple and shrines of the goddess Latona. " Who is this Latona that she should place herself above me? " she asked. " Why should my people not offer sacrifices to *me* and load *my* altars with gifts? Am I not quite as beautiful as this goddess? And have I not fourteen children, while Latona has only two?" The order went forth to cease the worship of Latona and to leave the temple of the goddess deserted.

When Latona heard of this command, she at once summoned Apollo and Diana. Such an insult, they all felt, should not go unpunished. Apollo took his stand on the high walls of Thebes and stretched his powerful bow. One by one the seven sons of Niobe, who were exercising on the plain below, fell dead, pierced by the arrows of the god. But though her grief was boundless, the queen's pride was not yet humbled. " I still have my seven daughters," she said, "and I am still superior to Latona." Then Diana drew her bow. Soon all the Theban princesses lay quiet, their girlish forms so beautiful even in death that the goddesses themselves could not help but be touched by the sight.

Uffizi Gallery, Florence

Fig. 6. Niobe tries in vain to protect one of her daughters from the arrows of Diana

Niobe sat alone in the midst of her dead, her face like stone. Through some kindly power she was finally borne away to a mountain in Asia Minor, where, in the form of a cliff over which water constantly drips, she continues to symbolize a stricken mother with stony features which grief can no longer move, and with tears ever falling from her eyes.

Like all the gods, who, as we have learned in the introductory chapter to this book, were more or less similar to mortals, exhibiting the same virtues and weaknesses, Apollo was revengeful at times and punished with great severity those who had offended him. This was the case with a Tro'jan princess.

King Pri'am of Troy had a daughter named Cas san'dra, who had attracted the admiration of Apollo. The god was ready to give her anything, so strongly was he moved by her beauty. It seemed to him that one of his greatest gifts to mortals was the power of prophecy, and this he bestowed upon the maiden. But on one occasion it happened that Cassandra failed to please him, whereupon he said, " I cannot take back the power I gave you, but it shall be your misfortune to prophesy truly, only to be laughed at in return. No one will give heed to your words." Accordingly, when she declared that the destruction of Troy was at hand and that the Greeks would succeed in winning the long ten-year war which had been waged around the walls of the city, people only smiled and said, " Oh, it's just Cassandra talking again ! "

The misfortune of Cassandra

Apollo was equally cruel, and for the same reason, in his treatment of a Sibyl (another name for a prophetess) who lived at Cu'mae, a spot on the western coast of Italy where Apollo had a temple.

When the Sibyl was young and beautiful, Apollo tried to win her love, promising her any gift which it was in his power to bestow. Pointing to a heap of sand on the shore, the maiden said, " Let me live as many years as there are grains of sand in that pile." The god at once granted her request. But, having neglected to ask for eternal youth together with length of life, the girl could look forward only to centuries of time during which she must bear the burdens of old age. In spite of the fact, however, that she might have gained from her ardent suitor this priceless gift of youth, the

Sad fate of the Cumaean Sibyl

Sibyl preferred to do without it rather than marry one whom she did not love.

But Apollo was not always angry at rebuffs. Once he highly honored a maiden who had rejected his love, by making her name famous for all time.

Daph'ne, a graceful nymph, had long sought to discourage Apollo's advances, since she could not return his affection.

Daphne's strange escape Whenever he approached her she ran away as fast as she could. On one occasion, however, although she was wonderfully fleet-footed, she found herself unable to outdistance her pursuer. Nearer and nearer came the god until it seemed that he had only to extend his hand in order to grasp her. But at this instant a marvelous thing happened. Even Apollo was astounded at the sight which met his eyes — the maiden was changing into the form of a laurel tree! Bark was encircling her figure; her arms were becoming graceful branches; and foliage was appearing where just an instant before he had seen Daphne's beautiful hair. Then Apollo remembered that he had heard the girl's voice crying out in terrified accents. Now he knew the explanation. The maiden had called upon some woodland

Bessie Potter Vonnoh   Courtesy of the Art Institute, Chicago

Fig. 7. Daphne

divinity for help, and the transformation which he saw was the answer to her prayer.

There was nothing left for Apollo to do except to embrace the tree and utter fond words. " If I cannot have you for my wife,"

Bernini (Villa Borghese, Rome)   *Photograph by Alinari*

Fig. 8. Daphne is being transformed into a laurel tree

he said, " at least I can make the laurel tree sacred. Hereafter it shall be my favorite tree and be forever associated with the name of Apollo."

It was not often that a god found himself defeated by a mortal in a contest for the hand of a maiden. But on one occasion this happened to Apollo. The god had made **A mortal lover preferred** persistent efforts to win the love of a girl named Mar pes'sa, offering her every gift which as a divinity he could bestow upon her. " Think what you might do as wife of the sun-god to make the lot of mortals happier," he said. " Consider how you could bring light into the dark and unlovely places of earth and how, by the aid of my healing powers, you could help men and women and little children when they are sick and in pain."

It chanced, however, that Marpessa had another lover, a man named I'das, who had

R. Marschall   Courtesy of the Metropolitan Museum, New York

Fig. 9. The laurel wreath, a reward for worthy achievement

no claims whatsoever to divinity. When the time came for him to present his case, he could only say, " I cannot vie with a god in offering you gifts, but even Apollo cannot outdo me in the measure of love which I bring you." Marpessa thought it all over and wisely decided that she would be happier with a husband who was mortal like herself.

One of the best-known stories connected with Apollo is the account of the way in which he punished King Mi'das. Pan, the rough, shaggy, and playful god of the country, once made a musical instrument called the syrinx, upon which he played with wonderful skill.   He thought it would be rather good fun

The punish-
ment of
Midas

to challenge Apollo to a contest in music.   The god acccpted, and a king named Midas was appointed judge.   The prize was awarded to Pan, an insult which Apollo could not overlook.

Midas waited with some apprehension to discover just what form his punishment would take, and was greatly relieved when he realized that he was not to be put to death.   Of course he did not at all enjoy having his ears changed into those of a donkey, as is said to have happened, but it occurred to him that he might wear his hair in such a way as to hide the ears, or find some kind of cap which would cover them up entirely.   But although he concealed his deformity from the public, he could not hide the secret from his barber.

The latter tried very hard not to betray his master, but the temptation to talk was too great.   Finally the barber said to himself, " I just must tell somebody or something about it." Accordingly, after some thought, he dug a hole in the ground and whispered the story into it.   Then he covered up the hole and went away.   But very soon a growth of reeds sprang up on the spot and began to murmur the words of the tale; and so it was not long before everybody knew about the king's shame.

This was the same Midas who was rewarded for a favor shown to the god Bac'chus by being allowed to ask for any gift which he most wanted, with the promise that it should be his.   The king did not hesitate.   " I should like," he said, " to have the power of turning everything that I touch into gold." " Granted," said the god.   Midas at once began to test his fortune by touching various things in his house.   He found that the power was really his, and for a time he quite enjoyed going about and turning his belongings into shining gold.   But when dinner time came, he began to realize that he should very soon starve to death. One cannot eat or drink gold, and he would soon have died had not the kindly Bacchus come to his relief. " Wash your body in the river Pac to'lus," said the god, " and the charm will disappear." This Midas hastened to do. He felt only joy as he saw the sands of this stream turning into gold and realized that the strange power which had almost destroyed him was his no longer.

The ordinary person may perhaps break his word, but not so with a god who has sworn by the waters of the Styx. For this reason Apollo probably regretted that he was not a mortal when his young son Pha'e thon insisted upon his keeping a promise which he had once rather carelessly made, namely, to grant whatever request the boy might make. But who would have thought that any youth, even though his father was a divinity, would have dared to ask permission to drive the sun-chariot across the sky! And yet this was Phaëthon's wish.

A bold adventure ends in death

Apollo knew that to yield meant death for the boy, if not disaster to the world. No arguments were left untried in his efforts to dissuade his son from so reckless an adventure. " You cannot possibly manage the horses," he said. " Even I, a god, can barely keep them under control. And just suppose that you can hold them, how will you make your way safely through the dangers of the sky — the outstretched claws of the crab, the poisonous fangs of the serpent, and the many similar perils with which the horrible monsters of the sky will threaten you? (He was referring to some of the constellations.) Release me from my promise. Ask anything else and you shall have it! " But Phaëthon could not be induced to change his mind. There could never be anything, he thought, which he would like to do quite so much as to step into his father's chariot and feel the fire-breathing steeds dash forward into the open spaces of the sky.

But no sooner had he mounted the chariot and taken the reins in his hands than the horses knew it was not their master who was behind them. Moreover, they felt the difference in the weight of the chariot — a god is much larger than a mortal — and this, too, added to their excitement. Away they dashed, quite beyond the control of the boy, who could only cling helplessly to the chariot as it swayed from side to side, and look with increasing terror at the vast spaces around him. The horses soon left the track and went plunging here and there, now high in the heavens, and again so near the earth that the heat of the sun's rays dried up the rivers and the seas and destroyed vegetation. Had Jupiter not come to the rescue, the whole world would have been wrapped in flames. With his powerful thunderbolt he dashed the helpless Phaëthon to the earth, and so put an end to this mad adventure.

Tradition says that Phaëthon's body fell into the Po River, a stream in northern Italy, and that his sisters, who wept long and bitterly over his fate, were changed by kindly gods into the poplars that now fringe the banks of this river. Their tears were thought to have hardened into electrum (amber), a substance in which the properties of electricity were first discovered. Phaëthon's young friend, Cyc'nus, was also overcome by grief, and dying, was changed by kindly gods into a swan. The myths account for a common belief that the swan does not fly, by the theory that Cycnus, remembering how Phaëthon had been dashed to the ground by Jupiter's fiery thunderbolt, always feared to trust himself to the sky.

In this story of Phaëthon's wild drive across the heavens, the Greek myths find the origin of deserts and the reason for the color of the negro. So close to the earth's surface in Africa did the sun-chariot pass that all moisture in the land was dried up and the skins of the inhabitants were burned to a dusky hue.

The Greeks connected this story about Phaëthon with the sun-god He'li os rather than with Apollo, but since the latter also performed the function of a sun-god, the poet Ov'id has associated the tale with Apollo.

IN THE WORLD OF TODAY

I. In Literary Allusion

See, led by morn with dewy feet,
Apollo mounts his golden seat,
 Replete with sevenfold fire;
While dazzled by his conquering light,
Heaven's glittering host and awful night
 Submissively retire.

 Thomas Taylor, *The Rising Sun*

Or view the lord of the unerring bow,
The god of life and poesy and light;
The sun in human limbs arrayed, and brow
All radiant from his triumph in the fight.

 Lord Byron, *Childe Harold*, Canto IV, 161

The Niobe of nations! there she stands,
Childless and crownless in her voiceless woe.

 Lord Byron, *Childe Harold*, Canto IV, 79

Note: Because Rome has seen so many civilizations come and go, and still remains, although in the ruins of the past, the poet has compared her to Niobe as she stood among the dead bodies of her children.

II. In Words and Expressions

The Greeks in later times thought of one day in the week as the day of Helios or Apollo. This honor to the sun-god we have preserved in our word **Sunday.**

Raphael (Vatican, Rome)

Fig. 10. Sunday

The English word **paean** comes from the Greek *paian*, a song of thanksgiving for deliverance from danger, said to have been sung by Apollo after his victory over the Python at Delphi. Later the name was applied to any chant of gratitude addressed to this god. In modern usage it means only a song of victory or thanksgiving.

Pae′on was the name of a physician whom the gods were accustomed to consult, and it is the idea of his healing powers which has come down to us in the name of the flower called **peony.** The juice of its roots was used by the early peoples of the Bal′kans to stop the bleeding of wounds.

A handsome young man is often called an **Apollo.**

Thorwaldsen   © *H. K. T.; Gramstorff Brothers.*

Fig. 11. Hygeia and Aesculapius

The idea of health was in characteristic Greek fashion personified as Hy gei'a, the goddess of health, daughter of Aesculapius and granddaughter of Apollo. From the same root come our words **hygiene** and **hygienic.**

The **Midas touch** is an expression often heard and frequently found in literature. It indicates that some people have a wonderful way of acquiring gold, or, in other words, of making money.

The expression **to win laurels,** meaning to gain honor by worthy achievement such as the Greeks associated with Apollo, who had made the laurel tree his own, is of common occurrence. In Figure 9 we see an illustration of this idea as it appears in art.

We sometimes hear of people who try to **work the oracle.** This is only another way of saying that they are attempting to influence some powerful agency to confer a favor.

Fig. 12. The French Croix de Guerre

Notice the laurel on the ribbon.

III. In Other Connections

How the Heliotrope Received Its Name

The flower which the Greeks called heliotrope (some say the sunflower) is connected with the fate of a girl named Cly'ti e. This unfortunate maiden loved Apollo with all her heart, but since her affection was not returned, she could only follow the sun-god with her eyes as he drove across the sky in his chariot. It is said that the god took pity upon her at last and changed her into a heliotrope, a word which in Greek means " to turn towards the sun."

The Hyacinth a Reminder of Grief

A flower which the Greeks called hyacinth (not the same as the one which we know by this name) is said to have borne upon its petals curious markings resembling the Greek word *ai*, meaning " woe." This came about from the fact that Apollo once accidentally killed a young boy named Hy a cin'thus as they were playing quoits together. The god loved him so deeply that he caused a flower, colored purple by the boy's blood, to bear the letters *ai* as a lasting reminder of his grief.

Legend adds that Zeph'y rus, the west wind, also loved the boy, and that it was he who deflected the course of the quoit thrown by Apollo, so that it struck Hyacinthus.

Why the Cypress Tree Is Gloomy

The Greeks connected the cypress with Apollo. They said that a boy named Cy pa ris'sus once had a pet stag which he loved dearly, but which he accidentally killed. In his deep grief he begged Apollo to allow him to mourn forever. As a result, the god changed him into a cypress tree, which with its dark and gloomy foliage has continued to be associated with mourning.

A Humble Descendant of the Sun-Chariot

The old-fashioned carriage known as a " phaeton " takes its name from the youth who attempted to drive the sun-god's chariot.

QUESTIONS FOR REVIEW

1. In what different capacities was Apollo regarded as the patron god?
2. Why was he called "Pythian"?

3. Why did Apollo serve King Admetus as shepherd?
4. Why was the worship of Apollo so widespread?
5. Where was Apollo born? Who was his mother?
6. Relate the story of Latona and Niobe. Why is Niobe described by Shakespeare as "all tears"?
7. Why did not the Greeks believe what Cassandra said?
8. How do the Greek myths explain Apollo's association with the laurel tree?
9. Why was the Cumaean Sibyl doomed to eternal old age?
10. By what human maiden was Apollo's offer of marriage rejected?
11. How was King Midas punished by Apollo, and how was his secret revealed?
12. Relate the story of the "golden touch." If you met in your reading the phrase "a Pactolian flood," which seemed to be connected with the income of a wealthy man, would you understand its origin?
13. What myth explains why, according to a common belief, the swan does not fly?
14. Account for the origin of the deserts and the color of the negro, as the creators of the myths explain it.
15. Give the meaning of the following words and expressions: *paean, Sunday, phaeton, to win laurels, to work the oracle.*
16. What stories are connected respectively with the heliotrope, the hyacinth, and the cypress tree?
17. What decorative designs suggest Apollo?

QUESTIONS FOR CONSIDERATION

1. What did the writer in the *New York Times Magazine* for June 13, 1926, mean, when in speaking of the author of the song, "My Old Kentucky Home," he said, "His laurels stay green"?
2. Why should a magazine published by the American Medical Society be called "Hygeia"?

OPTIONAL

FOR THOSE WHO HAVE TIME FOR FURTHER STUDY

A. ADDITIONAL READING

(Gay. = Gayley's *Classic Myths;* B. = Bulfinch's *Age of Fable*)

I. **In Textbooks Dealing with Classical Mythology**

1. How Amphion built Thebes, Gay., pp. 75–77 (sec. 62).
2. Story of the famous "Gordian Knot," associated with Gordius, father of King Midas, B., 48; Gay., p. 507 (sec. 113).
3. How the myths explain the creation of frogs, Gay., pp. 91–92 (sec. 73); B., 36–38.
4. Interesting details of Phaëthon's ride, B., 38–45.
5. How a poet, inspired by Apollo, was murdered, and how the cranes gave evidence against the assassins, B., 198–201.
6. The Sibyl's story of her life as she told it to Aeneas, B., 274.

For other references see the Appendix, pages xxviii ff., under the headings of subjects mentioned in this chapter.

II. **In Books in General**

1. *The Perilous Seat,* a novel about Apollo's oracle at Delphi, by Caroline Snedeker (Doubleday, Page and Company).
2. "The Golden Touch," by Nathaniel Hawthorne in *The Wonder Book,* pp. 22–47 (Everyman's Library, E. P. Dutton and Company).
3. Passages from Ovid's *Metamorphoses,* translated in the Loeb Classical Library (G. P. Putnam's Sons):
   (1) Apollo and the Python, I, pp. 33–35.
   (2) Daphne, I, pp. 35–43.
   (3) The story of Phaëthon, II, pp. 1–83.
   (4) Clytie's unrequited love for Apollo, IV, pp. 195–197.
   (5) The tragedy of Niobe, VI, pp. 299–309.
   (6) Midas and the "golden touch," XI, pp. 127–131.
4. Seymour's *Life in the Homeric Age,* pp. 428–431 (The Macmillan Company).
5. An account of a very famous institution connected with the worship of Aesculapius, where people went to recover their health, in some respects the forerunner of the modern sanitarium and also of the

" faith cures." Van Hook's *Greek Life and Thought*, pp. 265–267 (Columbia University Press).

6. Poems listed on page 30, the titles of which are marked with an asterisk.

B. LINES TO BE MEMORIZED

Then I arise, and climbing Heaven's blue dome
I walk over the mountain and the waves,
Leaving my robe upon the ocean foam;
    My footsteps pave the clouds with fire; the caves
Are filled with my bright presence, and the air
Leaves the green Earth to my embraces bare.

The sunbeams are my shafts, with which I kill
    Deceit, that loves the night and fears the day;
All men who do or even imagine ill
    Fly me, and from the glory of my ray
Good minds and open actions take new might,
Until diminished by the reign of Night.

SHELLEY, *Hymn of Apollo*, II, III

C. FURTHER STUDY OF LITERARY ALLUSION

If you are interested in seeing more at length how good English writers make use of the myths, look up the following references:

Apollo: R. L. Stevenson's *Across the Plains*, p. 113 (Scribners); Alfred Noyes' *Sherwood*, p. 170 (Stokes); Milton's *Comus*, 190. **Clytie:** Thomas Hood's *Flowers*. **Daphne:** Meredith's *Ordeal of Richard Feverel*, p. 41 (Scribners). **Delos:** Byron's *Don Juan*, Canto III, 689–692. **Midas:** Stephen Leacock's *Arcadian Adventures with the Idle Rich*, p. 62 (John Lane); Shakespeare's *Merchant of Venice*, Act III, Sc. 2, 21–22. **Narcissus and Hyacinth:** Shelley's *Adonais*, xvi. **Niobe:** Shakespeare's *Hamlet*, Act I, Sc. 2, 149. **Oracles:** Editorial in the *New York Times*, October 13, 1926.

D. PROJECTS FOR INDIVIDUAL OR GROUP WORK

To be selected from the list of projects on pages xx–xxv, in case the subject matter of this chapter lends itself readily to any one of them.

POEMS FOR REFERENCE

Since many of the poems for reference mentioned in this book are well known, it has not seemed necessary in every case to mention the title of the volume in which it appears or to give the name of the publisher.

The poems in which pupils will presumably be the most interested are marked with an asterisk.

CARMAN, BLISS	* Daphne; *also* * The Lost Dryad (*Pipes of Pan;* L. C. Page and Company, Boston)
CATHER, WILLA	Winter at Delphi (*April Twilights;* Alfred A. Knopf, N. Y.)
CHALMERS, PATRICK	* Daphne (*Green Days and Blue Days;* Norman, Remington Company, Baltimore)
CHAUCER, GEOFFREY	The Maunciple's Tale
CLARKE, J. I. C.	Laurels (*Literary Digest,* Nov. 9, 1918)
HOLMES, OLIVER WENDELL	Last Prophecy of Cassandra
JONES, THOMAS S.	Daphne (*Verse of Our Day;* D. Appleton and Company, N. Y.)
KEATS, JOHN	Hymn to Apollo
LOWELL, JAMES RUSSELL	* Daphne and Apollo (*A Fable for Critics*)
MEREDITH, GEORGE	Daphne (*Poems;* Charles Scribner's Sons, N. Y.)
MORRIS, LEWIS	Marsyas, Apollo (*Epic of Hades;* Kegan Paul, Trench, Trübner and Company, London)
NOYES, ALFRED	Ride of Phaëthon (*Collected Poems;* Frederick A. Stokes and Company, N. Y.)
PHILLIPS, STEPHEN	* Marpessa (John Lane Company)
SAXE, JOHN G.	* Choice of King Midas; *also* * Phaëthon or The Amateur Coachman
SHELLEY, PERCY BYSSHE	* Hymn of Apollo
TENNYSON, ALFRED	Amphion
THOMAS, EDITH M.	Apollo, the Shepherd; *also* Marsyas

Guido Reni (Rospigliosi Palace, Rome)

Fig. 13. Aurora

Aurora and Phosphor prepare the way for Apollo. Maidens, known as the Hours, surround the sun-god's chariot.

AURORA
(E'os)

WHEN the Greeks saw the beautiful coloring in the eastern sky just before sunrise, they thought that the goddess of the dawn,

Goddess of the dawn the " rosy-fingered Au ro'ra," was opening the gates of day and driving back the stars so that everything might be ready for A pol'lo as he started out upon his long ride across the sky. The conspicuously brilliant star which lingered longest — we call it the " morning star " — they regarded as Aurora's son Lu'ci fer (Phos'phor in the Greek), who by his torch heralded the coming of his goddess mother. It is interesting to know that both the Greek and Latin names of this star mean " light-bringing."

It is said that the young hunter, Ceph'a lus, was Phosphor's father, and that his meeting with Aurora eventually brought him great unhappiness. Here is the story which has come down to us.

Aurora was radiantly beautiful and mortal men as well as gods sought her love. Among the former was Cephalus, a young

hunter who was married to a king's daughter named Pro'cris.
Cephalus and Procris Led by his love for the goddess, Cephalus deserted his wife, although the myths say that Aurora was more to blame in this matter than the young husband.

Procris was very lonely after Cephalus left her and would have been still more so if she had not joined the group of Di a'na's maidens and learned to delight in the chase. The goddess received her kindly and gave her a dog that never grew tired no matter how long the chase, and a javelin that could never fail to hit the mark at which it was aimed.

But Cephalus was never quite happy with Aurora, for he still loved his wife dearly and was unable to forget her. Finally he returned to her. Procris, however, could never again believe in her husband's loyalty. One day in order to spy upon Cephalus she concealed herself in some bushes. Cephalus, who had become the possessor of the wonderful javelin, hearing the rustling of the leaves, at once aimed the weapon towards the bushes, thinking that some wild beast lay concealed within them. True to its magic power, the javelin found the mark, and Procris was killed.

IN THE WORLD OF TODAY

I. IN LITERARY ALLUSION

Like to rosy-born Aurora,
Glowing freshly into view.

GEORGE MEREDITH, *Daphne*

AURORA

Shunting fleecy clouds about,
Spreading rosy bunting out,
   Deftly in the eastern windows
   Ranging her display.

Rosy-fingered early riser,
Phoe'bus' ready advertiser,
Draping, in the eastern showcase,
Pearl and gold and gray.
In her oriental shop
Luring early birds to stop,
Archetype of window dressers,
Up before the day.

KEITH PRESTON, *The Chicago Tribune*

II. IN WORDS

The word **auroral** is descriptive of something that has the colors of the sky at dawn, with which the goddess Aurora was associated.

Such words as **phosphorus** and **phosphorescent** go back for their origin to the same root as that in the name Phosphor. This fact makes their meaning clear because, like Aurora's son, they " bring light."

III. IN OTHER CONNECTIONS

How the Grasshopper Recalls a Story about Aurora

Although Aurora could have married a god had she wished to do so, she preferred a mortal for a husband, a man named Ti tho'-nus. When she realized that he would grow old and die as other men do, she determined to make him immortal. This she accomplished through her influence with the gods. But unfortunately she forgot to ask at the same time for eternal youth. And so, while she herself as a divinity remained always young, Tithonus as a mortal grew old and gray and feeble. Finally nothing seemed to be left of him but a thin, quavering voice, and he became a great burden both to himself and to Aurora. Since his life as a man was no longer of any use, the goddess one day changed him into a grasshopper or, as some scholars say, a kind of locust.[1]

Why We Have Dew

After the death of her son Mem'non, who was slain by A chil'les in the Tro'jan War, Aurora wept unceasingly.   So great was her grief that, according to the myths, we see her tears shining every morning in the dew.

The Aurora Borealis

A wonderful coloring which we occasionally see at night in the northern sky is known as the " aurora bo re a'lis." This name is suggested by the rosy tints associated with Aurora, goddess of the dawn, and the place where they are seen, recalling the name Bo're as, god of the north wind.

As the Name for a Town

Like some other characters from classical mythology, Aurora has given her name to certain towns.   A large atlas lists twenty-six places having the name Aurora.

QUESTIONS FOR REVIEW

1. How did the Greeks explain the dawn?
2. Tell the story of Cephalus and Procris.
3. Who was Tithonus?   How did Aurora dispose of him?
4. What story did the Greeks make up to account for the dew?
5. Explain the term *aurora borealis* in the light of the myths.
6. What was Aurora's Greek name?
7. Look up the strange story about a colossal statue in Egypt which

[1] The Greeks used a word which probably referred to the cicada, an insect which cannot be identified closely with the grasshopper or locust.   But the version given above has long been known.

is called Memnon, and explain its connection with the goddess of the dawn.

POEMS FOR REFERENCE

DOBSON, AUSTIN   The Death of Procris (*Collected Poems;* Dodd, Mead and Company, N. Y.)

MOORE, THOMAS   Cephalus and Procris

NOYES, ALFRED   At Dawn (*Collected Poems;* Frederick A. Stokes Company, N. Y.)

SEEGER, ALAN   Tithonus (*Poems;* Charles Scribner's Sons, N. Y.)

TENNYSON, ALFRED   Tithonus

Vatican, Rome

Fig. 14. Head of Bacchus

BACCHUS
(Di o ny'sus)

A KING of Thebes, Cad'mus by name, had a marvelously
beautiful daughter called Sem'e le. Unfortunately she had
The birth of attracted the attention of Ju'pi ter and had thus
Bacchus aroused the jealousy of Ju'no. Wishing to destroy
the maiden, who was fast becoming a rival in her husband's
affections, Juno visited her one day in the form of Be'ro e,
Semele's aged nurse. Eager to confide her happy secret to
friendly ears, the girl poured forth the story of her good fortune
in having as her lover no less a person than the king of the gods
himself. "He may indeed be Jupiter," said Beroë, "certainly I
hope so. But I should advise you to prove it by asking him to
appear to you some day in his royal garb, wearing the divine

armor and equipped with his powerful thunderbolt." The idea pleased Semele and she at once determined to carry out her old nurse's suggestion.

On the occasion of Jupiter's next visit the girl said, " Grant me a favor, Jupiter, even though you know not what it is to be." Her lover assented. No sooner, however, had Semele started to express her wish than Jupiter realized his mistake. He tried to prevent her from putting her desire into words, but it was too late; she had already conveyed the meaning of her request.

Although Jupiter knew that no mortal could withstand the heat of his thunderbolt, and that Semele would surely perish if exposed to it, he dared not break a god's word. Accordingly he appeared to the maiden in all his awful splendor as king of heaven and, as he foresaw, Semele was instantly burned to ashes by the flames. But Jupiter rescued the

Vatican, Rome

Fig. 15. Silenus with the infant Bacchus

girl's unborn babe and cared for it as his son. He called it Bac'chus.

When Bacchus grew up, he was worshiped as the god of vegetation, who loved all the cool, moist places of shady glens and mountain sides where plants and trees flourish. But it was as the divinity that presided over wine that Bacchus was best known. Tradition says that he introduced the vine into Greece and went about encouraging its cultivation. By this gift he contributed to the prosperity of the country, just as Mi ner'va did by bringing the olive tree to Greece. In this act of service lay his real importance in the life

The god of vegetation and of wine

of the Greeks. While, then, he is most often thought of in connection with the wild orgies attendant upon his worship, Bacchus should in no sense be regarded as the god of drunken revelry as the expression is understood today.

Bacchus was constantly attended by a train of followers. These might be strange-looking women called bacchantes, often **Attendants of** under the influence of religious frenzy, at which times **Bacchus** they took part in wild and savage orgies in honor of the god. Or they might also be creatures half-human and half-animal, known as satyrs, fauns, and sileni. The satyr was shaggy, like an animal, and had the ears and tail of a goat and sometimes also horns and hoofs; but the upper part of the body was like that of a man. Fauns and sileni had the ears of animals and sometimes the tails, but in general they resembled men.

IN THE WORLD OF TODAY

I. IN LITERARY ALLUSION

Bacchus, that first from out the purple grape
Crushed the sweet poison of misused wine.

MILTON, *Comus*, 1, 46–47

So did he feel who pulled the boughs aside
That we might look into the forest wide,
To catch a glimpse of fauns and dryades,
Coming with softest rustle through the trees.

KEATS, *I Stood Tiptoe upon a Little Hill*

II. IN WORDS

Such words as **bacchic** and **bacchanalian,** meaning wild and drunken reveling, are derived directly from Bacchus, the wine-

god.   But the derived meaning is hardly fair to this divinity, who
stood for much that was good in Greek life.

One might not suspect that the word **tragedy** comes from the
worship of Bacchus, but there are grounds for thinking that it
really does, although the point is still a matter of controversy.
Scholars who uphold the theory see the explanation in the fact

Fig. 16. Theater of Dionysus in Athens

that those who took part in the rude choral dance about the
altar of the god imitated the satyrs — creatures half-man and
half-goat.   Thus their song came to be called " the goat-song "
from the Greek words *tragos*, goat, and *oidos*, song.   As the
performance passed over into the drama, the name " tragedy "
became connected with it.   Whenever we go to the theater,

therefore, it may be interesting to remember that the first " plays " may have centered about a Greek god.

The largest theater in Athens was the theater of Dionysus, much of which still remains.

It is common to speak of the animals of a country as the **fauna,** a name derived from an I tal'ic goddess (sister of Faunus) and connected with the fauns of classical mythology.   In a similar way the word **flora,** which designates flowers and plants, comes from Flo'ra, the goddess of flowers.

III. In Other Connections

Why We Have Dolphins

Bacchus was once lying asleep on an island, when some pirates found him and carried him off to their ship, thinking that so beautiful a youth could be sold for much money.   When they refused to listen to his entreaties to be carried to the island of Nax'os, a wonderful thing happened.   The ship seemed to be rooted in the sea and vines adorned the masts and sails.   Everywhere was the pleasant odor of wine and the decks swam with this delicious drink.   The captive disappeared and in his place was a savage lion, which so frightened the pirates that in their terror they jumped into the sea, where they were at once changed into dolphins.

As Titles for Musical Compositions

Bacchus has been a favorite theme for musical compositions, and at least thirty operettas bear his name.   Watch concert programs for mention of this god.

A Modern Novel

Hawthorne's *Marble Faun* is an interesting story and will recall much about the fauns of classical mythology.

Favorite Theme for Artists

Fauns, satyrs, and sileni are favorite themes for artists who wish to embody in their work some suggestion of the country. Therefore representations of these rude followers of Bacchus are often seen, not only in elaborate gardens and parks but also in paintings and decorative designs.

QUESTIONS FOR REVIEW

1. (1) Over what realms was Bacchus the patron divinity?
(2) In what capacity was he best known to the Greeks? Why?
2. Who were his parents?
3. Describe his attendants.
4. In what connection are Bacchus and his attendants favorite themes?
5. Explain the words *tragedy, bacchanalian, fauna, flora.*
6. Why, according to the myths, do we have dolphins?
7. How may Bacchus be recognized in art?
8. Mention one of our states, the name of which comes from the same root as that in the name of the goddess of flowers.

POEMS FOR REFERENCE

BENÉT, WILLIAM ROSE	*Night Watchers *and* Song of the Satyrs to Ariadne (*Merchants from Cathay;* Yale University Press, New Haven, Conn.)
BYNNER, WITTER	Never a Faun (*Caravan;* Alfred A. Knopf, N. Y.)
CARMAN, BLISS	*The Dead Faun (*Pipes of Pan;* L. C. Page and Company, Boston)
CAWEIN, MADISON	The Faun; *also* The Dead Oread (*Poems;* The Macmillan Company, N. Y.)
EMERSON, RALPH WALDO	Bacchus

GARRISON, THEODOSIA   The Faun (*The Earth Cry;* Mitchell Kennerley, N. Y.)

GORMAN, HERBERT S.   * The Satyrs and the Moon (*Poems for Youth;* E. P. Dutton and Company, N. Y.)

HOVEY, RICHARD   * The Faun (*Along the Trail;* Charles Scribner's Sons, N. Y.)

NEWBOLT, HENRY   * The Faun (*Poems Old and New;* John Murray, London)

NOYES, ALFRED   * Bacchus and the Pirates (*Collected Poems;* Frederick A. Stokes Company, N. Y.)

SHERMAN, FRANK D.   * Bacchus (*Modern American Poetry,* anthology by Louis Untermeyer; Harcourt, Brace and Company, N. Y.)

THOMAS, EDITH M.   * Evoe (*Home Book of Verse;* Henry Holt and Company, N. Y.)

TIETJIENS, EUNICE   * The Bacchante to Her Babe (*The Golden Treasury of Magazine Verse;* Small, Maynard and Company, Boston)

Fig. 17.   A young satyr as he is represented in modern art

CERES
(De me′ter)

CE′RES was the goddess of the green things of earth, the plants, the grass, and the trees, and particularly of the produce of the

A goddess of agriculture fields. She looked after the farmers' crops and saw that they flourished and yielded abundantly at harvest time. In fact, it was she who first taught men to sow the fields and to cultivate them, and to become skilled in all the arts of husbandry. In return for her care, the farmer never failed to load her altars with gifts of fruit and grain on the occasion of some rural festival, nor did the farmer's wife forget on " baking day " to set aside some particularly delicious loaf for the kindly Ceres.

Vatican, Rome   *Photograph by Alinari*

Fig. 18. Ceres

The goddess had a lovely daughter named Pro ser′pi na (Per seph′o ne), and one of the best-known stories of classical mythology is connected with the misfortune that befell this maiden.

Once on a sunny day Proserpina chanced to be picking flowers with her companions in a field in Sicily. Care-free and happy, the girl wandered here and there as some blossom unusually perfect in form or coloring caught her fancy. It happened that

43

Fig. 19. Pluto carries Proserpina away

her eye fell upon a narcissus, a flower which she greatly liked, and she stooped at once to pick it. As she did so, she saw to

Pluto carries Proserpina away to become queen of the Lower World
her amazement and horror that the ground was opening! Almost before she could cry out the chasm widened. Coal-black steeds of gigantic size sprang forth and a chariot appeared, in which stood Plu'to, the dreadful king of the Lower World. In an instant she was seized in the god's strong arms. Horses and chariot plunged downward into the black depths and the earth closed over them.

By such violence did Pluto obtain a wife and a queen for the gloomy realms over which he presided, and the unhappy Proserpina was lost to the Upper World.

Since Ceres was away from Sicily when Proserpina disappeared, she

A mother's search is rewarded
had no way of knowing what had become of her daughter. For nine days and nine nights she searched unweary-ingly but could find no trace of her. Finally, when she was about to give up all hope, the sun, which of course sees everything, or, as some writers say, the nymph A re thu'sa (who had been changed into a stream that ran under the earth) gave her a hint; Proserpina had been seen in the dark and unlovely Lower World seated upon a throne by Pluto's side.

Courtesy of the Metropolitan Museum, New York

Fig. 20. Head of a goddess (perhaps Persephone)

Ceres at once went to Jupiter and begged that her daughter be returned to her. Jupiter was eager to grant the mother's request, and particularly so because the whole world was suffering from neglect. The goddess no longer cared for the grain of the field, nor did plants grow or fruit trees flourish. He therefore decreed that Proserpina might return to her mother provided she had eaten no food while in Pluto's kingdom. Unfortunately, it was discovered that she had consumed some pomegranate seeds, and she was therefore obliged to spend three months of each year in the world below, but the other nine she passed with Ceres upon the earth.

The Greeks accounted for the seasons by saying that when Proserpina is in the Upper World, the earth smiles, and so we have spring, summer, and fall. But when she is gone, Ceres grieves and vegetation ceases to flourish.

Proserpina's story has been very beautifully told by Jean Ingelow in a poem entitled " Persephone." These stanzas are quoted from it. But read the entire poem to discover how the poet has treated the incident as a whole.

> She stepped upon Sicilian grass,
>   Demeter's daughter fresh and fair,
> A child of light, a radiant lass,
>   And gamesome as the morning air.
> The daffodils were fair to see,
> They nodded lightly on the lea,
>   Persephone — Persephone!
>
>
> Lo! one she marked of rarer growth
>   Than orchis or anemone;
> For it the maiden left them both
>   And parted from her company.
> Drawn nigh, she deemed it fairer still,
> And stooped to gather by the rill
>   The daffodil, the daffodil.

What ailed the meadow that it shook?
    What ailed the air of Sicily?
She wondered by the brattling brook,
    And trembled with the trembling lea.
"The coal-black horses rise — they rise;
O mother, mother!" low she cries —
    Persephone — Persephone!

"O light, light, light!" she cries, "farewell;
    The coal-black horses wait for me.
O shade of shades, where I must dwell,
    Demeter, mother, far from thee!
Ah, fated doom that I fulfil!
Ah, fateful flower beside the rill!
    The daffodil, the daffodil!"

*   *   *   *   *   *   *

She reigns upon her dusky throne
    'Mid shades of heroes dread to see;
Among the dead she breathes alone,
    Persephone — Persephone!
Or, seated on the E lys'i an hill,
She dreams of earthly daylight still,
And murmurs of the daffodil.

A voice in Ha'des soundeth clear,
    The shadows mourn and flit below;
It cries — "Thou Lord of Hades, hear,
    And let Demeter's daughter go!"
The tender corn upon the lea
Droops in her goddess gloom when she
Cries for her lost Persephone.

JEAN INGELOW

IN THE WORLD OF TODAY

I. In Literary Allusion

As when on Cêres' sacred floor, the swain
Spreads the wide fan to clear the golden grain.

POPE, Translation of the Iliad, V, 612–613

Dulcet-eyed as Ceres' daughter,
Ere the God of Torment taught her
How to frown and how to chide.

KEATS, To Fancy

II. In a Word

The word **cereal** is derived from the same root as that found in the name of the goddess of grain.

III. In Other Connections

Ceres is frequently represented in art and decorative design as a symbol for agriculture in its broadest sense. For example, the Legislative Library of the New York State Capitol at Albany is adorned with a wall painting by Will H. Low, in which this goddess typifies the agricultural resources of the state.

REVIEW QUESTIONS

1. What were Ceres' particular duties?
2. In what ways did the farmers show their gratitude to her?
3. How did a narcissus lead her daughter to a tragic fate?
4. Describe Ceres' search for her daughter and how it ended.
5. How did the Greeks account for the seasons?
6. Why are we often reminded of Ceres at breakfast?
7. How may one recognize Ceres in art?
8. What was the Greek name of Ceres?

OPTIONAL

FOR THOSE WHO HAVE TIME FOR FURTHER STUDY

A. ADDITIONAL READING

I. In Textbooks Dealing with Classical Mythology

1. Why Pluto fell in love with Proserpina, B., 52–53.
2. How Cyane and Arethusa helped Ceres to find her daughter, B., 55; Gay., p. 162.
3. How Ceres imparted to a youth a knowledge of agriculture so that he might teach men how to make the earth yield abundant harvests, B., 54–55; Gay., pp. 160–161; 164–165.

For other references see Appendix, pages xxviii ff., under the headings of subjects mentioned in this chapter.

II. In Books in General

1. "The Pomegranate Seeds" in *Tanglewood Tales* by Nathaniel Hawthorne, pp. 248–276 (Everyman's Library), and stories in books similar to this in character.
2. Translation of Ovid (Loeb Classical Library, G. P. Putnam's Sons); an interesting and detailed account of Proserpina's disappearance and Ceres' efforts to recover her daughter, *Met.*, V, pp. 265–277 (Latin lines, 385–571).
3. An account of a secret religious society connected with the worship of Ceres and known as the "Eleusinian Mysteries," W. S. Davis' *A Day in Old Athens*, pp. 228–231 (Allyn and Bacon); also Van Hook's *Greek Life and Thought*, pp. 260–263 (Columbia University Press).
4. Poem listed on page 50, the title of which is starred.

B. LINES TO BE MEMORIZED

Ceres was she who first our furrows plowed,
Who gave sweet fruits and every good allowed.

POPE, Translation of the *Iliad*

Sacred Goddess, Mother Earth,
Thou from whose immortal bosom
Gods, and men, and beasts have birth.

SHELLEY, *Song of Proserpine*, 1–3

C. Further Study of Literary Allusion

If you are interested in seeing more clearly how good writers make use of the Greek myths, look up the following references:

Ceres: Shakespeare's *Tempest,* Act IV, Sc. 1, 60–70; Pope's *Moral Essays,* IV, 176; George Eliot's *Adam Bede,* chap. v, p. 52 (Scribners); Thoreau's *Walden,* p. 145 (Everyman's Library). **Demeter:** Swinburne's *Laus Veneris,* p. 84 (David McKay). **Proserpina:** Milton's *Paradise Lost,* IV, 268–272.

D. Projects for Individual and Group Work

To be selected from the list of projects on pages xx–xxv, in case the subject matter of this chapter lends itself readily to any one of them.

POEMS FOR REFERENCE

Ingelow, Jean	*Persephone
LeDoux, Louis	The Story of Eleusis (Houghton Mifflin Company, Boston)
Rossetti, Dante G.	Proserpine
Shelley, Percy Bysshe	Song of Proserpine
Swinburne, Algernon C.	The Garden of Proserpine; *also* Hymn to Proserpine
Tennyson, Alfred	Demeter and Persephone
Woodberry, George E.	Proserpine (*Century Magazine,* July, 1909)

DIANA

(Ar'te mis)

Dı a'na loved the wilds, and nothing gave her more pleasure than to roam through and over the mountains far from the haunts

Goddess of the chase of man. Hunting was her favorite diversion, and it was no uncommon thing for men to hear, far away in the mountains and in the depths of the forest, the baying of the hounds and the cries of the nymphs as Diana's hunting parties followed in breathless chase the track of the wild boar and the stag.

But, while fond of hunting, the goddess was at the same time the friend and protector of the wild animals and avenged any wrong done to them.

As an unmarried goddess Diana exercised special care over girls,

Patron of girls and just as young men regarded A pol'lo, her twin brother, as their guide and

Louvre, Paris

Fig. 21. Diana with the stag

This statue is known as Diana of Versailles because a copy of it adorns a garden of the palace at Versailles, near Paris.

protector, so young women worshiped Diana and looked to her for help in all their difficulties. When it was time for them to marry and put away childish things, they brought their dolls to

Diana's altar and left them there as a gift for the gracious goddess who had shown them so many kindnesses.

Many stories are told of Diana's rescue of young women in times of danger. The one that follows is a notable example.

Ar e thu'sa was one of the nymphs in Diana's hunting train. One day after a particularly long and exhausting chase, she found herself separated from her companions on the shady banks of a mountain stream. The place was quite solitary and the water looked delightfully cool. Slipping off her clothes, she plunged her tired body into the river.

The strange tale of a maiden's escape

Soon she heard soft murmurs about her. At first she paid no heed to them, but as they became louder, she grew frightened. The thought flashed through her mind that the river-god might be trying to speak to her, and she knew that if this was the case she was in great danger. She swam quickly to the bank. As she did so, she heard these words uttered in rough and uncouth accents: "Do not run away, Arethusa! I, Al phe'us, love you. I mean you no harm!"

The nymph did not wait to hear more. Panic-stricken, she fled through the woods. Behind her, coming nearer and nearer, was the god, and although she was wonderfully fleet-footed, she knew that it was only a question of a moment before her pursuer would overtake her.

It was then that Diana, though far away, heard a cry for help. Almost at once a cloud of mist encircled the girl — so thick that Alpheus could no longer see her. And when it cleared away no Arethusa was there. A bubbling spring, however, was gushing from the ground. The river-god at once divined what had happened and instantly changed his human form into water, hoping thus to be united with the maiden whom he loved. Diana, however, was not lacking in resource, and opening a way deep

Fig. 22. Diana

Diana in her dress as a huntress. She has just shot an arrow from her bow.

down into the earth, she made a passage under the lands and the seas so that Arethusa might find her way to Sicily.

But some of the myths say that Alpheus still persisted in his wooing and accompanied the maiden in her flight, finally winning her love.   And the visitor in the city of Syr'a cuse on the eastern coast of Sicily may still see a beautiful spring marking the spot where Arethusa and Alpheus in the form of a sparkling stream came up to the light of day so many centuries ago.

This story has been beautifully told by Shelley in a poem called "Arethusa."   The lines that follow show us how he describes the journey of the nymph and the river-god under the land and the sea :

> Under the bowers
> Where the Ocean Powers
> Sit on their pearlèd thrones,
>   Through the coral woods
>   Of the weltering floods,
> Over heaps of unvalued stones;
>   Through the dim beams
>   Which amid the streams
> Weave a network of colored light;
>   And under the caves,
>   Where the shadowy waves
> Are as green as the forest's night :
>   Outspeeding the shark,
>   And the swordfish dark,
> Under the ocean foam,
>   And up through the rifts
>   Of the mountain clifts
> They passed to their Do'ri an home.

But in spite of such instances as that related above, Diana was sometimes very cruel.   The way in which she treated a young hunter named Ac tae'on is an illustration.

This youth, quite by accident, one day caught a glimpse of the goddess as she was bathing in a forest pool.   Diana's wrath was **Actaeon feels** swift and terrible.   Almost in an instant Actaeon was **Diana's wrath** changed into a stag.   As he fled in terror he heard the baying of his own hounds near by and realized that it would be but an instant before they would be upon him.   Again and again he called to them, hoping that they would recognize their master's voice.   But in the panting stag before them the hounds saw only their prey, and as Actaeon fell exhausted, they leaped upon his body and tore it to pieces.   This dreadful sight, however, did not move Diana in the least.   Not the slightest effort did she make to save the young hunter, innocent though he was, from a most painful death.

These lines from Alfred Noyes's poem called "Actaeon" picture the last scene in this tragic tale:

> Swift he leapt through the fern, Actaeon,
> Young Actaeon, the lordly stag;
> Full and mellow the deep-mouthed paean
> Swelled behind him from crag to crag;
> Well he remembered that sweet throat leading;
> Wild with terror he raced and strained,
> Swept through the thorns with soft flanks bleeding;

*   *   *   *   *   *   *

> Still with his great heart bursting asunder,
> Still through the night he struggled and bled;
> Suddenly round him the pack's low thunder
> Surged, the hounds that his own hand fed
> Fastened in his throat, with red jaws drinking
> Deep; for a moment his antlered pride
> Soared o'er their passionate seas, then, sinking,
> Fell for the fangs to divide.

Here is another story which has its origin in an offense against Diana. The King of Cal'y don in Ae to'li a was a man who
cared very little about hunting and life in the wilds. Therefore he was not always careful to pay proper respect to Diana, and one time at a great harvest festival he forgot her entirely although he had remembered other divinities. In revenge Diana sent a fierce boar to devour his people and lay waste his lands. Me le'a ger, the king's valiant son, decided to organize a hunt in order to rid the country of this pest. Heralds were accordingly sent far and wide to summon the bravest of the Greek heroes for this undertaking. In response, among others, came The'seus, Cas'tor and Pol'lux, Pe'leus (father of A chil'les), Ja'son, and, to the surprise of all, a beautiful woman named At a lan'ta [1] from the royal family of Ar ca'di a.

It was not easy to kill this monster, and several of the heroes were slain before he was even hurt at all. Atalanta was the first to inflict a serious wound with a well-directed arrow, although it was Meleager's spear that finally deprived the boar of life. With a fine sense of justice and inspired, too, with love for the huntress, the hero insisted that the skin should be given to the maiden as the prize rather than to himself. Of course some of the men did not like to see a woman win such a victory, among them Meleager's two uncles. They therefore tried to take the prize away from her, and in the fight that followed, for Meleager rushed to her defense, both of the uncles were killed.

When Meleager's mother, Al thae'a, heard that her brothers had been slain, she was seized with a fit of anger. Forgetting her love for her son, she thought only of punishing him. Now it had happened that when Meleager was only seven days old the Fates

---

[1] In the chapter entitled "Venus," a story is related of another Atalanta, a princess of Boe o'ti a, who was renowned for her beauty and her swiftness in running. The two characters are sometimes confused.

appeared to Althaea as she was sitting before the hearth with the infant. Pointing to one of the burning logs they said, "When that brand is consumed your child shall die." The mother at once pulled the brand from the fire. All the time her son had been growing up she had kept the fatal log concealed in a chest. It took only a moment now for the angry woman, filled with grief for the loss of her brothers whom she had greatly loved, to seize the brand and throw it into the fire. Just at the last, however, she seemed to realize what she had done and tried to save what was still unconsumed. But it was too late. Meleager was dead.

Although Se le'ne (or Lu'na) was looked upon as goddess of the moon, Diana also was so regarded. In this capacity she was often addressed as "Cyn'thi a." One of the best-known stories about Cynthia (or Diana as moon-goddess) is that connected with a handsome young herdsman named En dym'i on. So fair did this youth appear one night as he lay asleep in the moonlight on the mountain side that the goddess could not resist coming down to kiss him.

The moon-goddess kisses Endymion

One story says that Jupiter wished to remove temptation from Diana and therefore told Endymion that he must choose between death and perpetual sleep, but that in case he chose the latter he would also have perpetual youth. Endymion chose to sleep forever.

In some curious way Diana came to be worshiped as a divinity of the Lower World and in this connection was known as Hec'a te. Images of her as a triple-formed goddess were often seen at crossroads, and various secret rites associated with magic and things ghostly were performed in the dead of night before her altars.

A goddess of witches known as Hecate

Diana is usually represented as a young woman clad in a short

tunic and bearing a quiver of arrows.   Sometimes a stag or an
How Diana   animal indicative of the chase is seen near her.   A
may be
identified   crescent above her head identifies her as the goddess
of the moon.

IN THE WORLD OF TODAY

I. In Literary Allusion

Dian   .   .   .   golden-shafted queen,
Is turned not by thy smiles; the shadows green
Of the wild woods, the bow, ...
And piercing cries amid the fierce pursuit
Of beast among waste mountains — such delight
Is hers, and men who know and do the right.

SHELLEY, *Homer's Hymn to Venus*, ll. 13–18

Who is the same, which at my window peepes?
Or whose is that faire face that shines so bright?
Is it not Cinthia, she that never sleepes,
But walkes about high heaven al the night?

SPENSER, *Epithalamion*, ll. 372–375

II. In Words and Expressions

Raphael (Vatican, Rome)
Fig. 23. Monday or " Luna's Day "

Our English word **lunatic is**
connected by popular etymology with Luna because it was
once thought that sleeping
under the moon's rays produced a mild form of insanity.

The French call "Monday"
lundi, the Italians have named
it **lunedì,** and the Spanish,
lunes. All of these words have

come directly from the later Roman custom of designating this special day in the week as "Luna's Day." Raph'a el had this derivation in mind when he designed the picture called "Monday" (Fig. 23). We are sure that the goddess who is driving over the clouds is Luna (Cynthia) because we can see the crescent on her head.

Our word "Monday" is a shortened form of "moon-day."

The expression **Endymion sleep** means perpetual sleep which takes the place of death. In a cemetery at Baltimore there is a statue of the sleeping Endymion, the work of William Henry Rinehart, who designed it for his own grave.

III. In Other Connections

Why Orion Is in the Sky

Diana often took with her as a companion on her hunting expeditions a man named O ri'on. They became very great friends, for they had tastes in common, both being devoted to out-of-door sports and the chase in particular.

Apollo looked with some misgiving upon their intimacy and sought for some way in which he might get rid of Orion. For a long time no plan occurred to him as being feasible. One day, however, as he chanced to be on the seashore with his sister, he saw a tiny black spot far out on the water. Turning to Diana he said, "I challenge you to hit with your arrow that small black object in the distance." The goddess straightway aimed at the mark and shot. As the object disappeared from sight she knew that she had vindicated her skill as a marksman. But when she learned that it was the head of Orion which she had hit, she was overcome with grief. There was only one thing she could do for her friend now, since she could not bring him back to life, and that was to raise him to the sky. And so Orion appears today as one of the constellations.

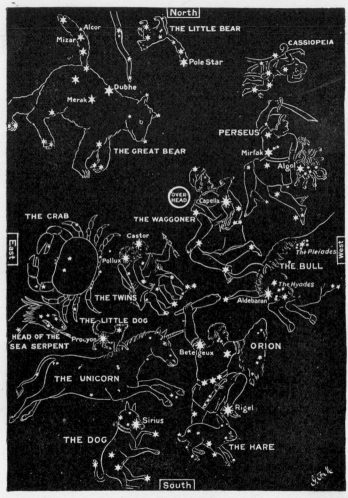

Fig. 24. A star map

Note, among other constellations, Orion, the Great Dog, and the Little Dog.

Orion, the Hunter, and Our "Dog-Days"

The brilliant star named Sir'i us was called the "Dog" by the Greeks and Romans because it seemed to be following the great hunter Orion. The constellation in which the star is found was known as the Great Dog and a smaller one near by was named the Little Dog. At one time in the year (between July 5 and August 11) Sirius shines with the sun. This part of the summer we call "dog-days," a term which has for its origin the story of Orion.

Arethusa Names a Plant

A certain swamp-orchid in North America is called "arethusa," perhaps in memory of the fact that this lovely maiden was connected with a fount. This plant, moreover, is extremely beautifu! and hides as much as possible in remote recesses. Both of these characteristics remind us of Arethusa.

Diana's Connection with the Early Days of Christianity

At Eph'e sus in Asia Minor there was a very splendid temple erected in honor of Diana, to which worshipers came from all parts of the world. When the early Christians began to preach in this city, they met much opposition from the gold- and silversmiths, whose trade in images of Diana was much hurt by the new ideas about religion. Of course people would not buy statues of a goddess in whom they no longer believed. So these tradesmen would gather at the meetings of the Christians and try to drown the words of the speakers by shouting, "Great is Diana of the E phe'sians!" Sometimes these early followers of Christ were even forced to leave the city. One should remember, however, that this Diana differed considerably from the one worshiped in Greece and Italy.

QUESTIONS FOR REVIEW

1. What was Diana's favorite diversion?
2. In what way was she particularly helpful?
3. Who was her twin brother, and what corresponding office did he exercise?
4. Was she married? No
5. What spot, marked by a beautiful spring in Sicily, recalls an instance of Diana's kindness?
6. On what occasion did Diana show cruelty to a young hunter? Did he deserve his fate?   Relate the story.
7. What were the circumstances of Meleager's death?
8. To whom did a kiss cause the doom of eternal sleep?
9. By what other name was Diana known and in what capacity?
10. How may Diana be identified in art?
11. Why is one of the constellations named "Orion"?
12. What connection did Diana have with the early days of Christianity?
13. What day in the week recalls Diana?
14. Explain in terms of the myths the word *lunatic* and the expressions *dog-days* and *Endymion sleep*.
15. What was Diana's Greek name?
16. Why name an automobile "Diana"?

OPTIONAL

FOR THOSE WHO HAVE TIME FOR FURTHER STUDY

A. ADDITIONAL READING

I. In Textbooks Dealing with Classical Mythology

1. The Pleiades, Diana's nymphs, Gay., pp. 123–124; B., 206.
2. Could Diana's maidens marry?   Gay., p. 30.
3. Interesting details of the story about Actaeon, B., 34–36.

For other references see the Appendix, pages xxviii ff., under topics mentioned in this chapter.

II. In Books in General

1. Stories about Diana and characters associated with her as they appear in the many books dealing with the Greek myths, which are interesting to younger pupils.

2. Ovid's account of the story about Actaeon, *Met.* III, pp. 135–143, as translated in the Loeb Classical Library (G. P. Putnam's Sons); also the tale of the Calydonian Hunt, VIII, pp. 425–445.

3. Seymour's *Life in the Homeric Age,* pp. 431–432 (The Macmillan Company).

4. Poems mentioned on pages 63–64, the titles of which are starred.

B. LINES TO BE MEMORIZED

That orbèd maiden with white fire laden,
Whom mortals call the moon.

SHELLEY, The Cloud

C. FURTHER STUDY OF LITERARY ALLUSION

In case you are interested in seeing more clearly how good writers make use of the Greek myths, look up the following references:

Actaeon: Shelley's *Adonais,* Stanza 31. **Atalanta:** Swinburne's *Atalanta in Calydon,* 45–46. **Cynthia:** Keats's *I Stood Tiptoe upon a Little Hill.* **Diana:** Milton's *Comus,* 441–446; Swinburne's *Atalanta in Calydon* (in first chorus); Wells's *The World of William Clissold,* Vol. I, p. 98 (Doran); Thackeray's *The Newcomes,* Vol. I, p. 220 (Everyman's Library); Tarkington's *Monsieur Beaucaire.* **Endymion:** Holmes's *Metrical Essay.* **Hecate:** Shakespeare's *Macbeth,* Act IV, Sc. 1, 1–47; Milton's *Comus,* 534–535. **Orion:** Scott's *Lay of the Last Minstrel,* Canto I, xvii.

D. PROJECTS FOR INDIVIDUAL AND GROUP WORK

To be selected from the list of projects on pages xx–xxv, in case the subject matter of this chapter lends itself readily to any one of them.

POEMS FOR REFERENCE

CLOUGH, ARTHUR HUGH	*Actaeon
ERSKINE, JOHN	*Actaeon (*Collected Poems;* Duffield and Company, N. Y.)
JONSON, BEN	*Hymn to Cynthia (from *Cynthia's Revels*)

KEATS, JOHN	Endymion
LANG, ANDREW	To Artemis (*Poetical Works ;* Longmans, Green and Company, N. Y.)
LONGFELLOW, HENRY W.	*Endymion
LOWELL, JAMES RUSSELL	Endymion
MORRIS, LEWIS	Actaeon, Artemis, Endymion (*Epic of Hades;* Kegan Paul, Trench, Trübner and Company, London)
NOYES, ALFRED	Actaeon (*Collected Poems,* Vol. II; Frederick A. Stokes Company, N. Y.)
PHILLIPS, STEPHEN	Endymion
SHELLEY, PERCY BYSSHE	*Arethusa
SWINBURNE, ALGERNON C.	Atalanta in Calydon, certain passages (*Poems;* David McKay, Philadelphia)
WILDE, OSCAR	Endymion (*Poems;* Brentano's, N. Y.)

THE FATES

THESE divinities were three in number and were sometimes called "Par′cae," meaning "sparers," although this was only a polite form of address, because these powers never "spared" anyone.

Ordinarily they were regarded as female beings in whose hands were the destinies of mankind, and as a personification of unalterable necessity — that which was destined to happen, no matter what gods or men might do in their efforts to prevent it. They were therefore supreme, and all that Jupiter could do was to act as their chief executive.

The picture on page 67 helps us to understand how they divided their duties in connection with man's life; Clo′tho, the youngest, seems to be putting the wool about the spindle, Lach′esis is twisting it, while At′ro pos, the eldest of the three, cuts off the thread of life when it is time for a man to die.

IN THE WORLD OF TODAY

I. IN LITERARY ALLUSION

Alas! forgotten or remembered still
Midst joy or sorrow, Fate shall work her will.

WILLIAM MORRIS, *The Earthly Paradise*

It is that power that rules us as with rods,
Lord above lords, and god behind the gods.

STEPHEN PHILLIPS, Prologue to *Ulysses*

Fig. 25. The Fates

"The Fates were kind to the capable singer, and last night's event will be memorable for those who were fortunate enough to secure admittance." *Daily News-paper*

II. In Words

Such words as **fate, fated, fatal** come from the same root as that in the name of the Fates and convey the same idea, namely, "that which has been spoken" and from which there is no appeal; it can never be altered. Some people today are "fatalists," that is, they believe that whatever happens has been ordained and that human beings are powerless to change the course of events.

Thumann   © *H. K. T.; Gramstorff Brothers*

Fig. 26. The three Fates

III. In Another Connection

The idea of the Fates survives in the folklore of modern Greece. The Greek peasant still believes in three spirits of great power, one of whom spins thread, while the other two give either good or evil fortune. They dwell in caves and their decrees are thought to be unalterable. Women, especially, worship these spirits.

JANUS

JA′NUS was one of the early Italian gods.   He is thought of as connected with the door or gate, and he is sometimes pictured as
The god of entrances   holding a key.   In statues he is represented with two faces, one in front and one behind, to typify the power of seeing forward and backward at the same time.

The Romans built a temple to Janus in the Roman Fo′rum, in the shape of a double arch with doors.   When these doors were closed, the state was at peace; but when they were open, everyone knew that war was being waged in some part of the Roman world.

IN THE WORLD OF TODAY

I. IN LITERARY ALLUSION

Janus am I; oldest of potentates;
  Forward I look, and backward, and below
I count, as god of avenues and gates,
  The years that through my portals come and go.

LONGFELLOW, *The Poet's Calendar*

II. IN WORDS

January, the month with which our year begins and which may ne thought of as the "gateway" to the year, takes its name from the god Janus.

Janus-headed means "double-headed," and **Janus-faced** conveys the idea of "two-faced," insincere, or deceitful. Sometimes it means that a question or situation has two sides to it, as in this quotation from the *Atlantic Monthly:* "This is a **Janus-faced** fact."

III. In Another Connection

As a Symbol for Open-Mindedness

Because Janus faced both ways he became a symbol for open-mindedness; for since he looks both forward and backward, he is able to take a just view of all questions.

Fig. 27. Janus

Fig. 28. Head of Juno

JUNO
(He'ra)

Ju'no was not only Jupiter's sister, but his wife as well. As queen of heaven she was naturally supreme among the goddesses of O lym'pus, although she often complained that lesser divinities could obtain favors from Jupiter which he would not grant to her.

Queen of heaven

While Juno was regarded by the Greeks as a beautiful and dignified queen whom they respected and honored, she is pictured in the poems of Homer as a very human person, who, on occasions, exhibited the same weaknesses that a mortal woman might display. For example, she was sometimes irritable, quick to resent a slight, and relentless in her anger towards those who had offended her. Quarrels with her husband were frequent. She upbraided him not only for keeping his affairs of state so much to himself instead of conferring freely with her, but also for the apparent disregard of the sanctity of marriage which he so often showed by his attentions to other goddesses and to mortal women.

Human characteristics

Perhaps, however, Juno should not be reproached for her indignation at Jupiter's many love affairs, inasmuch as it was part of her duty as a goddess to watch over the welfare of women and of wives in particular. The latter always looked to her for help and guidance and honored her with special ceremonies. Therefore, as the divinely appointed defender of the dignity of marriage, it was to be expected that, quite apart

A patron of wives

from any personal jealousy that she might feel, she would resent such illustrations of her husband's unfaithfulness as are related in the two paragraphs that follow and in several other places in this book.

Jupiter was once much attracted by a young woman named I'o. To prevent further acquaintance between them, Juno had **The many-** changed the girl into a white heifer and had placed **eyed Argus** a guard over it, a hundred-eyed creature named Ar'gus. No one had been able to set Io free until Mer'cu ry, at the suggestion of Jupiter, succeeded in putting Argus to sleep, thus allowing the heifer to escape.

Like all of Mercury's ideas, his plan on this occasion was very clever. He began by telling an interesting story. A second followed and a third. Still Argus was not tired but begged for more, for the god's tales were always charming. Gradually the accounts grew longer and less interesting. One by one the hundred eyes began to close until Argus was sound asleep. It was easy enough to kill him then and free Io from so unpleasant a guard.

In memory of the maiden whom Jupiter loved, the innermost of the satellites of the planet Jupiter is called Io.

Cal lis'to, a beautiful woman of Ar ca'di a, much loved by the king of the gods, had been changed by the angry Juno into a bear. **Callisto feels** One day when Ar'cas, Callisto's son, was hunting, he **Juno's wrath** saw the bear and aimed his spear for a deadly thrust. But Jupiter prevented what would have been an unnatural crime by raising the mother and son to the sky, where they appear as the constellations known as the Great Bear and the Little Bear.

When Juno perceived what had happened, she insisted that the victim of her unrelenting wrath should have no rest in the heavens. Accordingly, she saw to it that these constellations should always revolve around the pole and never set beneath the horizon.

Sabatelli (Pitti Gallery, Florence)   *Photograph by Alinari*

Fig. 29. **Meeting of Juno and Venus**

How may these goddesses be identified?

Not only was Juno often cruel towards those who had offended her, but she sometimes pursued for many years with most bitter

Hebe is deprived of office

persecution those whom she disliked, showing that it was difficult for her to forget an injury. For example, the sufferings of the Trojans, after the fall of their city in what is known as the Trojan War, were largely due to an insult to Juno's daughter, He'be.

Correggio (Imperial Gallery, Vienna)
© H. K. T.; Gramstorff Brothers

Fig. 30. Jupiter and Ganymede

Strange as it may appear to us, the divinities felt greatly honored when their sons or daughters were appointed to serve the nectar at the banquets of the gods, and it was only natural that Juno should feel a mother's pride when this office was conferred upon Hebe. She was greatly angered, therefore, when her daughter was deprived of this high privilege on the ground that she had been careless enough on one occasion to spill some of the nectar. Her resentment, moreover, was all the greater when she discovered that Jupiter had put in her daughter's place one of his young favorites, a Trojan youth named Gan'y mede, once a shepherd upon Mt. Ida's slopes. The beauty of this boy had so delighted the king of the gods that he had assumed the form of an eagle and, thus disguised, had borne the youth aloft to Olympus. That a maiden of such surpassing loveliness as Hebe should be supplanted by Ganymede seemed to the queen an insult.

Among the special attendants of Juno was the lovely I'ris,

a maiden who flew back and forth between heaven and
Iris, Juno's earth with a train of brilliant colors in her wake,
Messenger carrying messages for the queen and sometimes,
too, for the king.

Juno appears as a dignified matron wearing a long garment.
Juno in art Frequently she carries a scepter as symbolic of her
queenly power. The peacock, her favorite bird, is sometimes
seen beside her.

Photograph by Sidney N. Deane

Fig. 31. Temple of Hera at Olympia

IN THE WORLD OF TODAY

I. In Literary Allusion

And thou, great Juno, which with awful might,
The laws of wedlock still dost patronize.

SPENSER, *Epithalamion*, ll. 390–391

Hail, many-colour'd messenger, that ne'er
Dost disobey the wife of Jupiter.

SHAKESPEARE, *The Tempest*, Act IV, Sc. 1, 76–77

And wives still pray to Juno
For boys with hearts as bold
As his who kept the bridge so well
In the brave days of old.

MACAULAY, *Lays of Ancient Rome*, "Horatius," lxvii, 562-565

II. IN WORDS AND EXPRESSIONS

A beautiful woman is sometimes called a **Hebe.**

The term **argus-eyes** is often used to indicate unusual watchfulness. Thus at election times one frequently reads this statement in the newspaper: "The election board is planning to keep **argus-eyes** on the polls today."

Hal'cy on days are calm and peaceful, untroubled by any care. A story connected with Juno explains the term.

There was once a girl named Hal cy'o ne, whose husband perished in a shipwreck. Juno sent Iris to tell her the news. Moreover, to save her from her agony, the goddess changed the unhappy wife into a kingfisher. She did still more in the way of lessening Halcyone's grief, for she also caused the dead husband to live again in the form of a male kingfisher. Then, in order that their young might be hatched, Juno saw to it that at a certain time of the year the winds and waves should become quiet until the period of incubation was over.

Fig. 32. The kingfisher

The Romans called the brilliant star at the end of the Little Bear's tail "Cy no su'ra" (after the Greek), but it is commonly known today as the Pole Star. It is the one at which we look when we want to be sure of our direction, for it always means "north."

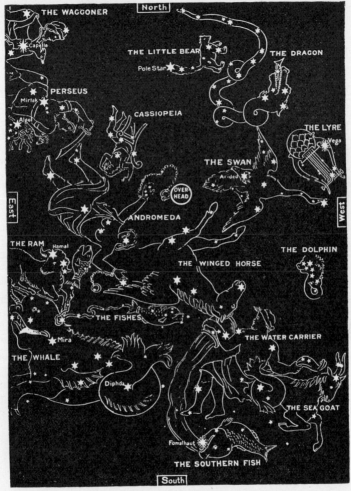

Fig. 33. A star map

Observe the constellation called the Little Bear, noting particularly the Pole Star. Also study Fig. 24 to discover the Great Bear.

The habit of gazing at this conspicuous point in the sky explains the meaning of our English word **cy′no sure,** defined in the dictionary as "something very striking, the center of attraction." A person, for example, may on some occasion be **the cynosure of all eyes,** meaning, of course, that everyone is looking at him.

Fig. 34. **The Argus pheasant**

III. In Other Connections

Why the Argus Pheasant Is So Called

Some one who knew the story of Argus was reminded of it when he saw the pheasant whose wings are quite covered with circular markings resembling eyes.

How the Greeks Accounted for the Rainbow

The Greeks explained the rainbow by saying that it was the path made by Juno's messenger, Iris, as she went back and forth between heaven and earth.

Why the Peacock Has Eyes on Its Tail

When Argus died, Juno is said to have gathered up his many eyes and put them in the tail of her favorite bird, the peacock.

Juno's Beauty Names Some Butterflies

A genus of strikingly beautiful butterflies has been called "Junonia" by scientists.[1]

[1] For colored pictures of butterflies, many of which are named from some character in the Greek myths, see The Nature Library, Vol. VI, *The Butterfly Book,* by W. J. Holland (Doubleday, Page and Company, 1920).

QUESTIONS FOR REVIEW

1. What was Juno's rank among the goddesses?
2. Of whom was she the patron divinity?
3. What very human characteristics did she possess?
4. Was she justified in her jealous attitude towards Jupiter?
5. Why is the satellite nearest the planet Jupiter called Io? Tell the story of Io.
6. Why, according to the myths, do the Great Bear and the Little Bear never set beneath the horizon?
7. Who was the cup-bearer of the gods after Juno's daughter Hebe was removed from office, and how did this change cause great suffering to the Trojans?
8. How can we tell from the stars which direction is north? Which is the Pole Star? What did the Greeks call it?
9. How did the Greeks account for the rainbow?
10. How did the Greeks explain the fact that the peacock has eyes in its tail?
11. Explain the meaning of the following words and expressions: *argus-eyes, halcyon days, cynosure.*
12. How may Juno be recognized in art?
13. What was Juno's Greek name?

A QUESTION FOR THE CURIOUS

When Rosalind in Shakespeare's *As You Like It* assumed the character of a young man, what name did she choose?

OPTIONAL

FOR THOSE WHO HAVE TIME FOR FURTHER STUDY

A. ADDITIONAL READING

I. In Textbooks Dealing with Classical Mythology

1. Where Juno spent her youth; also details about her marriage, Gay., p. 22 (sec. 26), including a mention of her wedding presents; B., 145.

2. How Juno presented her "best" gift to the sons of Cydippe, Gay.,
    pp. 80–81 (sec. 64).
3. Details of the story of Halcyone, Gay., pp. 175–177; B., 69–76.
4. Io's way of disclosing her identity to her father, B., 29.

For other references, see the Appendix, pages xxviii ff., under topics
mentioned in this chapter.

II. In Books in General

1. Many passages in the *Iliad*, translated by Lang, Leaf, and Myers.
   Examples:
   (1) Juno quarrels with Jupiter, I, pp. 18–20; IV, pp. 64–65.
   (2) Juno goes forth to battle in her war-chariot, V, pp. 104–106.
2. Many passages in Vergil's *Aeneid*, translated by John Conington
   (Scott, Foresman edition). Examples:
   (1) Why Juno hated the Trojans and sought to prevent their
       settlement in Italy, I, ll. 14–39.
   (2) Juno causes the destruction by fire of four of Aeneas' ships, V,
       ll. 633–677. Books VII–XII contain many illustrations
       of Juno's attempts to thwart the plans of the Trojans.
3. Passages in Ovid's *Metamorphoses*, translated in the Loeb Classical
   Library (G. P. Putnam's Sons). Examples:
   (1) Details of the story about Io and Argus, I, pp. 45–51 (Latin
       lines 601–698).
   (2) How Juno punished Callisto, II, pp. 93–95 (Latin lines 466–
       507).
4. Seymour's *Life in the Homeric Age*, pp. 425–426 (The Macmillan
   Company).
5. Poems on page 81, the titles of which are starred.

B. Memorize One of These Quotations

And godlike Ganymede, most beautiful
Of men; the gods beheld and caught him up
To heaven, so beautiful was he, to pour
The wine to Jove, and ever dwell with him.

> HOMER, *Iliad*, XX, 293–296, Bryant's Translation

Immortal Hebe, fresh with bloom divine,
The golden goblet crowns with purple wine.

> HOMER, *Iliad*, IV, 4–5, Pope's Translation

C. FURTHER STUDY OF LITERARY ALLUSION

In case you are interested in seeing more clearly how good writers make use of the myths, look up the following references:

Argus: Dickens' *Our Mutual Friend*, p. 349 (Hamilton Book Company, 1908). **Callisto:** Hewlett's *Leto's Child*, p. 41 (Scribners). **Cynosura** (the star): Milton's *Comus*, 341–342. **Ganymede:** Tennyson's *Palace of Art*, 121–122. **Hebe:** Dumas's *Count of Monte Cristo*, p. 316 (A. L. Burt); George Eliot's *Adam Bede*, chap. ix, p. 100 (Scribners). **Iris:** Keats's *Endymion*, p. 234 (Everyman's Library). **Juno:** Locke's *Septimus*, p. 19 (John Lane); Alcott's *Little Women*, p. 480 (Little, Brown, 1910).

D. PROJECTS FOR INDIVIDUAL OR GROUP WORK

To be selected from the list of projects on pages xx–xxvi.

POEMS FOR REFERENCE

FULLER, S. MARGARET	* Ganymede to His Eagle
LOWELL, JAMES RUSSELL	* Hebe
MOORE, THOMAS	* Fall of Hebe
NOEL, RODEN B.	Ganymede
THOMAS, EDITH M.	* Homesickness of Ganymede; *also* The Kingfisher

Fig. 35. Juno's bird

Photograph by Alinari

Fig. 36.

Head of Jupiter, commonly called the " Otricoli Zeus "

JUPITER

(Zeus)

We have already read the account of how Ju'pi ter's father attempted to destroy his children, and how the mother succeeded **Jupiter's** in saving one of them without any suspicion on the **infancy** part of her husband. Knowing that she must guard most carefully the fact that the infant Jupiter had escaped death, she sent the child to the island of Crete, where he was nursed by a goat named Am al the'a and fed upon honey which the wild bees brought to his cave. When he cried, the mountain spirits drowned the noise by clashing their shields and weapons so that if Cro'nus, Jupiter's father, happened to be in the neighborhood, he might not discover the infant and so realize that he had been tricked.

As has been said in the introductory chapter on the gods, Jupiter was regarded as the supreme ruler of the world and, in **Supreme** addition to this general oversight, was charged par- **ruler and god** ticularly with responsibility for the sky. In fact the **of the sky** Greeks often spoke of him as " Father Sky." In the latter connection he gave day and night to men, sent the snow and the rain, and caused the winds to blow and the dark storm clouds to gather. The lightning with the crash of thunder that followed was but an expression of his anger.

But however interesting Jupiter may have been to mortals because of his control of the heavens, he meant much more to them as the god of human relationships in general. He was the protector of the state and the supporter of the law and order which makes its existence possible. Kings and rulers looked to him for guidance and feared his wrath when they betrayed their people or in any way violated justice. Men who cared for his respect were slow to break their oath or to deal unjustly, either in the market place or in the conduct of their business elsewhere. Travelers reverenced him, for he punished violations of hospitality, and people rarely forgot the rights of friendship when they thought of Jupiter. The family and indeed all social institutions were in his care. In fact, the Greeks looked upon this god as the protector of the human relations of civilized man.

Just how kindly Jupiter was on occasion and how greatly he esteemed the simple virtues of even the poorest of his subjects, is shown by the story of Phi le'mon and Bau'cis.

One day two seemingly weary travelers stopped for rest and refreshment in a small village. From house to house they went, **Philemon and** asking for hospitality but meeting only rebuffs; the **Baucis** doors were closed in their faces, or some rude words forbade their entrance.

At last they came to one of the poorest huts in the village, and notwithstanding the evidences of extreme poverty about the place, asked for food and drink.   An aged man named Philemon greeted them in the friendliest way, and behind him was his wife Baucis, equally eager to welcome them.   The best that the couple had was put before their guests, and although the table had to be propped up, and in spite of the fact that the dishes were of the cheapest sort, the strangers felt that no greater respect or more sincere kindliness could have been shown them if they had come in the garb of kings.

La Valley   © H. K. T.; Gramstorff Brothers

Fig. 37. Baucis and Philemon

Baucis and Philemon decide to kill their one goose in order to provide food for their guests; but Jupiter intervenes and saves the fowl.

Naturally Philemon and Baucis had not the least idea that their guests were gods, one Jupiter and the other Mercury.   Nor did they realize it until they saw a flood sweep away the town with its inhospitable inhabitants, and observed a stately temple appear where once their hut had stood.   And when they learned that for the rest of their lives they were to be attendants in this shrine, their gratitude to their former guests knew no bounds.

When the time came to die they were changed into trees, Philemon into an oak and Baucis into a linden; for by such a transformation had Jupiter answered their prayer that they might not be separated even in death.

While Jupiter's severity in destroying those who were regardless of the laws of hospitality is illustrated in the account given above,

there is another story which brings out even more clearly his
determination to have the world peopled by a just and god-
fearing race.

Long ago in the period of time called the Iron Age, men became
very wicked. Jupiter saw no remedy for the evil of the world
Deucalion except to destroy the human race. He therefore
and Pyrrha summoned the rain clouds and called upon Nep'tune
to send forth all of the waters under his command, the wide ocean,
the seas, and all the rivers. Soon the land was entirely sub-
merged and of all the people who had been living upon the earth
at that time only Deu ca'li on and Pyr'rha remained alive.

This pious man and wife had been warned by Pro me'theus of
the doom that was approaching and had thus been able to provide
beforehand for their safety. They had built a chest large enough
to hold them and the supply of food which would be necessary to
keep them alive until the waters should subside. When the flood
began, they stepped into the chest and let it drift where it would
on the limitless sea. Finally it touched ground and came to rest
on the summit of a mountain. Little by little the waters receded
and the land began to emerge.

Deucalion and Pyrrha, seeing the desolation on all sides and
realizing that there was not a human being upon the earth to
keep them company, were in great despair. It seemed that they
must die too. But as they had always been accustomed to look to
the gods for help, so now they prayed for guidance. This answer
came : "Throw the bones of your parent behind you." But what
could this possibly mean? Surely nothing so irreligious as to
disturb the resting place of their fathers and mothers! After
much reflection it occurred to them that the earth was the great
parent of every one. They therefore picked up stones and threw
them over their shoulders. At once those cast by Deucalion became men and those thrown by Pyrrha were changed into women.

Jupiter was delighted to have as ancestors of the human race persons who esteemed the gods so highly.

The Greeks held the king of the gods in great honor and built for him many huge temples, among them one at O lym′pi a in **Jupiter honored at Olympia** southwestern Greece. In this was a wonderful statue of the god, forty feet in height, made of ivory and gold by a great artist named Phid′i as. Men came from all parts of the Greek world to see this statue because, as one of them said, to look upon the image made one a better per-

Fig. 38. Zeus

This head is supposed by many to be a copy of the head of the famous statue of Zeus, made by Phidias for the temple of the god at Olympia.

son. So inspiring was it and so magnificent that it was regarded as one of the Seven Wonders of the ancient world.

In order to pay still greater tribute to Jupiter, the Greeks established the O lym′pic Games. These were held every four **The Olympic Games** years beginning in 776 B.C., and became increasingly important as time went on. Not only did the most famous athletes in the whole world compete, but great musicians, writers, sculptors, and painters contended for the distinction of being first in their special fields.

These occasions became politically important since they afforded opportunities for an interchange of opinion among the leading men of the Greek world. In fact, so much a part of the

Reconstruction by Gatteschi

Fig. 39. Temple of Jupiter

The Romans honored Jupiter by building for him this splendid temple on the
Capitoline Hill in Rome.

national life did these games become that, after the fourth
century B.C., time was reckoned by the intervals between them,
each four-year period being called an "O lym′pi ad."

The Romans, too, quite as much as the Greeks, held Jupiter
in the highest honor.   And if we had been living in Rome or near

Jupiter worshiped at Rome
it, especially in the earlier days of its history, we
should have seen men climbing the Alban Mount
once a year to take part in a celebration in his honor.
And even in later times we should have been quite familiar with
the splendid triumphal processions which made their way through
the Roman Fo′rum and up the slopes of the Cap′i to line Hill
to the doors of the great temple of Jupiter Op′ti mus Max′i mus,
where the victorious general, returning from war, alighted from

his chariot to offer sacrifice and to render thanks. Nor would it have seemed strange to us that Roman consuls and other officials of the state sought this temple on many occasions, for the Romans always felt that Jupiter had a special interest in their affairs and was guiding the destinies of the race.

Macaulay's lines help us to visualize the splendid pageant which was doubtless familiar to every inhabitant of Rome:

Blest and thrice blest the Roman
Who sees Rome's brightest day,
Who sees that long victorious pomp
Wind down the Sacred Way,
And through the bellowing Forum
And round the Suppliant's Grove,
Up to the everlasting gates
Of Capitolian Jove.

Lays of Ancient Rome, "Prophecy of Capys," xxx, 261-268

Notwithstanding the fact that Juno was his lawful wife, Jupiter frequently contracted alliances with mortals as well as divinities and many children were born to him. It seems strange that the Greeks and the Romans should have so highly honored a god who was so careless of the rites of marriage. The following theories have been advanced in explanation of these stories about him.

How explain Jupiter's many unions with both divinities and mortals?

The Greek nation was made up of various peoples who had not always lived together. Each tribe of course had its own account of the chief god and his wife, which was remembered long after the union with other tribes had been brought about. Therefore, when they began to call these gods Jupiter, they had many versions at hand of the story about his marriage.

Moreover, prominent families liked to have it thought that they had descended from divine ancestors, particularly from

Jupiter. So they cherished any tradition which connected them with the king of the gods.

Then, too, some of Jupiter's unions should be regarded as symbolical of certain facts of nature. For example, as god of the rain and the sun he had to marry Ce'res, the goddess of grain, so that the crops might flourish and provide man with food.

IN THE WORLD OF TODAY

I. In Literary Allusion

Great Jove, to whose almighty throne
Both gods and mortals homage pay.

BYRON, From the *Prometheus Vinctus* of Aeschylus, 1–2

Jove's thunder roars, heaven trembles all around.

POPE, *Rape of the Lock*, V, 49

II. In Words and Expressions

Jo'vi al comes from the word "Jove," one of the forms of the name Jupiter. It means, according to the dictionary, "born under the lucky planet, Jupiter, and hence happy and healthy."

People who are addicted to a mild form of swearing are often heard to say, **"By Jove,"** a form of expression which would be quite familiar to a Greek or a Roman.

It sometimes rains on the occasion of a football or baseball game. At such times the sporting page of the newspaper is very likely to refer to this misfortune as "the unkindness of **Jupiter Plu'vi us."** The Romans used this title for Jupiter as god of rain, deriving the word *pluvius* from the verb *pluit*, meaning "it rains."

In a certain district in central Greece, the peasants sometimes say during a drought, "Rain, grandfather!" This reminds the classical student of the prayer of the A the'ni ans of old, "Rain,

dear Zeus, on the cornlands of the Athenians and their pastures! "
But when we pray for rain, we ask that rain be sent and do not use a personal subject as did the ancient Greeks.

Raphael (Vatican, Rome)
Fig. 40. Thursday or " Jove's Day."

Our word "Thursday," coming to us in its present form from old English meaning "Thor's Day," is really adapted from the late Latin of "Jupiter's Day" — Thor and Jupiter representing a similar power. Since the name "Jove" is another form for the word "Jupiter," it is easy to see how the French **jeudi,** the Italian **giovedì,** and the Spanish **jueves** have continued to preserve the term "Jupiter's Day" for this fifth day of the week.

The Romans identified an I tal′ic god called Sat′urn with the father of Zeus, whom they spoke of as Cronus. Some details concerning him appear under the topic, "In Other Connections."
The expression **a sat′ur nine smile** (not a cheerful smile) perhaps finds its origin in the idea of melancholy which has become associated with the planet Saturn. At least, astrologers assert that persons born under the planet Saturn are far from lively in their dispositions.

Still another trace of this

Raphael (Vatican, Rome)
Fig. 41. Saturday or "Saturn's Day"

Italic god (associated by the Romans with agriculture) is found in our word **Saturday,** which in Rome was called "Saturn's Day."

Raph'a el's design on page 90 shows this divinity carrying a sickle to indicate his connection with the harvest.

When we have been boasting about our good fortune in some connection or other, we sometimes " touch wood " in order to avoid what the Greeks called **the vengeance of Nem'e sis.** This divinity, long wooed by Jupiter and at last won, was accustomed to elevate the lowly and to humble the proud. She did not like to see among men an excess either of misfortune or prosperity; it was her duty to preserve the golden mean. Therefore she sometimes compensated the poor for their sad lot and, on the other hand, punished those whom conspicuous success had rendered haughty and arrogant.

It is doubtless our fear of a change in our good luck that leads us to try to avert it by the foolish method mentioned above. But it would not have seemed foolish to a Greek or a Roman, for even though his method of propitiating Nemesis might differ from ours, he would understand at once the motive that prompted our act.

III. In Other Connections

The Roman Saturnalia and Our Mardi Gras

In February or March the Mardi Gras is celebrated at New Orleans. This is an occasion when the whole city gives itself over to pleasure. There are elaborate processions, dancing, feasting, and much license on the part of individuals who take part in them. Such a festival is the descendant of the celebration in Rome in honor of Saturn known as the Sat ur na'li a, a period of wild merrymaking in which the Romans indulged about the middle of December (we frequently speak today of a " saturnalia " of crime in some big city). The custom of exchanging gifts at this season doubtless survives in our habit of giving presents at Christmas.

A Name for a Planet

The largest body in the solar system, except the sun, is Jupiter. Its moons are called Io, Callisto, Europa, and Ganymede.

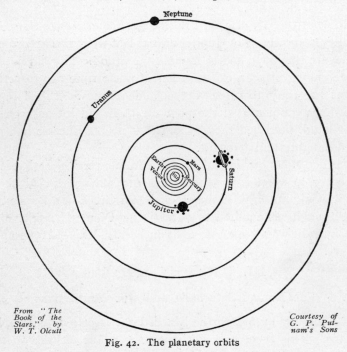

From "The Book of the Stars," by W. T. Olcutt

Courtesy of G. P. Putnam's Sons

Fig. 42. The planetary orbits

Why We Have Olympic Games

In commemoration of the Greek custom, it was proposed some thirty-five years ago to hold Olympic Games every four years, but not twice successively in the same place. The first ones were held in 1896 in Athens. However, only one feature of the Greek Olympic Games has been retained, namely, athletics. We have not imitated the ancient world in making the occasion interesting for rivalry along literary and artistic lines as well.

How the Continent of Europe Received Its Name

Eu ro'pa was a maiden whom Jupiter once saw as she was playing in the fields with her companions. So great was his admiration for her beauty that he determined to carry the girl

Veronese (Capitoline Museum, Rome)   *Photograph by Alinari*

Fig. 43. Europa and the bull

The white bull is really Jupiter in disguise; but Europa, who has climbed upon his back, does not know this.

away. In order to disarm any suspicion on her part of the plan which he had in mind, he changed himself into a white bull and by various devices tempted the girl to mount upon his back. He then ran swiftly away, finally reaching a land which in honor of the maiden he named Europa. Some details in connection with this story have been related in the chapter called " Cadmus."

In Decorative Design

Many decorative designs recall the story of Jupiter.

From the Raguenet drawings

Fig. 44. A building in Paris constructed for the Ministry of War bears this decorative design.   A glance shows the Gorgon's head — a symbol for war and only a modern representation of the head which appeared on Jupiter's aegis.   (For an illustration, see Figure 65.)

In connection with this picture, note the rods and fasces, a design which still stands for the authority of government as it did in Roman times.   Our newer ten-cent piece bears out this statement.   A conspicuous survival of this emblem is also seen in the fact that the ruling party in Italy, known as the " Fascisti," has adopted it as its insignia.

The oak leaves represent another classical symbol associated with the power of government.   This comes from the myth that the oak tree was sacred to Jupiter, king of gods and men.

QUESTIONS FOR REVIEW

1. In addition to being supreme ruler, for what particular duty was Jupiter responsible?

2. What relation did he have with human kings?

3. Relate the story which shows how Jupiter rewarded or punished human beings according to the way in which they observed the laws of hospitality.

4. What event somewhat similar to that of Noah and the Ark occurred in the Iron Age?

5. What famous sculptor made a wonderful statue of Jupiter, and where was it set up?

6. What were the Olympic Games, and why were they so important to the Greeks?

7. In what way did the Romans honor Jupiter?

8. What day in the week recalls Jupiter? What do the French, the Italians, and the Spanish call it?

9. What Roman celebration was the forerunner of our modern Mardi Gras? What was the nature of it?

10. How is the name of the continent Europe connected with classical mythology?

11. Account for the following words and expressions: *jovial, Jupiter Pluvius, Saturday.*

12. What were the emblems of Jupiter?

13. What decorative designs recall the story of Jupiter?

14. Reread the introductory chapters dealing with the gods in general, in order to gather up details about Jupiter's birth and the way in which he became king of gods and men.

15. What was Jupiter's Greek name?

OPTIONAL

FOR THOSE WHO HAVE TIME FOR FURTHER STUDY

A. ADDITIONAL READING

I. In Textbooks Dealing with Classical Mythology

1. Details concerning the story of Europa, Gay., pp. 68–70 (sec. 59).
2. Story of Antiope, Gay., p. 75 (sec. 62).
3. Saturn and the Golden Age, Gay., pp. 10, 52, 59; B., 9–10.
4. Oracle at Dodona, Gay., pp. 19–20 (sec. 24).
5. The Graces described, B., 8.
6. Details of the story about Philemon and Baucis, B., 49–51.
7. Account of the giants who warred against Jupiter, Gay., p. 7.

II. In Books in General

1. "The Miraculous Pitcher" in *The Wonder Book* by Nathaniel Hawthorne, pp. 96–113 (Everyman's Library) ; a story about Philemon and Baucis.

2. "The Dragon's Teeth" in
Tanglewood Tales by Na-
thaniel Hawthorne, pp.
194–226 (Everyman's Li-
brary) ; Europa's story
mentioned.

Fig. 46. The Distinguished Service
Medal

From the Raguenet drawings

Fig. 45. This eagle, designed for
Napoleon, represents imperial power
and continues the tradition of Roman
times. Notice that it grasps the thunderbolt — a symbol for Jupiter's power to
destroy his enemies.

This medal bears the insignia of the
United States. The eagle is still the symbol for governmental power. Note that
the bird is not only grasping arrows (a
representation of war as embodied in the
thunderbolt), but that he is also holding
the olive branch of peace.

3. Passages from the translation of Ovid's *Metamorphoses* (Loeb Classical
Library, G. P. Putnam's Sons).
   (1) Jupiter's palace in the sky, I, p. 15 (Latin lines, 168–176).
   (2) Story of the flood in detail, I, pp. 21–31 (Latin lines 253–415).
   (3) Story of Baucis and Philemon, VIII, pp. 449–457 (Latin lines,
   624–724).

4. Many passages in the *Iliad*, translated by Lang, Leaf, and Myers,
Pope, Bryant, and others. For a striking example, see Bryant's
translation, XV, 216–275, containing an account of the way in

which Jupiter comes to the assistance of the Trojans at a critical moment.

5. Seymour's *Life in the Homeric Age*, pp. 421–424 (The Macmillan Company).

6. An account of the Olympic Games in *Greek Life and Thought*, pp. 69–71, by La Rue Van Hook (Columbia University Press). See also Gardiner's *Greek Athletics, Sports, and Festivals* (The Macmillan Company).

B. Lines to Be Memorized

He whose all-conscious eyes the world behold,
The eternal Thunderer sat, enthroned in gold.
High heaven the footstool of his feet he makes,
And wide beneath him all Olympus shakes.

HOMER, *Iliad*, Pope's Translation

C. Further Study of Literary Allusion

If you are interested in seeing more clearly how good writers make use of the Greek myths, look up the following references :

Europa: Tennyson's *Palace of Art*, 117–120. **Jove:** Spenser's *Faerie Queene*, I, Canto IV, 11 ; Shakespeare's *Hamlet*, Act I, Sc. 2, 56 ; Christopher Morley's *Thunder on the Left* (Doubleday, Page). **Jupiter:** O. Henry's *Four Million*, p. 165 (Doubleday, Page) ; Alcott's *Little Women*, p. 162 (Little, Brown) ; Dumas's *Count of Monte Cristo*, Vol. I, p. 390 (A. L. Burt). **Nemesis:** Thackeray's *The Newcomes*, p. 323 (Everyman's Library) ; Jacob Riis's *How the Other Half Lives*, p. 16 (Scribners).

D. Projects for Individual or Group Work

To be selected from the list of projects on pages xx–xxvi, in case the subject matter of this chapter lends itself readily to any one of them.

POEMS FOR REFERENCE

DUNSANY, LORD   Nemesis (*Saturday Review of Literature*, July 17, 1926)
SAXE, JOHN G.   * Jupiter and His Children
SWIFT, JONATHAN   * Baucis and Philemon (burlesque)

Fig. 47. Mars in repose

MARS

(A´res)

MARS was the god of war. The Greeks looked upon him as young, impetuous, and ever thirsting for blood. He took a savage delight in slaughter, and the hordes of slain upon the battlefield filled him with a fierce joy. In the poems of Ho´mer we find such epithets as these applied to him: " scourge of mortals," " piercer of shields," " the blood-stained one." Even his own father, Jupiter, shrank from him in horror. " Most hateful to me art thou of all the gods that dwell in O lym´pus; thou ever lovest strife and war and battles," he once said to his son, and this attitude on the part of the king of heaven was reflected in the feelings of most of the other gods and goddesses.

The god of war

But there was one of the O lym´pi an divinities who did not share the opinion of the others, and that was Venus. In fact she was so strongly attracted to Mars that she allowed him to become her lover, in spite of the fact that she was already wedded to Vul´-can. Undoubtedly, as the myths lead us to suspect, the goddess yielded the more easily to the persuasions of Mars, because she was tired of her union with her lame and unsightly husband.

Such a picture of Mars as is indicated in the first paragraph of this chapter is hard to reconcile with the way in which the Greeks in later centuries represented him in art. For example, the illustration on page 98 shows a handsome and somewhat thoughtful young man. Perhaps this change is due to the fact that as the Greeks became more cultured, they saw in this war-god something finer than mere delight in the carnage of the battlefield.

The Romans were preëminently a warlike people; therefore it is not strange that Mars became their patron god. They built temples for him and honored him by many celebrations during the year. One of the most famous parts of the city of Rome was called the Field of Mars (Campus Martius, pronounced Mar'shius in English), and it was here that the army was reviewed and the spoils of war dedicated after the return of the soldiers from some successful campaign.

How the Romans regarded Mars

A second reason for the devotion of the Romans to the god of war is suggested in the story of Rom'u lus and Re'mus, for Mars was their divine ancestor.

After the Greeks had destroyed Troy, the survivors of the Trojans under the leadership of Ae ne'as came to Italy, where their descendants in the course of time built a city called Alba Longa. One of their kings was named Nu'mi tor. He had a brother, A mu'li us, who was ambitious and desired the throne for himself. His first step in securing it was to deprive Numitor of his kingly power. Next he took precautions against future trouble by seeing to it that his brother should have no heirs who might sometime or other claim their rights to the kingship. A son was killed and a daughter, named Rhe'a Sil'vi a, was made a priestess of Vesta; for in this way Amulius thought to prevent her from bearing children.

Romulus and Remus and the founding of Rome

But the scheme of Amulius was ruined by an unexpected occurrence. The god Mars fell in love with Rhea Silvia and became the father of her twin sons, Romulus and Remus.

When this fact was learned, Amulius resolved to destroy the infants. Therefore he had them put into a rudely constructed box or trough, which was cast adrift upon the Ti'ber River. The thought that they might escape drowning never occurred to the king. But the gods who were looking after the destiny of Rome saw to it that the box drifted to the banks of the stream. Here the children were finally found by a shepherd named Faus'tu lus.

Rubens (Palace of the Conservatori, Rome)   Photograph by Alinari

Fig. 48. The shepherd discovers Romulus and Remus

To discover two sturdy infants in this wild region was surprising enough, but Faustulus was still more astonished to see that they were nestling close to the body of a wolf, which was feeding them as though they were her cubs. He took them to his home, where they lived until they reached manhood.

Legend says that they finally gained possession of their grandfather's kingdom and later founded the city of Rome on the Seven Hills not far from Alba Longa.

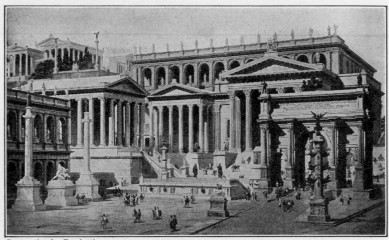

Restoration by Becchetti

Fig. 49. Northern end of the Roman Forum much as it looked in the time of the Empire

Macaulay in his *Lays of Ancient Rome* tells the story of Romulus and Remus. The lines that follow are quoted from it.

> The troubled river knew them,
>   And smoothed his yellow foam,
> And gently rocked the cradle
>   That bore the fate of Rome.
> The ravening she-wolf knew them,
>   And licked them o'er and o'er,
> And gave them of her own fierce milk,
>   Rich with raw flesh and gore.
>
> *   *   *   *   *   *   *
>
> "From sunrise unto sunset
>   All earth shall hear thy fame;
> A glorious city thou shalt build,
>   And name it by thy name.

> And there, unquenched through ages,
>   Like Vesta's sacred fire,
> Shall live the spirit of thy nurse,
>   The spirit of thy sire."
>   "The Prophecy of Capys," V, 33–44; XV, 125–132

IN THE WORLD OF TODAY

I. IN LITERARY ALLUSION

> The mailed Mars shall on his altar sit,
> Up to the ears in blood.
>   SHAKESPEARE, *Henry IV:* Part I, Act IV, Sc. 1, 116–117

During the World War current literature contained countless allusions to Mars.   The poem from which the following lines are quoted, although written just before the war, is characteristic of others.   The young English officer who wrote it was afterwards killed.

ARES, GOD OF WAR

> Here from the wooded haunt of nymph and faun
>   The hidden guns peer forth across the hills;
>   Their wheels are on the trampled daffodils,
> And so they wait the coming of the dawn.
> In dappled shadows where the fairy weaves
>   On grasses tall his web of sparkling lace,
> The gunners lie, their heads upon the sheaves:
>   White falls the moon on many a sunburnt face
>   That ere the day shall feel another god's embrace.
>   *   *   *   *   *   *   *
> The other gods are weaker; thou alone
>   Dost break the king and bend the emperor's knee:
>   Lower than unto Christ they bow to thee,
> Lord of the slave and guardian of the free,

Steel-hearted A're̲s, shaker of the throne :
Young god of battle, restless lover, hail !
For once a man has seen thine eyes aflame,
And mounted on the horses of the gale,
Death is a nothing, life an empty name ;
Arise and lead us ere our blood be tame,
O Lord of Thunder, Ares of the Crimson Mail !

LIEUTENANT HERBERT ASQUITH, *The Volunteers*

II. IN WORDS AND EXPRESSIONS

The word **martial,** pertaining to war, comes from Mars, the god of war.

Very few people stop to think that the word " Tuesday " really means " Mars' Day." It comes about in the following

Raphael (Vatican, Rome)

Fig. 50. Tuesday or " Mars' Day "

way. Our English ancestors of Teutonic stock coined a name for Tuesday in their language, which meant " the day of their chief god." Since they always conceived their most powerful divinity as a war-god, and since the Romans long before had associated Mars with the day in question, the Anglo-Saxons came to look upon it in the same way, namely, as a day belonging to this war-god. The French, Italians, and Spanish, who have continued to use derivations of the Latin name, call this day **mardi, martedì,** and **martes,** respectively.

One of the famous places in the world is the A re op'a gus at Athens, otherwise known as Mars' Hill. In ancient Greek times cases of murder were tried there, and on other occasions, too, it served as a seat of justice.   The word has come to mean with us a tribunal whose decisions carry great weight.   It is not unusual, for example, to speak of the " **Areopagus** of public opinion." But it is probable that the word is not derived from Ares, the Greek name for Mars (although those who translated it " Mars' Hill " thought that it was), but from the Greek word ἀρά, meaning " spirit," or Ἀρά, a " curse " or a Fury.   From early times a cave upon this hill was associated with the Furies.

The month of **March** was so named because Mars, the patron god of the Romans, was a war-god, and spring campaigns usually began about that time.

The Roman year once began with this month, and a poet explains in quite another way just why it stands for " war."

> I Martius am !   Once first and now the third !
>   To lead the year was my appointed place ;
> A mortal dispossessed me by a word,
>   And set there Janus with the double face.
> Hence I make war on all the human race ;
>   I shake the cities with my hurricanes ;
> I flood the rivers and their banks efface,
>   And drown the farms and hamlets with my rains.
>
> LONGFELLOW, *The Poet's Calendar*

III. IN OTHER CONNECTIONS

A Name for a Much Discussed Planet

One of the planets is called Mars.   We hear a great deal about this planet, because some people think it is inhabited and that some day we shall be in communication with its inhabitants.

The almanac, in which we look up the location of the planets at certain times of the year, uses signs to indicate these heavenly bodies. Here is the symbol for the planet Mars, ♂. The design is popularly supposed to represent the shield and spear of the war-god.[1]

Romulus and Remus in Italy

In Italy, and especially in Rome, the design of the bronze wolf with the infants Romulus and Remus is still much in evidence, and the Italian government actually keeps some live wolves on the Cap'i to line Hill at Rome in memory of the tradition concerning the founding of the city. Other specific illustrations of the survival of this legend are seen in the statuary at the city gates of Si e'na, in which Romulus and Remus appear with the wolf, and in the design on the postage stamps of the new state of Fiu'me.

QUESTIONS FOR REVIEW

1. What were the characteristics of the god of war?

2. What difference was there in the way he was regarded by the Greeks and by the Romans?

3. (1) Give a full account of the founding of Rome as the myths give it.

(2) In what way was Mars connected with the important event?

4. What illustrations of the tradition of the founding of Rome may be seen today in that city and elsewhere in Italy?

5. What month is associated with Mars and why was it so named?

6. How did Tuesday receive its name?

7. Explain the word *martial* by using it in a sentence.

8. How is Mars represented as a rule in pictures and statues?

---

[1] See Funk and Wagnalls's Dictionary under "Mars."

MARS

107

OPTIONAL

FOR THOSE WHO HAVE TIME FOR FURTHER STUDY

A. ADDITIONAL READING

I. In Textbooks Dealing with Classical Mythology

Ceremony at Rome in connection with Mars' shield, Gay., p. 471 (sec. 28).

For other references, see the Appendix, pages xxviii ff., under topics mentioned in this chapter.

II. In Books in General

1. Many passages in the *Iliad*, translated by Lang, Leaf, and Myers, Pope, Bryant, and others.
2. Seymour's *Life in the Homeric Age*, pp. 436–438 (The Macmillan Company).

B. LINES TO BE MEMORIZED

But thy father loves the clashing
Of broadsword and of shield;
He loves to drink the stream that reeks
From the fresh battlefield;
He smiles a smile more dreadful
Than his own dreadful frown,
When he sees the thick black cloud of smoke
Go up from the conquered town.

MACAULAY, *Lays of Ancient Rome*, "The Prophecy of Capys," XIX, 157–164

C. FURTHER STUDY OF LITERARY ALLUSION

If you are interested in seeing more clearly the way in which good writers make use of the Greek myths, look up the following references:

Mars: Shakespeare's *Hamlet*, Act I, Sc. 2, 57; also Act III, Sc. 4, 57; Keats's *Endymion*, p. 231 (Everyman's Library); Byrne's *Blizzard Snow*, Literary Digest, April 24, 1926; Black's *Judith Shakespeare*, p. 207 (Harpers). **Romulus and Remus:** Thoreau's *Essay on Walking*.

D. PROJECTS FOR INDIVIDUAL AND GROUP WORK

To be selected from the list on pages xx–xxvi, in case the subject matter of this chapter lends itself readily to any one of them.

Fig. 51. Mercury descends to the earth

MERCURY
(Her'mes)

MER'CU RY, son of Jupiter and Ma'ia, was eager and enthusiastic, the prince of story-tellers, an eloquent orator, and a wonderful athlete. He had the reputation also of being **A versatile god** very shrewd at a bargain and not above telling a few white lies when the occasion seemed to demand it. The Greeks also worshiped him as the god of shepherds, the protector of heralds and travelers, and as the guide of souls in their journeys to the Lower World. But it is as messenger to the gods that he is chiefly remembered today.

Mercury was only a few hours old, so the myths say, when he walked out of the cave on Mt. Cyl le'ne in Ar ca'di a where he **A precocious child** was born, to see whether he could find anything interesting to do. Just outside he found a tortoise, from the shell of which he straightway constructed a lyre, although very crude in shape. This was the first instance, the Greeks thought, of a marked tendency in this god toward inventiveness, and an illustration of his practical bent of mind.

The god was extremely fond of playing jokes and very skilful in avoiding unpleasant results from them. He was still an infant **A fondness for jokes** when he conceived the notion of stealing some of the cattle belonging to his brother A pol'lo. Choosing a time when the owner was away, he not only drove off the animals, but killed and roasted two of them. Apollo was very angry and could obtain satisfaction only by securing the aid of Jupiter.

But such was the charm of the boy that even the stern father had to laugh at his witty excuses. The matter was finally settled by making a gift of the lyre to Apollo, in return for which Mercury was allowed to become keeper of the cattle. Apollo, moreover, extorted a promise from his young brother that never again would he try to play such a trick upon him, and expressed his

A. Idrac (Luxembourg Museum, Paris)

Fig. 52. The origin of the caduceus

A myth thus explains the origin of the caduceus: Mercury found two serpents in real or playful combat and, in order to separate them, placed his wand between them. Immediately the serpents ceased fighting and coiled themselves around the staff.

pleasure in Mercury's apparent change of heart by presenting the boy with the ca du′ce us (pronounced ca-du′shius), a magic wand which became one of the symbols of this god. However, this explanation regarding the origin of the caduceus is not the only one that has come down to us.

The practically-minded Romans honored Mercury principally as the god of trade and commerce. They associated with him the

qualities of strength, keenness of wit, power of persuasion,
ability to entertain, and a liking for adventure. All
these characteristics they thought were conducive
to success in business. They also regarded him as
skilled in trickery and sometimes as a mischievous thief.

Mercury among the Romans

Mercury is generally represented as a handsome young man,
wearing winged sandals and often a winged cap, and
carrying the caduceus — a staff about which conven-
tionalized serpents are twined.

Mercury in art

IN THE WORLD OF TODAY

I. In Literary Allusion

The herald Mercury
New lighted on a heaven-kissing hill.

SHAKESPEARE, *Hamlet*, Act III, Sc. 4, 58–59

Foot-feather'd Mercury appear'd sublime
Beyond the tall tree tops; and in less time
Than shoots the slanted hail-storm, down he dropp'd
Toward the ground; but rested not, not stopp'd
One moment from his home; only the sward
He with his wand light touch'd, and heavenward
Swifter than sight was gone.

KEATS, *Endymion*, IV, 331–337

II. In Words and Expressions

We often say that a person has a **mercurial** temperament.
This means that, like Mercury, he is light-hearted, active,
changeable, and sometimes, too, a little tricky.

It is interesting to know that such words as **merchant** and **commerce** come from the same root as that in the name of Mercury.

Raphael (Vatican, Rome)
Fig. 53. Wednesday or "Mercury's Day"

The word "Wednesday" comes to us in its present form from an old English form meaning "O'din's day." But this day was just the same as the one which the Romans called "Mercury's day." The French, Italian, and Spanish words for Wednesday, namely, **mercredi, mercoledî,** and **miércoles,** preserve their Latin origin.

III. IN OTHER CONNECTIONS

As a Scientific Term

There is a silvery-white substance called "mercury" which is used in thermometers and in other ways. It is interesting to speculate as to why it was so named. Perhaps the resemblance to the god lies in the fact that Mercury as a messenger was "mobile," that is, able to move rapidly from one place to another, a characteristic which this substance possesses in a marked degree.

A Well-known Symbol of the Medical Department of the United States Army

The World War made every one familiar with the wand or ca du'ce us of Mercury as the emblem of the Medical

Fig. 54. The symbol of the Medical Department of the United States Army

Department of the United States Army. It was adopted in
America in 1902. Its use in England dates
considerably farther back.

Just why the wand of Mercury with its
two serpents (Aes cu la'pi us, god of healing,
had only *one*) was selected as a symbol of
the medical staff of the army is hard to
understand, and no one seems to be able
to explain it to the entire satisfaction of
scholars.

Fig. 55. The seal of
the American Women's
Hospital Association

As a Name for a Planet

The planet nearest the sun is called Mercury. Did the astron-
omer who named it happen to remember that Mercury was
Apollo's brother?

In Art and Decorative Design

Various illustrations in this chapter give
evidence that Mercury is a favorite subject
for decorative design.

A Name for Magazines

A well-known magazine published in England is called *The London Mercury*, and there
is a similar publication in France known as
Mercure de France. In America also we have
a journal called *Mercury*.

From the Raguenet drawings

Fig. 56. This is an
architectural decoration
on a Chamber of Com-
merce. This is exactly
the place for Mercury,
the god of trade, repre-
sented in this case by
his symbol, the ca-
duceus.

In England, newsboys were formerly
called " mercuries," because, like the messenger of the gods, they carried the
" news."

An Inventor of Signposts and the "Herm"

Mercury is said to have been the first to suggest setting up "signposts" at the crossroads as a convenience for travelers. They took the form of pillars narrower at the bottom than they were at the top, and because of their connection with the god

[*Praxiteles (Museum at Olympia, Greece)*   *Photograph by Alinari*

Fig. 57. The head of a famous statue of Mercury, always known as the "Hermes of Praxiteles"

(whose head they often bore) were known as "herms." The A the′ni ans were accustomed to have such pillars in front of their houses in order to speed the traveler on his way. The word "herm" is not in common use today, but those who are familiar with the world of art know that pillars similar in shape to the ones described above and bearing the head or bust of some person are often seen in art galleries or elaborate gardens, recalling the "herms" of the Athenians.

A Pioneer in Aviation

Mercury suggests the idea of flying through the air, and, in the early days of aviation, papers and magazines contained many references to him. The connection with this messenger of the gods became still closer when airplanes began to carry mail. Here is a poem from the *Chicago Tribune*, written on the occasion of the first attempt in America to carry letters through the air.

THE AËRIAL MAIL

Hail! hail! to the aërial mail
    As it speeds through the vast blue dome,
Where the winds are wild and the clouds up-piled
    Roll away from the planes like foam.
A fig for the dove with her missive of love,
    And the train on the track below,
And the liner churning the sea to yeast,
    They are all of them now too slow.

The messenger fast of the gods of the past
    Has taken the wings from his feet
And tied them, behold! to a wonderful car,
    Shining, and splendid, and fleet.
Twenty-four cents for an airplane stamp
    Shatters the time-table's fetters,
And Mercury capped and goggled and strapped,
    Is waiting to carry our letters.

Minna Irving

QUESTIONS FOR REVIEW

1. Who was Mercury and what were his particular duties?
2. What were his individual characteristics?
3. In what capacity did the Romans chiefly honor him?
4. How is he generally represented in art?
5. Mention several of his inventions.
6. How does the airplane suggest Mercury?
7. What is the position of the planet named for him?
8. What day in the week is associated with his name?
9. What is meant by a "mercurial" temperament?
10. What connection has the fluid substance in thermometers with Mercury?
11. What decorative designs suggest Mercury?

QUESTIONS FOR CONSIDERATION

1. Why did a writer in *Harper's Magazine* (1921) call Paul Revere the "Hermes (Mercury) of the American Revolution"?

2. Why should the New York Athletic Club have Mercury's foot as its seal?

3. What merit badge of the Boy Scouts bears the foot of Mercury as a decorative design?

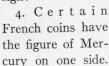

Courtesy of the New York Athletic Club

Fig. 58. The seal of an athletic club

4. Certain French coins have the figure of Mercury on one side. What does it mean in this connection?

From the Raguenet drawings

Fig. 59. Mercury as an architectural design for a bank building

5. In choosing Mercury as a design for a postage stamp, what idea did the modern Greeks have in mind?

6. How does the American Library Service make use of Mercury in its advertisements? Ask the librarian in your public library or watch the papers.

OPTIONAL

FOR THOSE WHO HAVE TIME FOR FURTHER STUDY

A. ADDITIONAL READING

I. In Textbooks Dealing with Classical Mythology
How Mercury fashioned the lyre, B., 7–8.

For other references see the Appendix, pages xxviii ff., under topics mentioned in this chapter.

II. In Books in General
1. Many passages in the *Iliad;* for example, XXIV, pp. 488–489 ff. in the translation by Lang, Leaf, and Myers (Mercury is sent to guide

the aged Priam to the tent of Achilles, where the Trojan king hopes to recover the body of his son Hector).

2. Mercury carries a message from Jupiter to the Trojan Aeneas, who is lingering at Carthage forgetful of his mission to establish his race in Italy; Vergil's *Aeneid*, IV, ll. 248–310 in the translation by Conington (Scott, Foresman edition); lines in the Latin text, 222–278.

3. Seymour's *Life in the Homeric Age*, pp. 435–436 (The Macmillan Company).

4. Poem listed below, the title of which is starred.

B. Lines to Be Memorized

See where the child of Heaven, with wingèd feet,
Runs down the slanted sunlight of the dawn.
> Shelley, *Prometheus Unbound*, Act i, 437–438

Giovanni da Bologna   *Photograph*
(National Museum,   *by Alinari*
Florence)

Fig. 60. Mercury

C. Further Study of Literary Allusion

If you are interested in seeing more clearly how good writers make use of the myths, look up the following references:

Maia's son: Milton's *Paradise Lost*, V. 285.
Mercury: Alcott's *Little Women*, p. 205 (Little, Brown); Shakespeare's *Hamlet*, Act I, Sc. 2, 58; Hardy's *Far from the Madding Crowd*, p. 300 (Harpers); Dickens' *Our Mutual Friend*, p. 277 (Hamilton Book Company); Walpole's *Harmer John*, p. 58 (George Doran); Dumas's *Count of Monte Cristo*, p. 212 (A. L. Burt).

D. Projects for Individual or Group Work

To be selected from the list of projects on pages xx–xxvi, in case the subject matter of this chapter lends itself readily to any one of them.

POEMS FOR REFERENCE

Lowell, James Russell   * The Finding of the Lyre
Shelley, Percy Bysshe   Homer's Hymn to Mercury

Fig. 61. Minerva (Athena)

MINERVA
(A the′na) [1]

MANY strange tales have come down to us about the birth of
some particular god or goddess, but certainly none of them are

The birth of
Minerva

more curious than that which is concerned with the
birth of Mi ner′va. It is said that Jupiter once felt
a severe pain in his head for which he was unable to account.
Soon, however, the goddess Minerva sprang forth, radiant in
beauty and wearing the full armor of a warrior. On her head was
a helmet and in her hand a spear, which she shook in so warlike
a fashion that all O lym′pus trembled with dread.

It may have been due to the unusual circumstances of her
birth that Jupiter felt that the goddess was peculiarly his own,
and accordingly honored her above all the other divinities. He
even allowed her to wear his awful aegis, a kind of covering for
the breast with the head of Me du′sa in the center, which was so
dreadful a sight to look upon that even the stoutest foe shrank
from it in terror.

Minerva was a stately and beautiful goddess, gray-eyed and
yellow-haired, and with all the dignity and grace that befitted the
patron divinity of the chief city of the Greeks. She represented
the finest ideals of the Greek race — learning and wisdom,

[1] That the Greek gods were never entirely identical with the Roman ones and
sometimes differed considerably has been pointed out in the introductory pages of
this book. While in most cases this fact has not made the use of the Roman names
unsuitable in connection with the stories related, it is somewhat difficult in this
particular chapter to speak of "Minerva" rather than "Athena," inasmuch as the
goddess was so closely identified with the city of Athens and the Athenians. But
in the interests of uniformity the former name has been used. We can still think
of Athena, however, as we read some of the paragraphs.

justice, righteous warfare, and all those qualities of men and nations which make for the development of civilization.   The arts
A stately goddess, typifying the highest ideals of the Greeks
of peace especially were her particular care.   Through her, men were trained in handicrafts, agriculture was made to flourish, and arts and letters were encouraged.   It was no wonder, then, that the Greeks should have held her in the highest honor and should have erected for her on the summit of one of the hills of Athens a temple so beautiful that the world has never ceased to admire it.   It is

Courtesy of the Metropolitan Museum, New York
Fig. 62.   The Parthenon (a model)

known as the Par'the non (a word which in Greek means " maidens' apartments," from παρθένος, " maiden "), and was so called because Minerva was an unwedded goddess.

Perhaps the most important festival that took place in Athens was the one known as the Great Pan ath"e nae'a, celebrated every fourth year in July in honor of this goddess.   The occasion was marked by contests in music and athletics and on the twenty-eighth of the month, the birthday of Athena, by a splendid procession through the city, formed for the purpose of carrying to the A crop'o lis a costly embroidered garment for the goddess,

upon the weaving of which the most skilful matrons and maidens
of At'ti ca had been engaged for nine months.

This procession forms the subject of one of the finest pieces of
Greek sculpture known, namely, the so-called " Parthenon
frieze." Many years ago, when the Turks were in possession of
Athens, an Englishman by the name of Lord Elgin took many
portions of this frieze to London,
where they may still be seen in the
British Museum.

Museum, Athens

But it was not only over the arts
of peace that Minerva presided;
A war goddess she was at the same
time a goddess of war.
Unlike Mars, however, she was associated with war only when it was
waged for righteous ends, and even
then her interests were primarily
concerned with the inventive power
and skill which brings victory,
rather than with the contests on
the battlefield in which strength
and valor are the dominant factors
in success.

Fig. 63. Athena mourns for the
soldiers who have died in battle

Minerva's great gift to Greece
was the olive tree, for it was by
its cultivation that the people be-
came prosperous. The story that follows explains how the first
olive tree was produced and why Minerva became the patron
goddess of Athens.

Nep'tune, the ruler of the waters, very early contested the
right of the goddess to Attica (that part of Greece in which
Athens was later the center). The question was decided in

this way: After agreeing that the country should belong to the one who could give to the inhabitants the more useful gift, Neptune and Minerva went up to a lofty hill.   Here the god struck a rock with his trident and at once a spring gushed forth; but Minerva caused an olive tree to sprout.   The twelve gods to whom the decision was left agreed that the gift of the goddess would benefit the country more than Neptune's, and therefore

The greater gift, water or the olive

the land fell to Minerva.   (Some say that the sea-god's present was a horse and not a spring.)

The hill upon which this incident took place was called the Acropolis, and it came to be regarded as the most important part of the city of Athens.

Many stories are told of Minerva's experiences with mortals.   One of them is concerned with a contest of skill in the art of spinning and weaving, a field over which the goddess of handicrafts of course presided.

Civic Museum   Photograph by
(Bologna)   Alinari

**Fig. 64. Head of the so-called
" Lemnian Athena "**

It happened that a Lyd'i an princess by the name of A rach'ne had become widely known for her work at the loom.   In fact, the myths say that even the nymphs came from their haunts in the forests and streams to gaze upon it.   It seemed that no one who had not been taught by a goddess could have acquired such amazing skill as this maiden possessed, and some wondered if Minerva herself could surpass it.   Arachne finally became so confident of her powers that she actually challenged Minerva to compete with

Arachne's punishment

her. While the goddess was offended at the girl's presumption, she accepted the challenge, and after winning the contest was generous enough to praise the work of her rival.

When Arachne, overcome by humiliation, attempted to hang herself, the goddess prevented the disaster by changing the maiden into a spider. Accordingly, Arachne, in the form of this insect, continues to spin even to this day.

The Romans regarded Minerva (perhaps identified with an old E trus'can divinity) as the patron of handicrafts and as the

Minerva's worship at Rome goddess of wisdom, especially along practical lines. Later they thought of her as the protector of cities and the teacher of men in the arts of military strategy. Her statue was set up in the great temple of Jupiter on the Cap'i to line Hill, together with those of Juno and Jupiter.

Minerva is represented as a tall figure clad in long garments. Usually **How Minerva may be identified** she wears a helmet (sometimes surmounted by a sphinx and griffins) and carries a spear. On many statues the breast

National Museum, Naples   Photograph by Alinari

Fig. 65. Head of Minerva (Athena)

This picture helps us to understand what is meant by the " aegis."

is covered by the aegis. Since the owl was her particular bird, it frequently appears at her side, as well as a serpent which in some curious way was associated with this goddess.

IN THE WORLD OF TODAY

I. IN LITERARY ALLUSION

I sing the glorious power with azure eyes,
Athenian Pal'las, timeless, chaste, and wise,
   . . . . From his awful head
Whom Jove brought forth, in warlike armour dressed,
Golden, all-radiant!

SHELLEY, Homer's Hymn to Minerva, ll. 1–6

Can tyrants but by tyrants conquered be,
And Freedom find no champion and no child,
Such as Columbia saw arise when she
Sprung forth a Pallas, arm'd and undefiled?

BYRON, Childe Harold, Canto IV, 96

II. IN WORDS AND EXPRESSIONS

A certain wooden statue of Pallas Athena at Troy was called the "Pal la'di um." The Trojans held this in the greatest reverence and thought that the safety of their city depended upon its

© H. K. T.; *Gramstorff Brothers*

Fig. 66. Diomede with the Palladium

preservation. During the siege of Troy the Greeks stole this statue, but there seems to have been a second one, inasmuch as when the Trojans came to Italy under the leadership of Ae ne'as they brought with them a palladium, which the Romans continued to look upon as essential to their security as a nation. We have inherited this word and its traditions, for we still speak of our constitution as the **palladium of our liberty,** meaning that it insures our existence as a democracy.

The story of the part played by the Palladium in the fall of Troy is related in the chapter entitled " The Trojan War."

The **olive branch of peace** is a common expression.   It comes about probably from the fact that Minerva was intimately connected with the olive, and that she presided over the arts of peace. During the World War a writer in the *New York Times* spoke of a proposed plan for ending the struggle as " the olive-branch policy."

III. IN OTHER CONNECTIONS

In Art and Decorative Design

The head of Minerva is very often seen over the entrances to schools, libraries, and museums.   The owl, too, the favorite bird of the goddess, is frequently found as a symbol for wisdom and learning.

In the English schools a tuition fee or a gift to an instructor was formerly spoken of as a " minerval." (This may still be the case in some places.)

Fig. 68. Trade mark of Henry Holt and Company, Publishers

A Scientific Term Recalls Arachne's Story

A member of the class of animals to which the spider belongs is known in science as an "arachnid." And while the story which we have read is only one which the Greeks made up to account for the activities of this insect, it is interesting to have it in mind when we meet this strange word in a science textbook.

Fig. 67. Seal of the Archaeological Institute

The Name of a Prominent Greek City

We ought not to forget that the city of Athens, which for so many years led the world in civilization, still flourishes. Athens is today, as in ancient times, the leading city in Greece.

Fig. 69. Athena's city as it appears today

Moreover, the fame of Athens of old accounts for the fact that towns today are still named "Athens." The Century Atlas lists thirty of these.

Libraries and Societies

"Athenaeum" is a well-known name for a library which contains mainly books of a scholarly nature.   There is one in Boston. The same name has also been chosen for learned societies, such as the famous "Athenaeum" of London.

QUESTIONS FOR REVIEW

1. In what manner was Minerva born, and how did she appear?
2. (1) Of what city was she the patron goddess?
   (2) What ideals and arts did she represent?
3. How did the Greeks regard her, and for what particular reason?
4. In what way did Minerva differ from Mars in respect to war?
5. (1) What was Minerva's great gift to Greece?

(2) Relate the story of her contest with Neptune.

(3) On what famous hill did this event take place?

6. Over what particular fields was Minerva regarded as patroness by the Romans?

7. (1) How may Minerva be identified?

(2) Describe her dress in detail.

8. Account for the name *Athens*.

9. Why is the owl associated with wisdom?

10. (1) According to the Greeks, why does the spider spin?

(2) What name in modern science reminds us of this story?

National Museum, Naples

Fig. 70. Athena

11. Over the entrances of what buildings may a bust of Minerva be seen?

12. What was the Palladium, and with what important event was it connected?

13. Explain the expression *the olive branch of peace*.

14. What is the Parthenon, and what is the meaning of the word?

OPTIONAL

FOR THOSE WHO HAVE TIME FOR FURTHER STUDY

A. ADDITIONAL READING

I. In Textbooks Dealing with Classical Mythology

1. Story of Procne and Philomela, Gay., pp. 249–250.
2. Minerva's contest with Mars, translation from the *Iliad*, XXI, 390 ff. quoted by Gayley on pp. 86–87.
3. An account of the procession known as the "Panathenaea," B., 154–155.
4. Details of the story of Arachne, B., 107–110.
5. Athena assists a hero to capture Pegasus, B., p. 125.

For other references, see the Appendix, pages xxviii ff., under headings connected with subjects mentioned in this chapter.

II. In Books in General

1. Many passages in the *Iliad* translated by Lang, Leaf, and Myers; such, for example, as that in Book V, p. 105, where Minerva is described as she arms herself for battle against the Trojans.
2. Passages in the *Odyssey*, translated by Butcher and Lang. Throughout the story of the Odyssey the goddess appears as the hero's friend and protector, and there are many vivid accounts of her appearance at critical moments. One of these is found at the beginning of the poem, I, pp. 4–11.
3. A vivid and interesting account of the Acropolis and the Parthenon as seen by a visitor in ancient times, Davis' *A Day in Old Athens*, pp. 213–224 (Allyn and Bacon).
4. Seymour's *Life in the Homeric Age*, pp. 426–428 (The Macmillan Company).

5. An account of the festival known as the " Panathenaea," Van Hook's *Greek Life and Thought*, pp. 73–74 (Columbia University Press); also Davis' *A Day in Old Athens*, pp. 235–237 (Allyn and Bacon).

B. Lines to Be Memorized

Minerva, child of Jove, who loves too well
Fierce war and mingling combat, and the fame
Of glorious deeds.

Shelley, Homer's Hymn to Venus, ll. 10–12

C. Further Study of Literary Allusion

If you are interested in seeing more clearly how good writers make use of the Greek myths, look up the following references:

Aegis: Byron's *Childe Harold*, Canto II, 14. **Athena:** Byron's *Childe Harold*, Canto II, 2 and 91 ; Black's *Judith Shakespeare*, p. 323 (Harpers). **Minerva:** Byron's *Childe Harold*, Canto I, 54 ; Hawthorne's *Marble Faun*, p. 181 (Houghton Mifflin) ; Pope's *Dunciad*, I, 10 ; O. Henry's *Voice of the City*, p. 21 (Doubleday, Page).

D. Projects for Individual and Group Work

To be selected from the list of projects on pages xx–xxvi, in case the subject matter of this chapter lends itself readily to any one of them.

POEMS FOR REFERENCE

Arnold, Matthew	* Philomela
Byron, Lord	The Curse of Minerva
Shelley, Percy Bysshe	* Homer's Hymn to Minerva

Ginn and Company
Athenæum Press

The Atlantic Monthly Advertiser
Courtesy of the publishers

The Ladies' Home
Journal

Fig. 71. Minerva is still a symbol for literature, as is shown by these seals

Fig. 72. The Muses dancing with Apollo

THE MUSES AND PEGASUS

THE Mu'ses were nine in number and were the daughters of
Jupiter and the goddess of Memory, whom the Greeks called
The nine   Mne mos'y ne. All the graces of civilization are
Muses   connected with their names — literature, art, music,
rhythmic dancing, and learning in general. Their names and the
particular field over which each presided are indicated in the list
that follows : Cal li'o pe, epic poetry and rhetoric ; Cli'o, history ;
Er'a to, love songs ; Eu ter'pe, lyric poetry ; Terp sich'o re,
dancing ; Tha li'a, comedy ; Mel pom'e ne, tragedy ; Pol y hym'-
ni a, religious hymns ; U ra'ni a, astronomy.

The Muses were born upon the northern slopes of Mt. Olympus,
facing Mt. Pi'e rus, where they were accustomed to play and from
Birthplace   whose springs they were said to have derived inspiration for their songs. Later, however, they frequented Mt.
Hel'i con and Mt. Par nas'sus, leading choral dances in honor
of Apollo or resting by the cool waters of the fountains of Hip po-
cre'ne or Cas ta'li a.

Associated with these patrons of letters was a famous winged
steed named Peg'a sus, which had been presented to the Muses

by Minerva and which even today is connected with the idea of
Pegasus   literature.   An interesting story about Pegasus is
related under the topic " Bel ler'o phon."

IN THE WORLD OF TODAY

I. In Literary Allusion

Of man's first disobedience and the fruit
Of that forbidden tree . . .
Sing, heavenly Muse.

MILTON, *Paradise Lost*, I, ll. 1–6

NOTE.   Modern poets as well as ancient, in beginning their work, like to call
upon the Muses for inspiration.

A little learning is a dangerous thing,
Drink deep or taste not the Pi e'ri an spring.

POPE, *Essay on Criticism*, II, ll. 15–16

During the latter part of the World War and immediately after,
such important changes in governments took place and such
startling events occurred in other connections, that the world
could scarcely keep up with the news.   A writer in a current
magazine expressed the situation by saying, "Clio's pen moves
rapidly in these days," an allusion to the fact that Clio was the
muse of history and kept the record of historical events.

II. In Words and Expressions

The word **mu se'um** is connected with the Muses.   In their
shrine on Mt. Helicon various prizes for excellence in art, poetry,
and music were collected and formed the first "museum" (in
Greek, *mouseion*).   Our word has come directly to us from the
name of the famous "Museum" at Alexandria in Egypt, named
from an earlier one at Athens.

Music, as one of the arts over which the Muses presided, takes its name from these divinities.

We often speak of **terp si cho re'an feats** in connection with some dancer. This is because the Muse who presided over the art of dancing was named Terpsichore.

Mounting Pegasus is a common expression for describing the efforts of some one who aspires to write poetry or deliver orations.

III. In Other Connections

In Art and Decorative Design

The Muses are constantly represented in art and decorative design as symbols of music, literature, science, and learning in general. Pegasus, too, is very commonly used in connection with the same ideas, as the various illustrations in this chapter clearly show.

Fig. 73. Pegasus

As the steed of the Muses, Pegasus has become the seal of the Frederick A. Stokes Publishing Company.

A Name for Butterflies

Perhaps some suggestion of grace or delicacy about the small white or yellow butterflies which flit about the garden led scientists to apply the name "Pi'er is" to them, in allusion to the beautiful maidens called the "Pi er'i des" who haunted the Pierian spring in Thes'sa ly.

In the Sky at Night

The story goes that Pegasus finally mounted to Olympus. This, however, is not the reason why the Greeks named a constellation for him, but rather because they were accustomed to associate their famous characters with the heavenly bodies. See Fig. 33.

Fig. 74. The deification of Homer

The central design on this Wedgwood vase of the eighteenth century shows Homer as he is about to be deified. Notice Pegasus at the top, a symbol for poetry.

A Pioneer in Aviation

Pegasus, the winged steed of classical mythology, has often been mentioned in connection with aviation. Literature which appeared during the World War frequently referred to the airplane or the dirigible as the "Pegasus" of modern times.

The Origin of the Calliope

The memory of the beautiful voice of Calliope is, rather humorously, connected with the name of a musical instrument much used to draw the attention of crowds. Everyone has heard the cal li'o pe in circus parades and elsewhere, but its raucous tones would hardly suggest the dignified source from which the name originates.

Why Magpies Chatter

King Pi'e rus in Thessaly named each of his nine daughters after one of the Muses. These maidens were once daring enough to challenge the Muses to a contest in song. As mere human beings they were bound to lose, for the nymphs who were the judges could not fail to award the prize to the daughters of Jupiter. Moreover, as a punishment for their presumption, the maidens were changed into magpies, in which form they still continue their idle chatter.

Well-known Names for Clubs

Thalia, muse of comedy, has given her name to many organizations devoted to the drama; Clio is a familiar title for associations interested in history; and there are many clubs called "Pierian."

QUESTIONS FOR REVIEW

1. Name the Muses and tell over what field of civilization each one presided.

2. What places did they frequent?

3. Why do poets sometimes call upon the Muses before they write their poems?

4. In what way are the words *music* and *museum* connected with the Muses?

5. (1) What is meant by the expression *mounting Pegasus?*

(2) Of what modern invention may Pegasus be called the forerunner?

6. Use the word *terpsichorean* in a sentence which will bring out its meaning.

QUESTIONS FOR THE CURIOUS

1. Why should a book of college prose and verse issued by the Dial Press be called "The Young Pegasus"?

2. A book by Percy Mark, published by Harcourt, Brace and Company, deals with the defects in our system of academic education. How may its title, "Which Way Parnassus?" be explained? Does your answer also account for the name of "The Parnassus Book Shop" on Fifth Avenue, New York?

POEMS FOR REFERENCE

BLAKE, WILLIAM	To the Muses
BYRON, LORD	Farewell to the Muses
HOLMES, OLIVER WENDELL	Musa
THOMAS, EDITH M.	The Muses (*Home Book of Verse;* Henry Holt and Company, N. Y.)

Fig. 75. Neptune

NEPTUNE
(Po sei'don)

Nep'tune had not only the sea but all the waters of the earth for his special province. His wonderful palace was far down in **God of the waters** the depths of the ocean. Here he lived with his wife, the lovely Am phi tri'te, and from this place he ruled his wide realm.

The god sometimes appeared upon the surface of the sea, especially when the waves were high and a storm was raging. At such times he could be seen, trident in hand, driving over the water and calming the angry billows.

Neptune had a son named Tri'ton. It was his task to see that his father's com- **Triton** mands reached all parts of the ocean. The Greeks often used to think that they could hear the silvery tones of his horn as he transmitted orders to some distant part of the sea.

Other divinities likewise lived in the ocean, among them Ne'reus and his family, and Pro'teus.

Nereus, a kindly old man, dwelt with his fifty daughters, the Ne're ids, in a shining cave far beneath the surface of the waters. The Nereids

Adriaen de Vries   Courtesy of the Metropolitan Museum, New York

Fig. 76. Triton

By means of his horn, Triton is conveying a message to distant parts of the sea.

were somewhat like the picture suggested to us by the word
"mermaid," that is, maidens whose bodies below the waist re-

Nereus and the Nereids sembled those of fishes. So wonderfully beautiful and graceful were they that they charmed everyone who
saw them. Their days were spent playing in the depths of the
sea, or, when the weather was warm and the sun shining, or the
light of the moon especially lovely, they might be seen sitting
upon the rocks at the surface of the ocean. They also delighted
in sporting with the Tritons (for Triton was not the only one
who bore this name) or riding on the backs of dolphins.

Two of the Nereids became very well known — Amphitrite,
wife of Neptune, and The'tis, the mother of A chil'les.

Proteus in some ways was more interesting than any of the
other sea divinities except Neptune himself. The curious crea-

Proteus, the prophet ture lived in caves beneath the surface of the sea, coming out only now and then to pasture his sea-
calves along the shore. On these occasions he was sometimes
seized and begged to prophesy; for, because of his age, he was
supposed to know all the secrets of nature. He would then make
every effort to escape, changing himself into a great many different shapes, a lion for example, or a serpent, or, as a last resort,
into fire or water.

There are many stories connected with Neptune, one of which
has been related under the topic "Minerva." Another tale gives
an account of a mortal's attempt to cheat the god.

Jupiter once became greatly offended with Neptune and
Apollo and forced both of them to serve a mortal as a punishment.

The treachery of King Laomedon They decided to help La om'e don build the walls of Troy in return for a price which the king gladly agreed
to pay. But after the work was finished, no reward
was forthcoming, Laomedon refusing to keep his promise. In
revenge, Neptune sent a monster from the sea to ravage the land

about the city.   None of the king's efforts to destroy the beast
was successful.   There was apparently only one way in which he
could appease it and free himself from this pest, and that was to
give over to the monster his
daughter He si'o ne.   This he
reluctantly decided to do.   But
to his great joy Her'cu les fortunately appeared in time to
deliver the girl from so horrible a fate.

Another well-known story is
connected with Neptune as
god of horses and horseman-
ship, for the Greeks thought
that he presided over this field
as well as over the waters of
the earth.

A certain king in E'lis named
Oen o ma'us,   extraordinarily
Pelops and   skilled   in   horse-
Hippodamia   manship and very
proud of his ability, had been
warned by an oracle that a
son-in-law would one day destroy him.   Accordingly the
king resolved that his daughter
Hip po da mi'a   should   never
marry, no matter how many

Kenyon Cox   *Courtesy of Wisconsin State
                        Department of Engineering*

Fig. 77.   **Neptune in a mural painting**

Soon   after   the   Panama   Canal   was
opened, this picture was painted upon the
wall of one of the rooms in the State Capitol at Madison, Wisconsin.   It is designed
to show the union of the two oceans, the
Atlantic, represented by Neptune, and the
Pacific, symbolized by the form of a goddess.
America, in the center, blesses the union.

suitors sought her hand.   Finding it difficult to explain the
reason for his refusal in the case of all of the girl's lovers, he
issued a decree to the effect that no one should aspire to be his
son-in-law who had not first defeated the king in a chariot race.

Moreover, the penalty of defeat was not only the loss of Hippodamia; it meant death to the loser as well. But the prize of victory was so attractive that young men continued to enter the contest, only to give up their lives at the end, for none was skilful enough to triumph over Oenomaüs.

Then came Pe'lops, a youth whom Neptune had endowed with unusual ability and to whom he had presented for this special race four winged steeds. Oenomaüs accepted the challenge of the newcomer as he had those of all the other candidates, never suspecting that Pelops was in any way different from those whom he had so easily outdistanced.

National Museum, Athens

Fig. 78. Neptune

Hippodamia, however, knew at once that the young stranger was something more than the average youth who came to seek her hand. In fact, she was so strongly attracted by his bearing that she bribed her father's charioteer, Myr'ti lus, to loosen a bolt in the wheel of the king's chariot before the race began, thinking in this way to make Pelops' victory certain.

Under such circumstances there could obviously be but one result of the race. Oenomaüs was killed and Pelops took Hippodamia away as his bride.

The Greeks built many temples to Neptune in regions near the sea to honor him as god of the waters. One of these temples was at Cor'inth, and it was in this region that the famous Isth'mi an Games were held every two years. The prize was a wreath of wild parsley.

How the Greeks honored Neptune

Neptune is usually represented as a dignified and elderly man,
either standing or seated in his sea-chariot. He bears a tri-
Neptune in dent in his hand as the symbol of his power. Some-
art times a dolphin or some other suggestion of the sea
accompanies the figure.

IN THE WORLD OF TODAY

I. In Other Connections

Will all great Neptune's ocean wash this blood
Clean from my hand?

> SHAKESPEARE, *Macbeth*, Act II, Sc. 2, 60–61

Whose mellow reeds are touch'd with sounds forlorn
By the dim echoes of old Tri'ton's horn.

> KEATS, *Endymion*, I, 205–206

Or where
Down through tress-lifting waves, the Nereids fair
Wind into Thetis' bower by many a pearly stair.

> KEATS, *Lamia*, I, 207–208

II. In Words

Vaudeville actors are often called **protean** because, like Proteus
of old, they can assume many different characters.

A person who fails to keep his word is sometimes called a
Laomedon.

III. In Other Connections

Neptune and the Stars

The outermost planet, third in size, is called Neptune.

How the Vale of Tempe was Made

In the realm of physical geography, too, the story of Neptune survives; for it is said that it was a stroke of his trident which opened the Vale of Tem'pe, a very famous valley in northern Greece, and thus drained the plains of Thes'sa ly, which had formerly been lakes.

A Modern Ceremony in Honor of Neptune

When ships cross the equator, the passengers indulge in a fantastic celebration in honor of Neptune. Accounts of these

ceremonies occasionally appear in the newspapers, and in *Scribner's Magazine* for August, 1926, there is an article on the subject entitled " Crossing the Line with Pershing."

Fig. 79. The seal of the Atlantic Monthly

In Decorative Design

Neptune is frequently represented in modern art and decorative designs.   (See Fig. 77.)

QUESTIONS FOR REVIEW

1. (1) In what capacity did Neptune rule, and at what times could he be seen?
   (2) What instrument of power did he wield?
2. Who was Triton and what was his especial duty?
3. (1) Who were the Nereids?
   (2) Describe their appearance and their pastimes.
4. What sea divinity was most interesting next to Neptune, and what made him interesting?
5. What happened when Laomedon refused to pay Neptune for his work?

6. Over what other field besides the sea did Neptune preside as god?

7. Relate the story of Pelops and Hippodamia.

8. Where and in what connection were the Isthmian Games celebrated?

9. How is Neptune usually represented in art?

10. How was Macbeth reminded of Neptune when he looked at his crime-stained hands?

11. On what occasion are ceremonies still performed in honor of Neptune?

12. How was the Vale of Tempe formed?

13. Why are vaudeville actors sometimes called "protean"?

14. What sort of person may be called a "Laomedon"?

15. What is meant by saying that "England wields the trident"?

16. Why does the name "Proteus" fit the fickle lover in Shakespeare's *Two Gentlemen from Verona?*

OPTIONAL

FOR THOSE WHO HAVE TIME FOR FURTHER STUDY

A. ADDITIONAL READING

I. In Textbooks Dealing with Classical Mythology

1. Glaucus, the guardian of fishes, divers, and those who go to sea, Gay., pp. 200–201 (sec. 142); B., 59. His love for Scylla, B., 60–61.

2. How Proteus was made to speak, Gay., pp. 202–203 (sec. 145); B., 189–191.

3. How Pelops' son, Atreus, took vengeance on a brother, Gay., p. 275 (sec. 193).

4. Two of Neptune's sons, Otus and Ephialtes, try to reach the sky by piling up mountains, Gay., p. 93.

For other references see the Appendix, pages xxviii ff., under the heading of subjects mentioned in this chapter.

II. In Books in General

1. Neptune's palace under the sea, *Iliad*, XIII, pp. 245–246 in translation by Lang, Leaf, and Myers. For Bryant's beautiful rendering, see lines 21–78 in his verse translation.

2. Neptune sends forth a flood at Jupiter's command, translation of Ovid, *Met.* I, pp. 21–23 (Loeb Classical Library, G. P. Putnam's Sons).

3. A tempest on the sea; Neptune's anger with King Aeolus, who loosed the storm winds without orders, Vergil's *Aeneid*, Bk. I, ll. 58–160 in the translation by John Conington (Scott, Foresman edition); the god helps in person to push the storm-tossed ships from the rocks, ll. 161–177.

4. Neptune's vengeance on a deceitful king, Ovid, *Met.* XI, p. 135 (Loeb Classical Library).

5. Seymour's *Life in the Homeric Age*, pp. 438–441 (The Macmillan Company).

B. LINES TO BE MEMORIZED

From the green heart of the waters
  We, old ocean's daughters,
Have floated up with mortal men to play;
  Out of the green translucent night
  Up to the purple earthly light,
To dance with creatures of a day!

STEPHEN PHILLIPS, Ulysses, Act I, p. 52

For lines about Neptune, see Keats's *Endymion*, III, p. 236 (Everyman's Library); also Stephen Phillips' *Ulysses*, Prologue, p. 15.

C. FURTHER STUDY OF LITERARY ALLUSION

If you are interested in seeing more clearly how good writers make use of the Greek myths, look up the following references:

Herald of the sea: Milton's *Lycidas*, 89. **Neptune:** Dana's *Two Years before the Mast*, p. 446 (Houghton Mifflin, Riverside Literature Series); Shakespeare's *Tempest*, Act V, Sc. 1, 35; Milton's *Comus*, 18–21; J. K. Bangs's *Mr. Bonaparte of Corsica*, p. 247 (Harpers); Kingsley's *Westward Ho*, p. 43 (Macmillan); Lucas's *Adventures and Enthusiasms*, p. 270 (George Doran). **Proteus:** Roosevelt's *The Strenuous Life*, p. 238 (Century). **Proteus and Triton:** Wordsworth's *Sonnet;* Holmes's *Chambered Nautilus*, 26. **Sea divinities:** Milton's *Comus*, 859–889.

D. PROJECTS FOR INDIVIDUAL OR GROUP WORK

To be selected from the list of projects on pages xx–xxvi.

Fig. 80. A satyr, a nymph, and a faun

THE NYMPHS

IT would not have surprised a Greek to meet at any time in the country a maiden so beautiful that a mere glance would be enough to assure him that she was something more than human. He would know at once that by a piece of good fortune he had seen a nymph. If a lovely face looked up at him out of a stream, he would recognize it as belonging to one of the Na'iads. Or if, as he was resting beneath a tree, he saw, or fancied that he saw, far up among the leaves, laughing eyes looking down at him, he would have no difficulty in believing that they belonged to a Dry'ad. Any climb in the mountains might give him a glimpse a girlish form which he would at once identify as an O're ad.

All of these terms, naiad, dryad, and oread, he would know were only particular names for the nymphs who lived in the streams, the trees, and the mountains, semi-divine beings in human form who made the world of nature alive.

The nymphs lived a care-free and, for the most part, a happy existence.   They found mortals amusing and had frequent intercourse with them.   But now and then this acquaintance brought them grief, especially when they fell in love.   A story in the next section is concerned with such an instance, and similar stories are found elsewhere in this book, as well as many details about the nymphs in general.

IN THE WORLD OF TODAY

I. In Literary Allusion

You nymphs, called Naiads of the winding brooks.
Shakespeare, The Tempest, Act IV, Sc. 1, 128

And once, above the edges of our nest,
An arch face peeped, an Oread, as I guess'd.
Keats, Endymion, I, 670–671

Whither wouldst thou lead my thought,
  Whispering wings of May?
Down dim glades with mystery fraught,
Emerald-veined, where long unsought,
  Nymph and Dryad play?   Life, May 5, 1921

II. In Other Connections

A Name for a Butterfly

Because of the fact that they are graceful and beautiful, as well as on account of their habit of frequenting the borders of woods, a group of butterflies has been called "Dry'a des." Still another illustration of this name in science is seen in Figure 82.

Fig. 81. Cupid and a nymph

The nymphs were always falling in love; this one, however, does not seem to want to listen to Cupid.

A Story about the Flower Called Narcissus

Nar cis'sus was a handsome young man who was so vain that he never tired of looking at his reflection in the clear waters of the forest pools. In fact, he seemed really in love with the image which he saw, often talking to it and even trying to embrace it. The legends say that because of his longing he finally pined away.

The water nymphs were very fond of the youth and wished to give proper burial to his body. But when they sought it in order to place it on the funeral pyre, they found nothing but a wonderfully beautiful flower, which even to this day bears the name "narcissus."

An interesting example of an allusion to Narcissus in current literature may be found in the title of a picture in *The National Geographic Magazine* for July, 1921, p. 84.

A Fanciful Explanation for the Echo

One of Di a'na's most beautiful nymphs was named Echo. Unfortunately she was so talkative that Juno deprived her almost entirely of the use of her voice, allowing her to repeat the last words of another person's sentence, but never to utter her own thoughts.

The maiden felt this misfortune most keenly when she fell in love with the young Narcissus, for she had no way of expressing her affection except to echo his final words. Not finding this habit particularly interesting, Narcissus would have nothing to do with her.

The unhappy nymph therefore spent the rest of her days in the lonely places of the mountains, compelled to find her only pastime in repeating sounds which she heard.

Fig. 82. Fungi which someone has named the " Dryad's Saddle "

Why Wild Olives Are Bitter

A Roman poet says that the wild olive tree, which bears very bitter fruit, was once a rude shepherd who persisted in insulting the nymphs. His transformation was a punishment for his bad manners, and his disagreeable nature lingers in the unpleasant taste of the wild olive.

QUESTIONS FOR REVIEW

1. What were the nymphs called who lived in the streams? Among the trees? Among the mountains?
2. What kind of existence did they lead?
3. What sort of experiences did they have with mortals?

4. Why are certain butterflies called "Dryades"?
5. Relate the story of Narcissus.
6. How did the Greeks explain the echo?

POEMS FOR REFERENCE

CAWEIN, MADISON	The Hamadryad (*Poems;* The Macmillan Company, N. Y.)
GOLDSMITH, OLIVER	On a Beautiful Youth
GUITERMAN, ARTHUR	* Echo (*The Light Guitar;* Harper and Brothers, N. Y.)
LEGALLIENNE, RICHARD	* The Dryad (*A Jongleur Strayed;* Doubleday, Page and Company, N. Y.)
LYTTON, EDWARD G. E.	The Oread's Song
SILL, LOUISE M.	* Pan and Echo (*In Sun and Shade;* Harper and Brothers, N.Y.)

Fig. 83. A nymph feeds the infant Jupiter
(some say the young Bacchus)

Fig. 84. Pan wishes to please Diana and therefore offers her the wool from his goat

Fig. 85. Pan shows a youth how to play upon the pipes

PAN

A QUEER-LOOKING creature this Pan must have been, this god of the country with his goat's legs, his horns, and his short tail! **God of the country** It is no wonder at all that the nymphs would have nothing to do with him as a rule, no matter how much he wooed them and notwithstanding the plaintive love songs which he played upon his pipes.

But the shepherds thought that there was no god quite so kindly as Pan. Whenever any of their sheep or goats were lost, they knew that the god would find and bring them back; and if disease came among them, it was to Pan that they looked for a remedy. They built altars to him and never failed to bring him gifts of honey and milk and cheese.

Pan slept at night in the caves of the hills, but in the daytime he roamed the forests and the mountains, dancing with the fauns and satyrs, wild creatures half-human and half-animal, and making the whole region resound with the weird music of his pipes.

E. Frémiet (Luxembourg Museum, Paris)

Fig. 86. Pan teases a bear

IN THE WORLD OF TODAY

I. In Literary Allusion

Oftenest in the dark woods I hear him sing
Dim, half-remembered things, where the old mosses cling
To the old trees, and the faint, wandering eddies bring
The phantom echoes of a phantom spring.

Fiona Macleod

Great Nature had a million words,
In tongues of trees and songs of birds,
But none to breathe the heart of man,
Till Music filled the pipes o' Pan.

Henry van Dyke

II. In a Word

Our word **panic** — an unreasoning kind of terror that takes possession of people at certain times — perhaps came about in this way : Travelers in wild and solitary places in Greece often had a strange feeling of fright even when there was no visible cause for it.   So, in order to account for it, men said that it must be due to Pan.   Therefore the usage of the word as we know it gradually came about, although we no longer confine it to terror in wild places.

III. In Miscellaneous Ways

A Far-away Origin of the Pipe Organ

Although Mer'cu ry is credited with the invention of the lyre, that of the pipes as a musical instrument is attributed to Pan.

It is said that Pan was once in love with a beautiful nymph named Sy'rinx, who, to escape him, was changed into reeds such as those that fringe the banks of streams.   Thus the god found that instead of holding Syrinx in his arms he had nothing but a clump of swaying reeds.   Sighing in disappointment, he was amazed to hear a soft murmur as the air stirred in the reeds, so musical in tone and so similar to the voice of the maiden — so it seemed to the lover — that Pan resolved to preserve the sound by making pipes from the stalks.   The instrument that resulted he called a "syrinx" in memory of the nymph.   The god became very skilful in its use, so much so that he even dared to challenge Apollo to a contest.   Our pipe organ, as we know, had its origin in some such simple device as this.

Poets have always been interested in the story of Syrinx.   A modern poet thus addresses the nymph :

A SONG OF SYRINX

Little lady, whom 'tis said
    Pan tried very hard to please,
I expect before you fled
    'Neath the wondering willow-trees,
Ran away from his caress
In the Doric wilderness,
That you'd led him on a lot,
Said you would, and then would not:
No way that to treat a man,
Little lady, loved of Pan!

I expect you'd dropped your eyes
    (Eyes that held your stream's own hue,
Kingfishers and dragon-flies
    Sparkling in their ripple blue),
And you'd tossed your tresses up,
Yellow as the cool king-cup,
And you'd dimpled at his vows
Underneath the willow boughs,
Ere you mocked him, ere you ran,
Little lady, loved of Pan!

So they've turned you to a reed,
    As the great Olympians could;
You've to bow, so they've decreed,
    When old Pan comes through the wood,
You're to curtsey and to gleam
In the wind and in the stream
(Which are forms, I've heard folks say,
That the gods adopt today),
And we watch you bear your ban,
Little lady, loved of Pan!

For in pleasant spots you lie
   Where the lazy river is,
Where the chasing whispers fly
   Through the bed of bulrushes,
Where the big chub, golden dun,
Turns his side to catch the sun,
Where one listens for the queer
Voices in the splashing wier,
Where I know that still you can
Weave a spell to charm a man,
Little lady, loved of Pan !

PATRICK R. CHALMERS

In Art and Decorative Design

No figure from classical mythology is more prominent in decorative design than Pan. Wherever music or poetry is to be represented or the idea of the country as distinguished from the city, one is likely to find some symbol of this god.

A Survival of Pan's Music

The Pan-pipes are the recognized accompaniment today of Punch and Judy shows and bear witness to the frolicsome side of the god's character, as well as to the ancient and rustic origin of this form of amusement.

From the Raguenet drawings

Fig. 87. Such representations of Pan as that shown above are often found in the architectural decorations of theaters.

Were Pan's Pipes Heard Only in the Country ?

The poet who wrote these lines seems to think that those who know how to listen for Pan's music can hear it even in the noisy city.

PAN PIPES

In the green spaces of the listening trees
  Pan sits at ease,
 Watching with lazy eyes
 Little blue butterflies
That flicker sidelong in the fitful breeze;
  While on his pipe he plays
  Quaint trills and roundelays
 With drooping cadences;
And shy red squirrels rub against his knees.

And through the city's tumult and the beat
  Of hurrying feet,
 Those whom the god loves hear
 Pan's pipes, insistent, clear;
Echoes of elfin laughter, high and sweet,
  Catch in the sparrow's cries,
  Those tinkling melodies
 That sing where brooklets meet,
And the wood's glamour colors the gray street.

          Punch

QUESTIONS FOR REVIEW

1. Describe Pan's appearance.
2. Where did he live as a rule?
3. What companions did he have about him?
4. How did Pan happen to invent the musical instrument called the "syrinx"?
5. What well-known shows preserve the memory of Pan?
6. Where are statues of this god most often found?

POEMS FOR REFERENCE

BROWN, ALICE   Pan (*Road to Castaly;* The Macmillan Company, N. Y.)

BROWNING, ELIZABETH BARRETT * A Musical Instrument

Browning, Robert   Pan and Luna

Burr, Amelia Josephine   * Syrinx (*Life and Living;* George H. Doran and Company, N. Y.)

Carman, Bliss   * Pipes of Pan; *also* A Young Pan's Prayer (*Pipes of Pan;* L. C. Page and Company, Boston)

Chalmers, Patrick   * Pan Pipes (*Green Days and Blue Days;* Norman, Remington Company, Baltimore)

Eaton, Walter Prichard   Pan on Change (*Echoes and Realities;* George Doran and Company, N. Y.)

Emerson, Ralph Waldo   Pan

Field, Eugene   * Pan Liveth (*Poems;* Charles Scribner's Sons, N. Y.)

Hewlett, Maurice   Pan and the Young Shepherd

Phillpotts, Eden   A Litany to Pan

Riley, James Whitcomb   * Pipes of Pan (introductory poem in volume with same title)

Shelley, Percy Bysshe   Hymn of Pan (Homer's *Hymn of Pan*)

Stedman, Edmund C.   * Pan in Wall Street (*Poetical Works;* Houghton Mifflin Company, Boston)

Story, William Wetmore   * Pan in Love

Swinburne, Algernon C.   Palace of Pan

Van Dyke, Henry   * Pan Learns Music (*Poems;* Charles Scribner's Sons, N. Y.)

Fig. 88. Hades

PLUTO

(Ha′des or Dis)

PLU′TO was the god of the Lower World — that vast and mysterious region under the earth to which the souls of men passed at death. This world, which the Greeks called Ha′des, was looked upon as his house. Here the stern god of death lived, and it was to this unlovely home that he brought his young bride, whose story is given under the topic "Ce′res."

While the Greeks did not know really what the Lower World was like, they had some kind of picture of it in their minds, drawn from their imagination. Certain accounts which we find in their literature will perhaps help to make this picture clear.

The realm of Hades knew no sun except in the part called E lys′i um.[1] The rest of it was wrapped in darkness, but not

A place of gloom and darkness so much so that people could not recognize one another and make their way about. There was always some light, but it was too faint to do more than relieve the blackness of night.

Although the Greeks thought of the Lower World as a "home" of Hades, they also considered it as a vast stretch of country

Some of the natural features with rivers, plains, hills, and other features characteristic of a landscape. Among these the rivers seem to have been the most striking, at least the writers have left vivid descriptions of them. There was the Ach′e ron, for example, whose dark waters all the dead had to cross before they

---

[1] The Greeks had very vague ideas as to the location of Elysium. But Vergil makes it a part of the Lower World.

entered Hades.   Then there was the Styx (often confused with the Acheron) and the Co cy'tus.   The Phleg'e thon, too, is always mentioned, a river of fire whose roaring flames encircled Tar'ta rus.   Another stream of this Lower World was called Le'the, and a very strange river it was, for those who drank from its waters straightway forgot everything that had happened to them.

People in Hades looked very much as they had when alive. But their bodies had no substance and were really not bodies at

What happened to men's bodies at death   all — only shadowy likenesses of their human forms. Men did not lose all of their physical selves, however, inasmuch as they could still use their voices, although they were thin and quavering just as we should expect a ghost's to be.   And they ate and drank (at least in Elysium) and in other ways seemed to continue the habits of their earthly life.   Certainly their bodies did not lose the capacity for feeling pain.   Otherwise the punishments about which we read in connection with Tartarus would not have meant much.

As the shade approached the Styx, it found that the banks were filled with an innumerable throng of other ghosts, " as many in

Crossing the Styx   number," says the poet Ver'gil, "as are the leaves that fall in the autumn."   All of them were crowding toward a boat in which stood the grim and powerful figure of a man with a mass of snow-white hair and a shaggy and unkempt beard.   This was Cha'ron, whose task it was to ferry the souls across the black waters.   However, not all of those waiting upon the banks could take this journey, but only those persons who had received the rites of burial and could present the small coin known as the *obol* in payment for their fare.   All the others were driven back by the ferryman's long oar.   These were obliged to wait one hundred years before they might at last hope to enter Charon's boat.

Just across the river and at the very entrance of Hades was a huge monster in the form of a three-headed dog, whose neck The hound Cerberus bristled with serpents and whose dreadful baying terrified all who approached. This was Cer'ber us, put here by Pluto to see that no shade escaped after he once entered the realms of the dead. But it was quite easy for those who were entering to get past this guard.

All who died were forced to appear before certain judges, among whom were Rhad a man'thus and Mi'nos. At this bar of justice The bar of justice their deeds in the world above were reviewed and sentence was passed upon them. The souls were then assigned to their proper places in Hades, some to suffer in Tartarus, and others to dwell happily in Elysium; while those whose lives had not been conspicuous either for good or for evil were condemned to wander aimlessly about, knowing neither pain nor pleasure.

Tartarus was the name given to that district in Hades where those who had sinned greatly, whether men or semi-divinities, Tartarus and its punishments were punished. It is sometimes described as a city with gigantic walls surrounding it, and strong gates of adamant which opened only to admit those sent there by divine decree. But other writers speak of it as a vast hole, sloping down to a center as far from the surface of the ground as Mt. Olympus towered above the earth.

No mortal, except a very great hero such as U lys'ses, for example, ever entered that part of Hades called Tartarus and returned to earth to describe the horrible sights; but Ae ne'as, the mythical founder of the Roman race, whom the gods had allowed to visit the Lower World in search of his father, passed by the spot. He heard the clanking of chains, the blows of whips, and shuddered at the shrieks and cries of anguish. And though he himself might not see them with his own eyes, he received from his guide a vivid account of the monsters within, the awful Hydra, the Chimaera breathing forth flames, the hundred-armed giant named Briareus, and the cruel Furies brandishing their scorpion-whips.

The punishments of certain characters in classical mythology have become so famous and are mentioned so frequently in literature that a brief account is given in the following paragraphs.

Tantalus

Tan′ta lus, son of Jupiter and father of Ni′o be, lived on intimate terms with the gods, even feasting with them and in close touch with their plans and activities. Once, however, he betrayed one of their secrets

Fig. 89. Tantalus, Ixion, and Sisyphus suffering in Tartarus

and was sent to Tartarus. There he was punished by having food and water ever before his eyes, but always just out of his reach; or, as some writers say, by having a part of a mountain placed above him which at any moment might fall and crush him.

Ixion

Ix i′on was a powerful king of Thessaly, well known for his inhuman cruelties. It is said that he once aspired to be the husband of Juno. Thinking he had some reason for suspecting that the goddess looked with favor upon him, he began to boast of his success. Jupiter punished him by having him bound to a wheel in Tartarus so that he might suffer eternally for his presumption.

Sis'y phus was a king of Corinth who indulged often in trickery and deceit. Once he even tried to cheat Death himself.
Sisyphus   Having given the gods various causes for offense, he
was compelled when he died to roll a huge stone uphill. As this
always slipped from him near the top and rolled down again, his
labor was never ended.

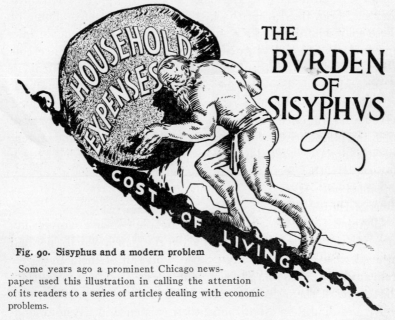

Fig. 90. Sisyphus and a modern problem

Some years ago a prominent Chicago newspaper used this illustration in calling the attention
of its readers to a series of articles dealing with economic
problems.

King Dan'a us had fifty daughters called the Da na'i des. It
happened that his brother Ae gyp'tus, having the same number
The Danaïdes   of sons, proposed that the Danaïdes become their
wives. The idea was not pleasing to Danaüs or to
his daughters. But not being able to prevent the union, the
king supplied the young brides with fifty daggers with which
to slay their husbands on the wedding night. All but one of

them carried out the plan.   As a punishment they were obliged to suffer in Tartarus by continually pouring water into sieves. The fiftieth daughter escaped this fate only because she fell in love with her husband.   (See Fig. 1.)

A certain region of Hades was set apart for the abiding place of those whose lives in the Upper World had been above reproach, **Elysium**   although even these had to undergo purification until they had been freed from the last stain of mortal life.   Some of those souls who came to Elysium might in time enter again into human form and so live once more upon the earth.   Since this happiness fell to the lot of only those who were preëminent in virtue and greatly loved by the gods, their number was very small.

A ghost coming to these realms from the gloom of Hades must have been astounded at the scene which met his eyes.   Here were hills, and plains bright with flowers, sparkling streams, and stately forests ; and over and above them all a rosy glow of indescribable beauty.   In the daytime there was a sun, and at night the sky was filled with stars — phenomena unknown in the desolate regions of Hades.

All about could be seen groups of people — some conversing, some feasting, and others taking part in the sports which they had enjoyed when they were alive.   But while all of them were free from any pain or trouble and so might be expected to enjoy perfect bliss, some of them greatly missed the excitements of the world above and doubtless often found their existence in Elysium lacking in interest.

IN THE WORLD OF TODAY

I. In Literary Allusion

Gloomy Pluto, king of terrors,
Arm'd in adamantine chains.

POPE, *Song of a Person of Quality*, 17 ff.

Lo! Tantalus, in his eternal thirst,
Still reaching for the fruit he may not grasp.

STEPHEN PHILLIPS, Ulysses, Act II, Sc. 2

See Sisyphus that in his anguish rolls
Upward, ever, the stone that still rebounds.

STEPHEN PHILLIPS, Ulysses, Act II, Sc. 2

By the streams that ever flow,
By the fragrant winds that blow
  O'er the Elysian flowers,
By those happy souls that dwell
In yellow meads of asphodel
  Or amaranthine bowers.

POPE, Ode on St. Cecilia's Day, V, 71–76

II. IN WORDS AND PHRASES

Sty′gi an darkness means profound night. The word comes from the name Styx as representative of a river of the dark underworld.

E lys′i an is a term applied to such joys as the blessed knew in the Lower World, and to the beauty of the region in which they dwelt. The French were thinking of the latter when they named one of their most famous streets in Paris " Champs É ly sées " (The Elysian Fields).

Plu to′ni an refers to Pluto and his realm, hence, subterranean and dark. Poe, for example, in his poem called "The Raven," speaks of " the night's plutonian shore."

To tantalize a person is to delude him with the thought that at last he is about to gain fulfillment of his wishes. According to classical mythology, it was only food and water that were kept before the eyes of Tantalus and just beyond his reach, but modern usage of the word does not confine the idea to these material ends.

The term **rhad a man'thine judgment** is applied to a final and solemn decision passed upon the guilty, recalling the impartial judge of the Lower World.

A **task of Sisyphus** is one which is seemingly endless. No sooner is it finished than it must be undertaken again — just as Sisyphus was compelled to roll his stone up the hill only to see it roll again to the bottom.

The expression **waters of Lethe** or the word **le the'an** is used to imply forgetfulness and complete oblivion such as overcame the souls who drank from this stream in the Lower World.

"The crews are worn out with their **Da na id'e an task.**" A writer in the *Century Magazine*, in describing the efforts of certain sailors to bail water from a leaky boat, thus refers to the punishment of the Danaïdes.

III. IN OTHER CONNECTIONS

Chemistry and the Story of Tantalus

For many years chemists tried to identify a certain rare metal occurring in combinations but scarcely known at all in separate form. Often they would feel that they were near the solution of their problem, only to be disappointed. When it was finally discovered, the name " tantalum " was given to it. The Oxford Dictionary says that the man who first identified this metallic element named it as he did, first, because it was customary to use names from classical mythology in such cases, and secondly, because he had observed that this metal remained a long time in acid without being saturated. The association with the Tantalus of the myths would seem, then, to lie in the idea that although food and water were close to him, he could neither eat nor drink. The non-absorbent quality of this metal makes it suitable for use in electric light filaments.

An Object Quite Out of Date

The "tantalus" is out of fashion with us now that the United States has prohibition. It is a stand for holding wine in which decanters, although locked up, are quite visible.

The Danaïdes and a Water Wheel

Just because these sisters were doomed to be forever pouring water through a sieve, a wheel for lifting water for irrigation purposes has been called "danaïde." One still sees it in Egypt.

Why Some Rocks Are Called "Plutonian"

Everyone knows a kind of rock called granite. Scientists say that this was formed by the agency of heat deep down in the earth ; they have therefore called such rocks "plutonian" because this realm was ruled by King Pluto. There is a theory, too, called the "plutonian," which explains the present aspect of the world's surface by asserting that it is due to subterranean fire.

A Mountain in Alaska

At the entrance to a remarkable volcanic region in Alaska known as the Kat'mai Valley is a mountain which looks like the crouching figure of an enormous beast. Explorers have named it "Cerberus." (For a picture, see *The National Geographic Magazine*, February, 1918, p. 130.)

QUESTIONS FOR REVIEW

1. (1) What was the home of Pluto called?
   (2) Describe its appearance and natural features.
2. What peculiar property was ascribed to the river Lethe?
3. What river were the shades obliged to cross before entering Hades?
4. According to the Greek idea, what happened to persons at death?
5. Describe the crossing of the Styx.
6. What was the watchdog of Hades, and what was his particular duty?
7. What happened to souls at the bar of justice in Hades?
8. What was the fate of souls condemned to Tartarus?
9. (1) Under what circumstances was a certain mortal permitted to go to Hades and return to earth?
   (2) What did he see and hear in Hades?
10. What punishment was inflicted upon Tantalus? Upon Sisyphus? Upon the Danaïdes?
11. What kind of existence was led by those whose mortal life had been above reproach?
12. Why is one of the streets in Paris named "Champs Élysées"?

A QUESTION FOR SOMEONE WITH A SENSE OF HUMOR

What mistake did the speaker make who, in introducing the new college president, said, "We feel sure that our institution will be safe with such an Ixion at the wheel"?

OPTIONAL

FOR THOSE WHO HAVE TIME FOR FURTHER STUDY

A. ADDITIONAL READING

I. In Textbooks Dealing with Classical Mythology

Where was the Lower World? Gay., p. 47 (sec. 44).

For other references see the Appendix, pages xxviii ff., under topics mentioned in this chapter.

II. In Books in General

1. The Lower World as seen by Aeneas, Vergil's *Aeneid*, Book VI, translated by Conington, ll. 139 ff. in the Scott, Foresman edition (lines in the Latin text, 268 ff.).

2. The Lower World as seen by Ulysses, translation of the *Odyssey* by Butcher and Lang, Book XI; also Stephen Phillips' *Ulysses*, Act II, Sc. 2.

3. Certain passages in Norton's translation of Dante's *Inferno*, to be selected under the guidance of the teacher (Vol. II, *Hell;* Houghton Mifflin Company).

4. *The House Boat on the Styx, The Pursuit of the House Boat,* and *The Enchanted Typewriter*, novels by John Kendrick Bangs.

B. Lines to Be Memorized

ELYSIUM

For them the night all through,
  In that broad realm below,
The splendor of the sun spreads endless light;
  Mid rosy meadows bright,
Their city of the tombs with incense-trees,
  And golden chalices
Of flowers and fruitage fair,
  Scenting the breezy air,
Is laden. There with horses and with play,
  With games and lyres, they while the hours away.

J. A. SYMONDS, Translation from Pindar

C. Further Study of Literary Allusion

If you are interested in seeing more clearly how good writers make use of the Greek myths, look up the following references:

Acheron: Locke's *Beloved Vagabond*, p. 236 (John Lane); Shakespeare's *Macbeth*, Act III, Sc. 5, 15. **Acheron, Styx, Cocytus, Phlegethon:** Milton's *Paradise Lost*, II, 575–586. **Cerberus:** Kingsley's *Westward Ho*, p. 37, (Everyman's Library). **Charon:** Shakespeare's *Richard III*, Act I, Sc. IV, 46. **Elysian Fields:** *Saturday Review of Literature*, Sept. 25, 1926; Tennyson's *The Princess*, III, 323–325. **Hades:** Thackeray's *The Newcomes,*

Vol. I, p. 295 (Everyman's Library); Byron's *Childe Harold*, Canto I, 52; II, 14. **Ixion:** Pope's *Rape of the Lock*, II, 133–134. **Lethe:** Eliot's *Silas Marner*, p. 11 (Crowell). **Tantalus:** Noyes's *Sherwood*, p. 143 (Stokes).

D. Projects for Individual or Group Work

To be selected from the list of projects on pages xx–xxvi, in case the subject matter of this chapter lends itself readily to any one of them.

POEMS FOR REFERENCE

Auslander, Joseph	Ixion (*The Cyclops' Eye;* Harper and Brothers, N. Y.)
Arnold, Matthew	Empedocles on Aetna, Act II, pp. 158-159 (*Dramatic Poems;* The Macmillan Company, N. Y.)
Browning, Robert	Ixion
Graves, Robert	* Escape (*Literary Digest,* Nov. 16, 1918)
Morris, Lewis	Sisyphus, Tantalus (*Epic of Hades;* Kegan Paul, Trench, Trübner and Company, London)
Morton, David	Napoleon in Hades (*Century Magazine,* October, 1917)
Phillips, Stephen	Christ in Hades
Rossetti, Dante G.	Proserpine
Story, William Wetmore	Tantalus

PROMETHEUS

Pro me'theus was not a god but a Ti'tan who had been endowed with the power of seeing into the future. Therefore, **A Titan helps the gods** when his father, I ap'e tus, took the side of Cro'nus in his struggle with Jupiter, as did most of the Titans, Prometheus, knowing how the battle would end, supported the Olympians and shared in their triumph.

To this Titan and his brother Ep i me'theus was assigned the task **Creation of man and the gift of fire** of creating both animals and man and equipping them with such faculties as would be necessary for maintaining life. Epimetheus provided animals with means of

Thorwaldsen (Copenhagen)   ©️ *H. K. T.; Gramstorff Brothers*
Fig. 91. Minerva gives a soul to man while Prometheus, the creator, looks on

defense — claws and horns, for example; he gave wings to birds and presented protective shells to the tortoise, the crab, and similar creatures. At the same time he endowed all animals with the qualities of courage, endurance, and shrewdness. In fact, so generous was he in presenting his gifts that when the time came to equip man, the creation of Prometheus, nothing seemed to be left which would contribute to his well-being. Finally Prometheus thought of a unique gift, one which, if skilfully used, would raise man far above the animals and make it possible for him to develop the arts of civilization. Accordingly he brought fire from heaven and presented it to him.

Jupiter, however, did not look with favor upon the race of men and grudged them the use of so powerful an instrument for progress as the heavenly fire. Therefore, when angered by an offense on the part of their champion, Prometheus, he deprived them of this priceless gift. But so great was the desire of Prometheus to further the welfare of man that he was bold enough to steal the fire a second time and bring it down to earth.

From an old print

Fig. 92. Prometheus on Caucasus

Jupiter was very angry at the theft and straightway had Prometheus chained to a rock on the wild and rugged Caucasus mountains. This alone would have been a most cruel punishment, but it was made much more dreadful by the fact that every day an enormous eagle devoured the liver of the Titan. Moreover, in some strange way, this liver was renewed each night, so that the torture never ceased. But Prometheus bravely endured the suffering although it lasted many centuries. Finally he was set free by Her'cu les.

A Titan's punishment

Some of the myths say that Prometheus might have obtained

his freedom long before he did, had he been willing to reveal to Jupiter a certain secret connected with the decrees of the Fates, which Jupiter had reason to think was of great importance to the continuance of his power. But the Titan steadfastly refused to give any information on the subject.

Jupiter was not satisfied with punishing Prometheus. Man as well must be made **Pandora** to suffer. And so a clay image of a beautiful maiden, the first woman, was fashioned and presented to Epimetheus, the brother of Prometheus. Since Mi ner'va had adorned her with very lovely raiment, Venus with beauty, and both Mercury and the Graces had helped to make her altogether charming, the former by giving her the gift of winning speech, and the latter by placing beautiful garlands upon her head, Epimetheus was much pleased to have her as his companion. She was called Pan do'ra, which means " gifts from all," and was so named because all the gods had contributed to her beauty.

Capitoline Museum (Rome)

Fig. 93. Pandora

The first thing she did, after coming to the house of Epimetheus, was to open a jar or box from which all the ills of life flew forth — disease, labor, pain, and many more. She closed it only in time to shut in hope. And so, according to this story, woman's curiosity is responsible for all the woes from which mankind suffers.

Another version of the story, however, says that Pandora brought the box with her and that it was the curiosity of Epimetheus that caused the escape of the ills within.

IN THE WORLD OF TODAY

I. IN LITERARY ALLUSION

Behold Prometheus, who stole fire from heaven ;
Now at his heart the eternal vulture eats.

STEPHEN PHILLIPS, *Ulysses*, Act II, Sc. 2

More lovely than Pandora, whom the gods
Endowed with all their gifts.

MILTON, *Paradise Lost*, IV, 714–715

II. IN WORDS AND EXPRESSIONS

The expression **Pandora's box** has become a symbol for troubles,
although it often typifies pleasant surprises too. For example,
an eastern newspaper once called the plan of daylight saving "a
Pandora's box of surprises and irritations."

III. IN ANOTHER CONNECTION

As a Symbol for Self-Sacrifice

Prometheus survives in the modern world as an ideal of unself-
ish conduct. He is thought of as a person who did not hesitate
to endure great suffering in an effort to benefit others.

Several famous poets have chosen Prometheus as a theme,
notably Shelley, Mrs. Browning, Byron, Longfellow, and Lowell.
The closing lines from Shelley's poem called "Prometheus Un-
bound" set forth in a very fine way the high ideals of life which
the story of the Titan suggests :

To suffer woes which Hope thinks infinite ;
To forgive wrongs darker than death or night ;
To defy Power, which seems omnipotent ;
To love, and bear ; to hope till Hope creates
From its own wreck the thing it contemplates ;

Neither to change, nor falter, nor repent ;
This like thy glory, Titan, is to be
Good, great, and joyous, beautiful and free ;
    This is alone Life, Joy, Empire, and Victory.

QUESTIONS FOR REVIEW

1. Who was Prometheus, and why did he fight on the side of the gods?

2. What task was assigned to him and his brother Epimetheus?

3. Account for the existence of fire on earth, according to mythology.

4. (1) Why was Prometheus punished, and in what manner?
    (2) How was he delivered?

5. Why was Pandora created and why was she so beautiful?

6. How did a woman's curiosity bring woe upon mankind, according to the story?

7. What ideals does Prometheus exemplify?

8. For what has the expression *Pandora's box* become a symbol?

POEMS FOR REFERENCE

BRIDGES, ROBERT	Prometheus, the Firegiver (*Poetical Works;* Oxford University Press, Oxford and N. Y.)
BYRON, LORD	* Prometheus
CHALMERS, PATRICK R.	* Promethea (*Green Days and Blue Days;* Norman, Remington Company, Baltimore)
GIBSON, WILFRED WILSON	* Prometheus (*Collected Poems;* The Macmillan Company, N. Y.)
HEWLETT, MAURICE	Prometheus
LONGFELLOW, HENRY W.	* Masque of Pandora; *also* Prometheus
LOWELL, JAMES RUSSELL	* Prometheus
ROSSETTI, D. G.	Pandora

Fig. 94. Venus

Head of the famous statue known as the Venus of Melos, regarded by many as the most beautiful statue that has come down from ancient times.

VENUS
(Aph ro di′te)

AMONG the goddesses on Mt. Olympus there was one who never failed to please, the "laughter-loving Venus." Not only was she beautiful beyond words, but in addition she possessed all the charms and graces associated with womanhood.

There are several stories about her birth; one that she was the daughter of Jupiter and the nymph Di o′ne. But another and **The birth of** more interesting account says that she rose from the **Venus** foam of the sea and was wafted first toward the island of Cy the′ra and later to Cy′prus, where she stepped out upon the shore. Here the Seasons met her, and clothing her in wonderful raiment fit only for the gods and adorning her with jewels, took her to the shining palace upon Mt. Olympus and there introduced her to the divinities of heaven.

To the Greeks and Romans she symbolized love between men and women, and in the world of animals and nature, the force **A symbol for** that reproduces life. Her worship, therefore, was **love** universal, and her altars heaped with roses were to be found everywhere.

Cupid was the son of Venus and constantly attended her. He always carried a bow and a quiver of arrows, and being a very **Cupid (Eros)** frolicsome boy, greatly enjoyed piercing the hearts of both gods and mortals whom he wished to inspire with love. The arrows which he used on these occasions were tipped with gold, but he also had others tipped with lead. The latter, far from making persons fall in love, produced exactly the opposite effect. For

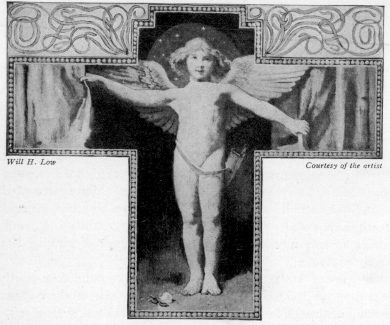

Will H. Low   Courtesy of the artist

Fig. 95. Cupid

example, it was because Daph'ne's heart had been pierced with a lead-tipped arrow that she so much disliked Apollo and therefore fled from him.

Although the above description of the god of love is the one that has come down to us from the Romans and presents the picture which most of us have in mind when we think of Cupid, it does not describe the being which the Greeks knew as E'ros. He was older — in fact, a young man — and far more serious and dignified than the character whom we think of under the name of Cupid.

The name of Venus is connected with many love stories, notably that of Paris and Helen, related in the chapter about the Trojan

War. But the accounts of how the goddess concerned herself
with the affairs of other and less famous lovers are also interesting.
Venus was kind-hearted as a rule and seldom failed to respond to a
call for help when it came to her from a despairing lover. An
instance of her immediate aid, rendered at a critical moment, is
shown in the story of a young man who won a king's daughter as
his bride.

Once upon a time there was a king in Greece who had a daughter named At a lan′ta, famed far and wide for her swiftness in
Fleet-footed running. So proud was the father of her ability that
Atalanta he allowed no one to become a suitor for her hand
who could not outdistance her in a foot race. Many attempted
it and lost their lives in consequence, for the king had decreed
death as the penalty for failure. But suitors continued to come,
willing to face such a fate for the mere chance of winning the
lovely Atalanta.

One day as Atalanta was running, she saw a handsome youth
regarding her somewhat scornfully from the side of the course,
looking as though he might be thinking to himself, "How foolish to risk one's life for the chance of winning a bride!" She was
greatly surprised when a little later she saw Hip pom′e nes [1] — for
that was his name — among the contestants, and she was quite
unable to account for her reluctance to race with him. "He is
such a boy," she said to herself. "It is a pity for one so young to
die." To tell the truth, she was really falling in love with Hippomenes, although she did not know it, and thought that her
efforts to dissuade him from entering the contest were prompted
by compassion only.

Early in the race Atalanta saw that she could run faster than
Hippomenes, and that there could be no doubt about the result of
the race. Accordingly, when a shining golden apple rolled across

[1] One Greek writer calls him Mi la′ni on.

the track in front of her, she stopped to pick it up, knowing that she could make up the time which she had lost. Soon a second one appeared, and this, too, she seized as she ran. But a third one was some distance from the track. Should she risk it? She felt that the delay would be dangerous, but she had never been defeated in a race and she very much wanted the glittering ball. She took the chance and lost. Hippomenes darted ahead and came in first amid deafening applause from the crowd of onlookers.

Legend says that Atalanta was not sorry to have been defeated, even by means of a trick, for it was the golden apples alone that brought victory to Hippomenes. They had been put into his hands by Venus in answer to his prayer for help, and she had instructed him in their use. The lovers were very grateful to the goddess for thus rendering timely help, and so making their marriage possible.

Venus was once very kind also to a young artist named Pygma'li on, who had made a marvelously beautiful statue of a
woman. This he had named Gal a te'a. So fond did he become of the image that he spent long hours adoring it as though it were a living being. On the occasion of one of her festivals, the goddess took pity upon the man's sufferings and, to his utter amazement, caused the hard marble to change before his very eyes into a lovely mortal whose womanly charms far exceeded anything he had dreamed of when he was shaping the statue.

A marble statue becomes alive

But Venus did not always bring happiness to lovers nor avert tragedy. It seems strange, however, that the goddess should have allowed one of her own priestesses to suffer from lack of her divine aid. But the story that follows seems to imply that in one case at least she failed to exert her power to prevent disaster to a bold lover.

At A by'dos on one side of the Hel'les pont (now the Dar da-
nelles') lived Le an'der, a youth who was deeply in love with a
Hero and maiden named Hero, an attendant upon the shrine of
Leander Venus directly across the straits. In spite of the fact
that they were forbidden to see each other, Leander every evening
after the coming of darkness swam across to the other side,

returning early the following
morning. But one night when
a fierce storm raged and the
waves were rough, he was
drowned. Hero watched in
vain for him during the long
hours, only to see his body
washed up at dawn upon the
beach.

Another instance of suffering
on the part of lovers which
Venus did not or could not relieve, is illustrated in the well-
known story of Pyr'a mus and
This'be.

In far away Bab'y lon lived
a young man called Pyramus

Bodenhausen   © *H. K. T.; Gramstorff Brothers*

**Fig. 96. Hero discovers the body of
her dead lover**

Pyramus and and in an adjoining
Thisbe house a girl named
Thisbe. They were deeply in love and had resolved to marry
in spite of the stern commands of their parents to the contrary.
Had they known that Venus favored the match, they would have
been greatly encouraged. But even without such assurance they
were daring enough to enter upon a very bold undertaking,
nothing less, in fact, than an elopement.

The lovers were not allowed to see each other, but a tiny crack in the wall which separated the two houses afforded them a means of communication. Through this small opening they held a whispered conversation and arranged the details of their flight. This was the plan they agreed upon: Thisbe was to slip out of her house when it grew dark and make her way to a certain spot which they both knew outside the walls of the city. Here Pyramus was to join her and together they were to make their escape.

Thisbe carried out her part of the program. She found the mulberry tree under the branches of which they had agreed to meet, and sat down to wait for her lover.

She had not been there long when in the bright light of the moon she saw a lion approaching. Greatly terrified, she fled for safety to a cave near by. The lion was on its way to a stream in order to get a drink and did not pause to pursue Thisbe. On its return, however, it saw the girl's cloak, which had fallen from her shoulders as she ran. This the animal tore to shreds, leaving the garment all stained from contact with his jaws, still wet with the blood of a bullock which he had recently devoured.

When Pyramus arrived, he looked in vain for Thisbe. The tracks of the lion, which he soon discovered, and the blood-stained cloak seemed to furnish the explanation of her absence — a lion had devoured her! Life without Thisbe would be unendurable, he thought, and in despair he fell upon his sword.

As Thisbe ventured timidly from the cave, her eyes at once sought the mulberry tree. Surely Pyramus would be waiting for her beneath its branches. But the tree seemed somehow unfamiliar; its berries were no longer white but were tinged with purple. While she stood in doubt, she saw the body of Pyramus upon the ground. Her lover had just strength enough to open his eyes as Thisbe took his head into her arms. Then all life left him.

Thereupon Thisbe, with a courage no less than that which had inspired Pyramus, resolved to die. Her lover's sword was at hand, and after a prayer to the gods that her body might be placed in the same tomb with that of Pyramus, she fell upon the sword and lay lifeless by her lover's side.

At this act the color of the mulberries took on a darker tinge, as though the tree were putting on deeper mourning for the sad fate which had befallen Pyramus and Thisbe.

We have seen that Venus did not always assist lovers, but we have had no conspic-

Cupid and Psyche   uous example of a determined attempt on her part to keep lovers apart. However, when her own son Cupid (we should keep E'ros in mind) fell desperately in love with Psy'che, she showed herself to be not only bitterly opposed to their marriage but very harsh as well. But those who knew the weaknesses of the goddess attributed her conduct to jealousy of Psyche's marvelous beauty rather than to any love of cruelty.

For a long time Cupid, who had at last become the victim of his own arts, worshiped Psyche, visiting her in an enchanted palace, but only at night when it was too dark for her to see him. In response to

Beyschlag   © H. K. T.; Gramstorff Brothers

Fig. 97. Psyche

the girl's reasonable desire to look upon him in the light, he said, "Never try to see me. Such an attempt will bring only misfortune." At the suggestion of her jealous sisters, however, Psyche was moved one night to light a candle when the god lay asleep and to look upon his manly beauty. Unfortunately a drop of burning oil fell upon him and Cupid vanished at once.

Psyche in her misery, for she was deeply in love, wandered about for a long time seeking aid from mortals as well as from Ce′res and Juno; but no one seemed able and willing to help her. Finally she resolved to go to the angry Venus herself to see if in any way she might placate the goddess and so regain her lover.

Courtesy of the Metropolitan Museum, New York

Fig. 98. Psyche placates Cerberus at the entrance to the Lower World

But she met only scorn and insulting words. Psyche, however, was very humble and promised to fulfil any condition, however cruel, in order to gain forgiveness. Venus so far relented as to assign her certain tasks to perform in the way of penance. These tasks were seemingly impossible, but just at critical moments some divine power came to her assistance; otherwise she could never have succeeded in accomplishing such difficult undertakings as the two which are here described.

An enormous amount of seeds and grain of various kinds was to be sorted out and arranged neatly in piles. Moreover, this work was to be finished before evening. Psyche was in despair, for she saw that she could not possibly accomplish it in one day. But as she looked at the grain before her, myriads of ants appeared and helped her in the task. When darkness came, the piles were ready for the inspection of Venus.

Another task was to bring to the goddess some of Pro ser′pi na′s beauty inclosed in a box which Venus brought for the purpose. To accomplish this, Psyche was forced to descend to Ha′des. She crossed the river Styx, encountered Cer′ber us, and through friendly assistance of one kind and another, was able to return to the Upper World with the urn tightly clasped in her hands. But she was tired and unhappy. "Why can I not have some of this divine beauty for myself?" she thought. "I will open the urn at any rate." But so sooner had she done so than deep sleep

Neide   © H. K. T.; Gramstorff Brothers

Fig. 99. Psyche returning from the Lower World

Charon carries Psyche across the Styx. She has succeeded in getting the divine beauty for which she came, and is holding it in an urn tightly clasped in her hand.

(for this is what the box contained) fell upon her. Thus Cupid found her lying upon the ground.

The gods were moved by Cupid's plea for pardon, and even Venus was touched. The lovers were allowed to be happy together.

While Venus had many lovers, the myths lead us to think that none were more dear to her than a handsome young shepherd **Adonis** named A do'nis. His death in a combat with a wild boar brought such grief to the goddess that she would not allow the body to be taken from her arms until the gods promised that he might continue to live with her during the spring and summer, and that she might spend the other half of the year with him in the Lower World.

This is one of the stories, Eastern in origin, by which the Greeks tried to explain the disappearance of vegetation in the winter and its return in the spring. The latter season was personified by Adonis, a beautiful youth whose life was short and at whose departure all nature put on mourning and ceased to bear fruit, only to rejoice again when spring returned to earth. Dirges were sung to lament his passing, and festivals were celebrated in honor of his return.

The Romans never forgot that Venus was the mother of Ae ne'as, and that it was partly due to her divine guidance that the Trojan race succeeded in establishing itself in Italy, thus laying the foundation for the Roman state. They built magnificent temples to her — especially Julius Caesar, who derived his name from I u'lus, Aeneas' son — and looked upon her as the divine ancestress of their race.

Worship of Venus at Rome

Among trees the myrtle was sacred to Venus, and among the animals the following were held in special reverence because of her — the dove, sparrow, ram, hare, swan, tortoise, and dolphin.

Sacred to Venus

IN THE WORLD OF TODAY

I. IN LITERARY ALLUSION

Lo, this is she that was the world's delight.

SWINBURNE, *Laus Veneris* (Praise of Venus), l. 9

And the anemones that April brings
Make purple pools as if Adonis came
Just there to die.

EUGENE JACOB LEE-HAMILTON, *Sonnets*, II

II. In Words and Expressions

The word "Friday" really means the "day of Venus." It comes to us, however, through our English ancestors, who in their language called it the "day of Odin's wife" — this person corresponding to Venus in classical mythology. The Romans called it "Venus' day," and their descendants, the French, Italians, and Spaniards, still use the same name. You will recognize it in **vendredi, venerdì,** and **vier-nes,** their words for Friday.

Raphael (Vatican, Rome)
Fig. 100. Friday or the "Day of Venus"

A young woman who excels in swift running is frequently called an **Atalanta.**

III. In Other Connections

Why Lovers Send Roses

When Adonis lay dying on the ground, Venus ran to help her expiring lover. In her haste she pricked herself on some white roses which chanced to be in her way; whereupon these flowers turned red, blushing with shame because they had been the cause of such an accident to the lovely goddess. But whether or not this tale is a true one, the rose at any rate was Venus' favorite flower, and florists know very well that the modern world has not forgotten this fact.

The Origin of the Red Anemone

This flower is said to have sprung from the blood of Adonis as he lay wounded on the ground.

The Fragrance of the Marjoram

The marjoram was a flower much used at weddings; the myths say that Venus created it and that the perfume is merely the fragrance of her rosy fingers.

Venus' Looking-Glass

Venus once lost a mirror which had the power of increasing the beauty of the object reflected in it. Her son Cupid, happening to find a rough shepherd gazing into it, struck it in anger from his hand. It fell to the ground, and at once a host of beautiful flowers sprang up where a moment ago there had been nothing but sod. This flower was called "Venus' Looking-Glass."

Why the Butterfly Reminds Us of Psyche

Psyche's name comes from a Greek word meaning "breath," "spirit," or "soul." She was looked upon as a kind of personification of the soul, which was symbolized by the butterfly. Sometimes she is represented in art with the lovely wings of this dainty creature.

Venus in the Sky

The most brilliant planet is Venus. So bright is it that even in the daytime it is sometimes faintly visible. At a certain time in the year we call Venus the "morning star," and at another the "evening star." This is the way in which a poet describes its loveliness as it appears just after sunset:

> Venus has lit her silver lamp
> Low in the purple West.

A Butterfly's Name

Any large dictionary contains scientific names connected with Venus or some of the characters associated with her. For example, there is a very beautiful butterfly named "Adonis."

Venus in the Operas

Of the many operas which have been written about Venus, the most famous is the one called " Tann'häus er." According to a medieval legend, a knight by this name was lured into a cavern in a mountain called "Ve'nus berg" where the goddess was holding her court — a place from which no one but Tannhäuser ever returned.

Will H. Low   *Courtesy of the artist*

Fig. 101. This picture shows how artists make use of cherubs, descendants in art of the boy Cupid

QUESTIONS FOR REVIEW

1. (1) What made Venus so charming?
   (2) Relate the circumstances of her birth.
2. Why was her worship universal?
3. (1) Describe her son Cupid both from the Roman and the Greek point of view.
   (2) What was his Greek name?
4. What different effects were produced when Cupid's arrows were tipped with gold and with lead?
5. Tell the story of how Venus helped a certain lover win a foot race and a bride.
6. How did it happen that a marble statue once became alive?
7. On what occasion did Venus fail to aid a lover who was swimming to his lady-love?
8. Relate in full the tragic story of two lovers and a lion.
9. When did Cupid become the victim of his own arts, and what was the outcome?
10. How was Venus associated by the Greeks with the disappearance of vegetation in the winter and its return in the spring?

11. Why was the worship of Venus of especial importance to the Romans?

12. What tree and what animals were sacred to Venus?

13. Why are roses the favorite flowers of lovers, according to mythology?

14. How do the myths account for the origin of the red anemone and the fragrance of the marjoram?

15. What is the meaning of Psyche's name, and how is she sometimes represented in art?

16. How does the name of Venus appear in the sky?

17. What famous opera has Venus for part of its theme?

18. Why did Shelley call one of his poems "Adonais"?

19. What name is appropriate for a fleet-footed maiden?

20. What day in the week is associated with Venus?

A QUESTION FOR THE CURIOUS

What was the name of the Greek maiden whose figure appears upon the front of a Studebaker car?

OPTIONAL

FOR THOSE WHO HAVE TIME FOR FURTHER STUDY

A. ADDITIONAL READING

I. In Textbooks Dealing with Classical Mythology

1. Details in connection with the story of Pygmalion, B., 62–63.
2. Atalanta and Hippomenes changed into lions, Gay., p. 141 (sec. 103).
3. Interesting sidelights on the story of Psyche, B., 80–89.

For other references see the Appendix, pages xxviii ff., under topics mentioned in this chapter.

II. In Books in General

1. Pyramus and Thisbe, Shakespeare's *Midsummer Night's Dream*, Act V, Sc. 1.

2. Many passages in the *Iliad*, of which the following from the translation by Lang, Leaf, and Myers, V., pp. 92–93, is an example : How Venus was wounded in battle while aiding her son. Those who are interested should collect references to this goddess from the poem as a whole.

3. Many passages from Vergil's *Aeneid*, translated by Conington, Williams, Fairclough, and others. Venus was the mother of Aeneas, the hero of this poem, and therefore is frequently mentioned in the poet's narrative. For two examples, see Bk. I, 229–260 (Latin text), ll. 255–295 in Conington's translation (Scott, Foresman edition) ; and Bk. I, 314–417 (Latin text), ll. 355–472 in Conington's translation.

4. Seymour's *Life in the Homeric Age*, pp. 434–435 (The Macmillan Company).

B. Lines to Be Memorized

And Venus loves the whisper
Of plighted youth and maid,
In April's ivory moonlight,
Beneath the chestnut shade.

Macaulay, *Lays of Ancient Rome*, "Prophecy of Capys,"
XVIII, 153–156

C. Further Study of Literary Allusion

If you are interested in seeing more clearly how good writers make use of the Greek myths, look up the following references :

Adonis: Kingsley's *Westward Ho*, p. 41 (Macmillan). **Aphrodite:** Willa Cather's short story, " Coming, Aphrodite ! " (*Golden Book*, Nov., 1926). **Atalanta:** Shakespeare's *As You Like It*, Act III, Sc. 2, 293. **Cupid:** Ben Jonson's *Runaway;* Shakespeare's *Tempest*, Act IV, Sc. 1, 90–91 ; Alcott's *Little Women*, p. 330 (Little, Brown). **Psyche:** Keats's *Ode to Psyche*, 21–24 et al. ; George Eliot's *Adam Bede*, p. 136 (Scribners). **Thisbe:** Shakespeare's *Merchant of Venice*, Act V, Sc. 1, 6–9. **Venus:** Byron's *Childe Harold*, Canto IV, 49, 433–434 ; Locke's *Tale of Triona*, p. 65 (Dodd, Mead) ; Thackeray's *The Newcomes*, Vol. I, p. 319 (Everyman's Library).

D. Projects for Individual or Group Work

To be selected from the list of projects on pages xx–xxvi, in case the subject matter of this chapter lends itself readily to any one of them.

POEMS FOR REFERENCE

BRIDGES, ROBERT	Eros and Psyche (*Poetical Works;* Oxford University Press, Oxford and N. Y.)
BYRON, LORD	* Poem Written after Swimming from Sestos to Abydos
COATES, FLORENCE E.	Of Love (*Lyrics of Life;* Houghton Mifflin Company, Boston)
DOW, DOROTHY	* To Atalanta (*Home Book of Modern Verse;* Henry Holt and Company, N. Y.)
HUNT, LEIGH	* Cupid Drowned
KEATS, JOHN	Ode to Psyche; On a Picture of Leander
LANDOR, WALTER SAVAGE	Hippomenes and Atalanta
LANG, ANDREW	* The New Pygmalion (*Poetical Works;* Longmans, Green and Company, N. Y.)
MARLOWE, CHRISTOPHER	Hero and Leander
MOORE, THOMAS	Hero and Leander; Cupid and Psyche; * Cupid Stung
MORRIS, LEWIS	Venus; Psyche (*Epic of Hades;* Kegan Paul, Trench, Trübne· and Company, London)
MORRIS, WILLIAM	Cupid and Psyche; Atalanta's Race; Pygmalion and the Image (*The Earthly Paradise;* Longmans, Green and Company, N. Y.)
SHAKESPEARE, WILLIAM	Venus and Adonis (parts)
SHELLEY, PERCY BYSSHE	Homer's Hymn to Venus
SILL, EDWARD ROWLAND	The Venus of Milo
SITWELL, EDITH	* Web of Eros (*Home Book of Modern Verse,* Henry Holt and Company, N. Y.)
SWINBURNE, ALGERNON C.	Eros
TAGGART, GENEVIEVE	Galatea Again (*Words for the Chisel;* Alfred A. Knopf, N. Y.)
TENNYSON, ALFRED	* Hero to Leander

Leroux

Fig. 102. School of the Vestals

(The artist has taken liberties as regards the number of maidens.)

VESTA
(Hes′ti a)

VESTA was the goddess who presided over the home. The hearth in particular was the center of her worship, and here sacri-
The goddess fices were made and food prepared. Spirits known
of the hearth as the La′res and Pe na′tes were associated with her, the former keeping watch over the welfare of the place in general, and the latter, in early times at least, looking after the store-houses in particular, but later serving in other ways also.

The Lares (or the Lar, for sometimes there was but a single " house spirit ") were represented as youthful male figures, often with a drinking horn in the upraised left hand and a pail in the right as though in the act of pouring a libation.

The Penates took the form of small images, among which were found the likenesses of such divinities as might be expected to serve best the interests of the particular family. So sacred were these spirits that it was considered a grave omission of duty when the master of the house forgot to make offerings of food to them at meal times, and in times of danger the protection of the images was the first thought.

Other spirits closely associated with the family hearth were known as " genii," who seem to have been somewhat like " guardian angels." Each man, for example, was supposed to be

Fig. 103. A Roman shrine

This shrine in a house at Pompeii shows the Lares painted upon the wall with the figure of the " genius " of the master (or perhaps that of the emperor) between them. The small images in front represent the Penates.

watched over throughout his life by such a divinity, while a woman had similar protection from her " Juno." The genius of the master of the house always received special worship. Rather curiously, this spirit was often represented in the form of a serpent painted upon the walls of the shrine, although in general it appears as the figure of a man clad in the toga.

The Romans paid special attention to the worship of Vesta, thinking that the preservation of the fire upon her altar was essential to their safety. They therefore built for her a very beautiful temple in the Forum, and near it constructed a house in which her attendants, the Vestal Virgins, lived.

The Vestal Virgins honored at Rome

This sisterhood was made up of six women who were chosen when quite young from the noblest families of Rome. Upon entering the order they were obliged to promise not to marry, and to serve the goddess faithfully for thirty years. At the end of this time they might marry or return to their families if they wished to do so.

The chief duties of the Vestals consisted in attending to the sacred fire and keeping guard over certain objects which were supposed to insure the safety of the Roman state, among which the most important was the wooden image of A the'na known as the Pal la'di um. There were other requirements, too, such as the instruction of the younger Vestals.

The Romans held these priestesses in the highest honor. They had many privileges not granted to other women and extraordinary powers were conferred upon them. For example, a criminal who chanced to meet a Vestal as he was being led to execution might obtain his freedom or have his death sentence deferred. On the other hand, the Vestals were strictly watched, and any neglect of duty was punished with the utmost severity. Sometimes they were even buried alive.

Those who are interested in knowing more about the Vestals should read Plutarch's *Life of Numa*, Chapters IX and X; the novel by Edward Lucas White, called *The Unwilling Vestal;*[1] and Rodolfo Lanciani's *Ancient Rome in the Light of Recent Discoveries*, Chapter VI.[2]

[1] George H. Doran and Company.   [2] Houghton Mifflin Company.

IN THE WORLD OF TODAY

I. IN LITERARY ALLUSION

Bright-haired Vesta.

MILTON, *Il Penseroso*, 23

II. IN WORDS AND PHRASES

The term **vestal** is frequently used today in connection with the idea of the hearth or domesticity.

Courtesy of the Metropolitan Museum, New York

Fig. 104. A Lar

The word **genius** seems to have retained something of the ancient meaning, as is seen, for example, in such expressions as " He proved to be my evil genius."

When people are moving they frequently say, " I am moving my **Lares and Penates**," so closely have these spirits become connected with the house and its possessions.[1]

III. IN OTHER CONNECTIONS

The Name Vesta in Science

A group of beautiful, gossamer-winged butterflies have been called " Vestals," perhaps because they suggest the white-robed priestesses of Rome.

---

[1] For a further illustration, see O. Henry's short story called " The Furnished Room," p. 239 (Doubleday, Page and Company).

In the Business World

Somewhat curiously, the name of Vesta has survived as a common term for objects associated with the hearth. For example, there are " Vesta " stoves and " Vesta " matches.

QUESTIONS FOR REVIEW

1. What was the center of Vesta's worship?
2. What spirits were associated with her, and what were their duties?
3. How were these spirits represented?
4. What were the "genii"?
5. Why did the Romans build a temple to Vesta?
6. (1) Who were the Vestal Virgins and what were their duties?
   (2) Why was their position both honorable and precarious?

A QUESTION TO THINK ABOUT

Remembering that the myths grew up in times when such conveniences as lucifer matches were unknown, can you think of any reason, other than one concerned with religion, why it was important to keep the fire on Vesta's hearth from going out?

Rubens (Prado Gallery, Madrid)

Fig. 105. Vulcan in his smithy

VULCAN
(He phaes'tus)

VULCAN was the patron god not only of workmen who by the aid of fire wrought out in their forges such objects as were neces-

Patron of artisans

sary to men in both war and peace, but of builders and artisans in general, all of whom looked to him for guidance and inspiration. He built the palaces upon Mt. O lym'-pus, fashioned the weapons used by the gods, and in general served the divinities in all ways requiring such practical skill as he possessed.

His workshops were under the earth, and the outlets to his forges were found in volcanoes. So when men saw smoke and flames pouring from the summit of Mt. Aet'na, for example, they thought that Vulcan and his assistants were hard at work down below.

Like Mi ner'va, he greatly assisted men in the arts of civilization. For as Prometheus brought fire down from heaven for

A teacher of men

men, so Vulcan taught them how to make this gift really useful.

Vulcan was not attractive in appearance; first, because he was very bulky, and secondly because he was lame. The gods

Vulcan's appearance and why he was lame

found these defects very amusing and did not hesitate to break into gales of laughter as they saw him bustling about in the palace on Mt. Olympus. And yet he was the husband of Venus, loveliest of all the goddesses.

There are two stories in explanation of Vulcan's lameness. According to one, he once took the part of Juno, his mother, in a

quarrel with her husband. Jupiter could not brook such interference and at once hurled him from Olympus. All day he fell
and finally plunged into the sea near the island of Lem'nos, from
which he escaped, although in a crippled condition.

According to another story he was born lame, and Juno, in dis-
gust, threw him from Heaven. In revenge he cunningly fashioned a golden chair which he presented to his mother. As soon
as Juno sat in it, she found herself bound fast by invisible chains
from which she could not escape. The entreaties of all the gods
were not sufficient to move Vulcan to undo his work. But finally
Bac'chus made him drunk and succeeded in inducing him to free
Juno.

In Rome he was looked upon as the god of fire who occasionally
brought much destruction to the wooden buildings of the city.
Worshiped in Rome To appease this divinity, a temple was erected in his
honor, although outside the city.

Vergil has given us a picture of Vulcan's workshop:

> Fast by Ae o'li an Lip'a re
>   And fair Si ca'ni a's coast
> An island rises from the sea
>   With smoking rocks embossed;
> Beneath, a cavern drear and vast,
> Hollowed by Cy clo pe' an blast,
>   Rings with unearthly sound;
> Bruised anvils clang their thunder-peal,
> Hot hissing glows the Chal'yb steel,
> And fiery vapor fierce and fast
>   Pants up from underground;
> The centre this of Vulcan's toil,
> And Vulcan's name adorns the soil.
> Here finds he as he makes descent,
> The Cy'clops o'er their labor bent:

Museum of the Conservatori, Rome   Photograph by Alinari

Fig. 106. The Cyclopes at work

The Cyclopes make a shield for Achilles under the direction of Vulcan.   Who are
the figures at either end?

Brontes and Ster′o pes are there,
And gaunt Pyr ac′mon, stripped and bare.
The thunderbolt was in their hand,
Which Jove sends down to scourge the land;

*   *   *   *   *   *   *

Elsewhere for Mars they plan the car
Wherewith he maddens into war
   Strong towns and spearmen bold,
And burnish Pallas' shirt of mail,
The Aegis, bright with dragon's scale
   And netted rings of gold:
The twisted serpent-locks they shape
And Gorgon's head.

*   *   *   *   *   *   *

Some make the windy bellows heave,
Now give forth air, and now receive:

The copper hisses in the wave:
The anvils press the groaning cave.
With measured cadence each and all
The giant hammers rise and fall:
The griping pincers, deftly plied,
Turn the rough ore from side to side.

Aeneid, VIII, Conington's Verse Translation, pp. 271–273 [1]

IN THE WORLD OF TODAY

I. IN LITERARY ALLUSION

The windlass strains the tackle-chains — the black mound heaves
  below,
And red and deep a hundred veins burst out at every throe.
It rises, roars, rends all outright — O Vulcan, what a glow!

SAMUEL FERGUSON, "The Forging of the Anchor," in *Lays of the Ancient Gael*

II. IN WORDS

The word **vulcanize,** meaning to treat rubber with sulphur at high temperature in order to yield elasticity and strength, comes from the name of this god. The word **volcano** is also associated with Vulcan, as has been shown earlier in this chapter. But the Greeks had another way of explaining the volcano.

World Wide Photos, New York

Fig. 107. Mt. Aetna in eruption

The flames and smoke would indicate to the Greeks that Vulcan was at work, or that some giant below was very uneasy.

III. IN OTHER CONNECTIONS

How the Greeks Accounted for the Volcano

According to one theory it was the fiery breath of some giant buried below that poured from the crater of a volcano, and it

[1] Longmans, Green and Company.

was the movement of his body from side to side that caused the awful rumbling which accompanies an eruption.

The Name " Vulcan " in the Business World

Any city directory will show indications of the fact that Vulcan's name is associated with the industrial world.

As a Synonym for Weapons of War

Because Vulcan made the weapons and armor of the gods, his name is often used in connection with war equipment. For example, the War Pictorial of the *Chicago Daily News* for February 18, 1915, has a picture of the former owner of the Krupp Works in Germany, entitled, " The Modern Vulcan."

QUESTIONS FOR REVIEW

1. Of whom was Vulcan the patron god, and what were his duties?
2. Where were his workshops, and what were the "chimneys"?
3. How were volcanic eruptions explained?
4. What service did Vulcan render to men?
5. Describe Vulcan's appearance and account for his lameness.
6. How was Juno punished for her treatment of Vulcan?
7. Why did the Romans build a temple to Vulcan?
8. Explain the meaning and significance of the word *vulcanize*.
9. In what other connections is the name Vulcan used today?
10. What was Vulcan's Greek name?
11. What is the answer to this charade?

> My first for naught has been employed,
> A verb the thrifty most avoid,
> And you and I must make my last;
> When Vulcan from my whole was cast,
> He had my second ever after,
> Provoking all the gods to laughter.
>
> WILLIAM BELLAMY

OPTIONAL

FOR THOSE WHO HAVE TIME FOR FURTHER STUDY

A. ADDITIONAL READING

I. In Textbooks Dealing with Classical Mythology

How Vulcan was waited upon in his forge and what he constructed for the gods, Gay., p. 25 (sec. 29); B., 4, 39, 41, 123.

For other references see pages xxviii ff., in the Appendix.

II. In Books in General

1. Such interesting passages in the translation of the *Iliad* by Lang, Leaf, and Myers as the following:

   Bk. I, pp. 19–20, Vulcan gives his mother good advice and relates the incident of his fall from the sky; Bk. XVIII, pp. 378–385, a description of the shield which Vulcan makes for Achilles at the request of Thetis. For an account of a shield made by Vulcan for Aeneas at the request of Venus, see the translation of the *Aeneid* by Conington (David McKay, publisher), Bk. VIII, pp. 329, 336–339.

   Bryant's verse translation of Bk. XVIII, ll. 462–588, presents an attractive picture of Thetis on the occasion of her call at Vulcan's smithy, and in the same translation, Bk. XIX, ll. 440–475, Achilles is shown trying on his new armor.

2. Seymour's *Life in the Homeric Age*, pp. 432–433 (The Macmillan Company).

B. FURTHER STUDY OF LITERARY ALLUSION

If you are interested in seeing more clearly how good writers make use of the Greek myths, look up the following references:

Vulcan: Milton's *Paradise Lost*, I, 740–746; *Comus*, 605; Shakespeare's *Hamlet*, Act III, Sc. 2, 89; *Twelfth Night*, Act V, Sc. 1, 57; Tennyson's *Princess*, III, 55–56.

C. PROJECTS FOR INDIVIDUAL OR GROUP WORK

To be selected from the list of projects on pages xx–xxvi, in case the subject matter of this chapter lends itself readily to any one of them.

POEMS FOR REFERENCE

LONGFELLOW, HENRY W.   *Enceladus

SAXE, JOHN G.   Venus and Vulcan

THE HEROES

So when the first bold vessel dared the seas,
  High on the sterr the Thracian raised his strain,
While Argo saw her kindred trees
  Descend from Pelion to the main.
Transported demigods stood round,
And men grew heroes at the sound.

POPE, Ode on Saint Cecilia's Day

Fig. 108. Bellerophon

Minerva has given Bellerophon a golden bit, and the hero is trying to entice Pegasus to come nearer so that he may put it in the horse's mouth. The figure near Pegasus is perhaps one of the nymphs.

BELLEROPHON

BEL LER'O PHON, a grandson of one of the early kings of Cor'-inth, had the misfortune accidentally at one time to cause a man's

A hero kills the Chimaera death. In order to obtain the purification thought necessary, he went to the king of Argos. In consequence of a false charge on the part of the king's wife, the hero was sent to her father, a monarch in far-away Lyc'i a, bearing letters from the king. In these were instructions to the Lycian ruler to kill the bearer, although of course Bellerophon did not know of this fact.

The king decided that the best way to carry out these instructions was to send the hero away on a journey from which he could not possibly return alive. Bellerophon was therefore sent to overcome the Chi mae'ra, a strangely formed fire-breathing monster with the body of a lion, a serpent for a tail, and a goat's head springing from its back.   This creature had long ravaged the country, and to kill it was looked upon as an impossibility. But contrary to the hopes of the king, Bellerophon, mounted on

Archaeological Museum, Florence

Fig. 109.   The Chimaera

the winged Pegasus, succeeded in slaying the monster.

After escaping from many difficult situations in which his enemy, the king, continued to place him, Bellero-

A mad adventure ends in death

phon, mounted upon the winged steed, Peg'a sus, finally died in a rash attempt to reach O lym'pus.

Although the horse, as he was immortal, succeeded in reaching the lofty heights of heaven, the hero fell headlong to the earth.

One version of the myth leads us to think that the hero was not killed in this adventure, but that he married a princess and later ascended her father's throne.

Hawthorne tells Bellerophon's story in a chapter in his *Wonder Book*, entitled " The Chimaera." [1]   It has been related at length in *The Earthly Paradise*, by William Morris.   Those who enjoy prose more than poetry will want to read a book by Madalen Edgar, called *Stories from the Earthly Paradise Retold in Prose*.[2]

IN THE WORLD OF TODAY

I. In Literary Allusion

There is that story of the golden bit
By goddess given to tame the lightning steed:
A mortal who could mount, and sit
Flying and up Olympus midway speed.

GEORGE MEREDITH, Bellerophon, IX

[1] Pp. 117–137.   Everyman's.   [2] George G. Harrap and Company, London.

II. In Words

Bel ler′o phon″tic is the name we apply to letters which carry the fate of the bearer, although the fact is quite unknown to him.

Certain ideas are called **chi mer′ic al,** meaning that they are pure fancy and outside the range of fact. When the League of Nations was first proposed, a great many people applied this adjective to it.

III. In Miscellaneous Ways

In Decorative Design

The Chimaera appears often in decorative design, especially in architecture, although in most cases greatly changed from the form known to classical mythology.

The Name "Bellerophon" in English History

One of England's war vessels in the most famous naval battle of the Na po′le on″ic wars, fought off Cape Tra fal′gar in 1805, was called "Bellerophon."

QUESTIONS FOR REVIEW

1. Who was Bellerophon?
2. What was the seemingly impossible task that he was commissioned to perform, and why was it assigned to him?
3. Describe the Chimaera.
4. In what way was Bellerophon a forerunner of some of our modern aviators?

POEMS FOR REFERENCE

MEREDITH, GEORGE   Bellerophon
MORRIS, WILLIAM   Bellerophon in Argos *and* In Lycia (*The Earthly Paradise;* Longmans, Green and Company, N. Y.)

CADMUS

A PRINCESS named Eu ro'pa once disappeared from her father's palace in Phoe nic'ia. Although people said that she had been **The building of Thebes** stolen by Jupiter (see the account given on page 93) and that it would therefore be quite useless to search for her, her two brothers, Cad'mus and Ci'lix, determined to make the attempt.

They traveled all over the world in their efforts to find some trace of their sister, but all to no purpose. Cilix finally abandoned all hope and settled down in Asia Minor, but Cadmus went on to Egypt and later to Delphi. Here he consulted the oracle, only to learn that he would never find Europa. He was somewhat cheered, however, when the priestess told him that he was destined to be the founder of one of the famous cities of the world. "When you leave this building," she said, "follow a cow, which will lead you to the site." Cadmus obeyed and later built the city of Thebes upon the spot designated. But before this happened, Cadmus had an amazing adventure.

While in search of water, Cadmus came upon a spring which was guarded by a dragon. After a long and bloody contest he **The dragon's teeth** killed the monster, and at Minerva's suggestion sowed the teeth in the ground. Immediately armed warriors sprang up, mighty in strength and enormous in size. Still following the advice of the goddess, he threw a stone into their midst, which produced a marvelous effect. The men at once began to fight one another and continued the contest until

at last only five remained alive. With the help of these five sur-
viving warriors, Cadmus built the city of Thebes.

For many years Cadmus reigned at Thebes, and it was
King of here that his daughter Sem'e le, whose story is
Thebes told in the chapter dealing with Bac'chus, met a
tragic death.

IN THE WORLD OF TODAY

I. IN LITERARY ALLUSION

These are the letters Cadmus gave.
Think you he meant them for a slave?

BYRON, *Don Juan*, Canto III, 86

NOTE: Because Cadmus came from Phoenicia, the country from which, according to tradition, the Greek alphabet was first brought to Europe, the hero's name
has been connected with literature.

II. IN WORDS AND EXPRESSIONS

The words **warriors of Cadmus** are sometimes used to describe
an army which comes into existence without any apparent preparation. During the World War, for example, a prominent newspaper in referring to certain military forces said, " It is not, therefore, a new army, sprung like warriors of Cadmus from the soil."

A **Cad me'an victory** is one in which the victor, in spite of the
fact that he has won the day, finds himself involved in even
greater danger than that from which he has just escaped. This
expression arose from the story that Cadmus had no sooner van-
quished the dragon than he was at once attacked by the armed
warriors who sprang from the ground.

Sowing dragon's teeth is a very common expression. It means
that by a certain act people are preparing trouble for themselves
— usually stirring up war. *The World of Tomorrow*, in its issue
for June, 1919, has an article with this expression as the title.

QUESTIONS FOR REVIEW

1. Why did Cadmus leave his home in Phoenicia?
2. What assistance did he receive from the oracle at Delphi?
3. Relate the circumstances that led to the founding of Thebes.
4. What was the name of the daughter of Cadmus who became the mother of a god?

OPTIONAL

FOR THOSE WHO HAVE TIME FOR FURTHER STUDY

A. ADDITIONAL READING

I. In Textbooks Dealing with Classical Mythology

1. Details of Cadmus' fight with the dragon, B., 92–93.
2. Story of Ino, daughter of Cadmus, who was changed into a sea divinity known as Leucothea, B., 174.
3. The marriage of Cadmus and Harmonia, and their transformation into serpents, B., 94; Gay., pp. 89–90.
4. Harmonia's necklace, Gay., pp. 265, 268.
5. Expedition known as "The Seven against Thebes," Gay., pp. 264–267; B., 182–183.
6. Oedipus and the Sphinx, Gay., pp. 261–264.
7. Story of Antigone, Gay., pp. 266–267.

II. In Books in General

1. "The Dragon's Teeth" in *Tanglewood Tales* by Nathaniel Hawthorne, pp. 194–220 (Everyman's Library), and similar books.

B. FURTHER STUDY OF LITERARY ALLUSION

In case you are interested in seeing more clearly how good writers make use of the Greek myths, look up the following references:

Cadmus and **Harmonia:** Milton's *Paradise Lost*, IX, 505–507. **Dragon's Teeth:** Holmes's *Autocrat of the Breakfast Table*, p. 16 (Everyman's Library); Churchill's *Mr. Crewe's Career*, p. 247 (Macmillan).

POEMS FOR REFERENCE

SOPHOCLES' *Antigone*, translated by E. H. Plumptre, and by F. Starr (Loeb Classical Library; G. P. Putnam's Sons, N. Y.). This story is connected with Thebes and the descendants of Cadmus.

HERCULES
(Her'a cles)

No Greek hero was more widely known in ancient times than Her'cu les, and even today his name appears frequently in our magazines and newspapers, an evidence of the fact that the world is slow to forget strong men and brave deeds.

A strong man who loved adventure

Juno was largely responsible for the fact that the hero's whole life was spent in the midst of danger and toil. She disliked him exceedingly and did her best to involve him in difficulties. Her relentless hatred was doubtless due to the fact that Hercules was the son of Jupiter and a distinguished woman named Alc me'ne, although Am phit'ry on, a mortal, was commonly known as the child's father.

But Hercules, who always loved adventure, did not complain about his fate. On the other hand, he seemed rather to enjoy the opportunity to overcome obstacles and to accomplish difficult tasks. Perhaps the thought that, by ridding the country of savage monsters and evils equally dangerous, he might make the world a better place in which to live, had something to do with his feeling. At any rate, the hero never tried to avoid labor, although a person as strong as he was need not have obeyed any master who was a mortal, had he not been willing to do so.

The extraordinary physical powers of Hercules showed themselves at a very early age. He was barely ten months old when he accomplished a feat which was nothing less than wonderful, and which proved beyond a doubt that he was no ordinary child.

Alcmene, the mother of Hercules, had put the infant and his half-brother Iph'i cles to sleep in a cradle made from Amphit-

An early evidence of physical strength

ryon's shield. Soon afterwards the whole household was wrapped in slumber. But in the middle of the night queer sounds were heard in the room in which the babes were sleeping. When Alcmene, carrying a light, entered the door, she saw a sight which caused her to cry

Capitoline Museum, Rome

Fig. 110. The young Hercules

Hercules, although an infant, finds no difficulty in strangling the serpents.

out in terror. Two huge serpents were near the cradle! The infants had evidently been awakened by the movement of the shield, for they were sitting up, and Iphicles was whimpering in fright. But when Amphitryon came rushing in, summoned by his wife's cries, the danger was over. There sat Hercules, clutching the necks of the serpents in his chubby hands and slowly strangling them to death. But what surprised the parents most was the fact that the child was laughing and seemed to be enjoying the adventure.

The outstanding achievements of Hercules were the famous "Twelve Labors," tasks so difficult that they seemed far beyond

The reason for the Labors of Hercules

the power of man to accomplish. These were exacted from the hero because of an act which he committed when made insane by Juno, and which Apollo thought should be expiated, namely, the murder of his own wife and children. Eu rys'theus, king of Ti'ryns, was charged with the execution of the punishment. How Hercules succeeded in the case of each Labor in carrying out the harsh commands of this master is related in the paragraphs that follow.

A savage lion, sent by Juno, was ravaging the country around Ne'me a, a region not far from Cor'inth. Hercules was ordered

The First Labor — the Nemean Lion

to destroy it. After a long and terrible struggle he succeeded in strangling the beast, and, as an evidence of the victory, he bore away the lion's skin, which he continued to wear as his mantle for the rest of his life. The myths say that no weapon could penetrate this pelt.

An awful monster with nine heads, a creature known as the Hy'dra, infested the Ler ne'an swamp not far from Ar'gos. At

The Second Labor — the Hydra

first Hercules thought that all he had to do in order to kill it was to destroy the heads. But he soon discovered that as fast as he did this, other heads grew in their places. He therefore directed his friend I o la'us to sear the bleeding necks with a blazing torch, and by such means he prevented the growth of new heads. One head, however, said to be immortal, he hid under a stone. Finally the Hydra was overcome.

Hercules was doubly glad of his victory over this monster because not only was he able to please the king by thus executing his commands, but he gained an advantage for himself as well, in that he was able to make his arrows deadly ever after by dipping them in the blood of the slain Hydra.

Some one has suggested that this story as a whole symbolizes the draining of some pestilential swamp in the early days of Greece.

A wild boar, which had escaped the efforts of all hunters to capture it, had long rendered Mt. Er y man'thus in Ar ca'di a

The Third Labor — the Erymanthian Boar

a most dangerous region. This beast Hercules was ordered to bring alive to King Eurystheus. After a long and hazardous chase, the hero finally entangled the creature in a net on the summit of the mountain. When the

John Singer Sargent   © Museum of Fine Arts, Boston

Fig. 111. Hercules kills the Hydra

king saw Hercules coming towards him dragging the boar, he
was very much frightened, so much so, in fact, that he tried to
conceal himself by climbing into a huge jar which happened to
be at hand. Hercules must have been amused as he saw the
king peeping out over the rim of the jar.

To capture an ordinary doe would have caused Hercules no trouble, but to catch one that never grew tired was quite a different matter. So when the hero heard that he was expected to bring alive to the king a doe with golden horns and brazen hoofs which roamed the hills of Cer y ne'a near Arcadia, an animal which could run continuously without fatigue, he realized that he had a most difficult task before him. But after pursuing the doe for an entire year, he caught it and presented it to King Eurystheus.

The Fourth Labor — the Cerynean Doe

The Stym pha'li an Swamp in Arcadia was the home of huge birds with arrow-pointed feathers and cruel claws — a source of great danger to men. By the aid of Minerva, who throughout the hero's life rendered him kindly assistance, Hercules scared them from their haunts by shaking enormous rattles, and then shot them with his arrows.

The Fifth Labor — the Birds of Stymphalus

King Au ge'as in E'lis was very wealthy and kept many herds and flocks. Among his possessions were twelve white bulls sacred to the sun-god. When Hercules learned that at the king's command he must in one day clean stables which had remained untouched for thirty years, he saw at once that success would be impossible by ordinary means. He therefore resolved to turn the waters of a neighboring river, called the Al phe'us, into the stables. This device proved successful, and the hero was able to report that he had accomplished the task assigned him.

The Sixth Labor — the Stables of King Augeas

Neptune had once presented to King Mi'nos of Crete a beautiful bull of enormous size, destined for sacrifice to the god. But when the king decided to keep the animal for himself, it began to show signs of a strange madness, which continued to increase in violence until the beast became a source of great danger to the inhabitants of Crete. Hercules was told to bring this brute to King Eurystheus.

The Seventh Labor — the Cretan Bull

Since Minos lived on an island far out in the Ae ge'an Sea, the hero was at first greatly puzzled as to how to get the maddened bull to Greece. The first step, he thought, would be to tame the creature so that it would obey his commands. This Hercules did. Then, leaping upon its back, he drove the animal into the sea and forced it to swim to the mainland. The rest of the task was easy, for it only remained to lead the tired bull to the palace of Eurystheus.

The myths say that the bull did not stay in Greece but made its way back to Crete. The chapter called " Theseus " relates other details concerning this famous bull.

A certain Di'o mede, king of Thrace, had been accustomed to feed a pair of horses on human flesh. So fierce were they that **The Eighth Labor — the Horses of Diomede** only bronze chains and iron stalls could hold them. But in spite of the difficulty involved in conquering such savage animals, Hercules succeeded, and in order to punish this cruel king as he deserved, he threw him into the stalls to be devoured by his own steeds.

The daughter of King Eurystheus very greatly desired a certain girdle belonging to Hip pol'y te, queen of the Am'a zons, warlike **The Ninth Labor — Hippolyte's Girdle** women who won much fame in olden times by engaging in battle with men on equal terms. Through the admiration which the queen felt for his brave deeds, Hercules succeeded in gaining this ornament.

Hercules was commanded to capture the cattle of Ge'ry on, a huge monster with three bodies, six arms, and six legs who lived **The Tenth Labor — the Cattle of Geryon** far to the West. In fact, this region was so remote that the hero might never have succeeded in reaching it if Apollo had not given him a golden bowl to use as a boat, and if Hercules' quick wit had not suggested to him the idea that the lion's skin would make a very good sail.

When he landed, the hero was surprised to see so many thousands of red cattle grazing in the pastures of Geryon. But he had little time to admire the splendid animals, for he was at once attacked by a powerful hound which guarded them, and by a herdsman of extraordinary strength. After subduing both of these, and after a terrible struggle with the giant himself, Hercules succeeded in driving away the cattle.

National Museum (Naples)

Fig. 112. An Amazon

Many exciting incidents happened in the course of the hero's return journey, one of which was concerned with the attempt of

The attempt of Cacus foiled

another giant, named Ca'cus, to steal some of the cattle. This took place on what was later known as the Av'en tine Hill in the city of Rome. Cacus thought himself very shrewd indeed in making a plan to deceive Hercules, for instead of driving the cattle which he had stolen into his cave, he dragged them in by the tails so that the tracks of the animals might indicate that they had gone out of, rather than into, the cave. ·

But as Hercules passed the cave, driving the herd before him, he noted that the lowing of the cattle was answered by a similar lowing within the cave. His suspicions were at once aroused, and it did not take him long to discover the facts in the case. Cacus was killed and the stolen animals restored to the herd.

Far off in the western ocean was a wonderful garden containing trees which bore apples of gold, of which At'las, the giant who **The Eleventh** supported the heavens upon his shoulders, was the **Labor — the** possessor. So precious did he consider these apples **Golden** that he had them guarded not only by a fierce **Apples of the** **Hesperides** dragon, whose eyes never closed in slumber, but by his daughters as well — stately maidens who were known as the Hes per'i des.

When Hercules learned that he must get this golden fruit for King Eurystheus, he saw that he must first of all secure the aid of Atlas. The giant consented to help him, but of course he could not possibly set forth on this errand while he was holding up the sky. Hercules, therefore, had to assume this burden. Atlas, however, so much enjoyed his freedom that when he came back from the garden, he proposed that he take the apples himself to the king. " But just hold the heavens a moment," said Hercules, " until I can fix a pad for my shoulders." The unwary Atlas consented, whereupon Hercules started home with his booty.

While engaged in the accomplishment of this Labor, the hero had several adventures.

In the course of his search for the garden of the Hesperides, Hercules met a terrible giant named An tae'us, who, as rumor **Antaeus, the** said, had killed many men. In fact, it was reported **giant** that a certain temple in the neighborhood was hung thick with the skulls of men whom he had challenged and then

Fig. 113. The architectural design known as the "Atlas," the figure of a man upholding a heavy weight, is frequently seen in any large city where the buildings are richly ornamented. The female figure in the center, however, is known as a "Caryatid."

overcome in combat.   But Hercules did not hesitate to encounter him.   He had little difficulty in throwing the giant down, but for some reason or other he could not keep him there.   Curiously enough, he seemed all the stronger by reason of the fall.   This was because Gae'a (Earth) was the giant's mother, and she renewed his strength each time that he touched her.   When Hercules realized this, he held Antaeus up in his powerful arms and strangled him while he was off the ground.

Another incident in the journey of Hercules, and one that brought him great fame, is concerned with Pro me'theus.   This **Prometheus is freed** Ti'tan, whose story is told earlier in this book, had been condemned by Jupiter to be chained forever to the Cau'ca sus Mountains while an eagle tore continually at his liver.   Hercules put an end to this torture by setting Prometheus free.

In spite of terrible dangers attendant upon the adventure, Hercules was able to bring the three-headed dog, Cer'ber us, **The Twelfth Labor** from the Lower World up to the earth.   Later he was returned so that Pluto's kingdom might not lack a guardian.   This was the last of the tasks which King Eurystheus exacted from Hercules.

In spite of the years of toil and hardship which Hercules had been obliged to spend in order to gain his freedom from servitude, **Once more a slave** he was reckless enough to bring once more upon his head the wrath of the gods, and in consequence to be condemned again to slavery.   His crime consisted in killing a man, who, as it seemed to Jupiter, should have had a guest's protection.   As a punishment the hero was obliged to serve a three-year sentence as a slave to Queen Om'pha le of Lyd'i a.

The duties which the queen exacted of Hercules were altogether different from anything which he had known when serving Eurystheus. Most of the time he spent in sitting about the court, wearing the garments of a woman and engaged in such feminine occupations as spinning. One might think that this life would have been intolerable to a person like Hercules. But the myths say that he did not find his days unpleasant, because he had fallen deeply in love with Omphale. Besides, he seized several opportunities to perform feats of strength not inferior to some which had brought him fame in previous years.

The account of the exploits of Hercules would not be complete without the strange tale of the hero's victorious contest with Death.

It chanced one time that Hercules stopped for rest and refreshment at the palace of King Ad me'tus in Thes'sa ly, where he was **An encounter** most graciously received. But in spite of the cour- **with Death** tesies extended to him, he could not help perceiving an air of gloom. This he tried to banish by his gay conversation, and it was only when a servant rebuked him with the words, " Such behavior does not befit a guest in a palace where the queen lies dead," that he found out the situation.

He learned that the doom of death which had been decreed for Admetus had been postponed by the aid of Apollo, on condition that some one be found to die in the king's place. But of all the relatives, friends, and followers of the king, none had been willing to make such a sacrifice. Al ces'tis, however, the king's young and beautiful wife, had not hesitated. " Gladly will I go to the house of Ha'des for you, my husband," she said, and although the king protested, he seems to have been not unwilling to accept the gift of life at her hands.

Hercules went away. When he returned he brought with him a veiled woman whom he asked the king to admit to his home. When Admetus objected, saying that no one should ever take the place of Alcestis, the veil was removed, and he saw to his astonishment his young wife standing before him. Hercules had wrestled with Death and forced him to give up his prey.

A centaur named Nes'sus had given De ja ni'ra, the wife of Hercules, a small bottle filled with his own blood, telling her that **How Hercules** if she ever found that her husband was ceasing to love **died** her, she could restore his affection by means of it. And so, when later her suspicions were aroused by the story of a

Capitoline Museum, Rome

Fig. 114. A centaur

princess whom Hercules had carried off as a captive, she sent her husband a garment which she had dipped in the blood. No sooner had he put it on than he felt as though his body were on fire. He attempted to throw off the garment, but so closely did it adhere to his flesh that his efforts only increased his agony. Realizing that death was near, he threw himself upon a huge funeral pyre which he had helped to construct on the top of a mountain, and perished in the flames.

As the smoke rolled up to the sky, lightning played about the pile and thunder crashed; for Jupiter, who was the father of Hercules, could not endure that his son should have an inglorious end.

The myths say that the hero was taken up to O lym'pus and there made a god. It is interesting to know, moreover, that he married Hebe, thus becoming the son-in-law of Juno, who had caused him so much trouble when he was a mortal.

IN THE WORLD OF TODAY

I. In Literary Allusion

Deep degraded to a coward's slave,
Endless contests bore Al ci'des brave.

Note: Alcides was one of Hercules' names.   Schiller, *Ideal and Life*

With At lan te'an shoulders fit to bear
The weight of mightiest monarchies.

Milton, *Paradise Lost*, II, 306–307

Note: "Atlantean" shoulders mean shoulders as strong as those of Atlas.

II. In Words and Expressions

We use the word **her cu'le an** to define any work which calls
for an extraordinary amount of strength. For example, when
our American engineers went to France during the World War, a
writer in a certain magazine spoke of the **herculean labors** which
they accomplished.

The term **hydra-headed** is used to describe an evil which, if
overcome in one place, breaks out in another.

Sometimes a difficult undertaking is expressed by the phrase
an Augean task, meaning that its accomplishment is as trying as
that which confronted Hercules in the kingdom of Augeas.

A person or a country which seems to thrive on defeat, becoming
stronger with each misfortune, is sometimes called **a modern
Antaeus.** Not long ago a writer in the *Atlantic Monthly* spoke
of Russia as a country "whose strength is renewed with every
fall, like **Antaeus** of old."

To say that **one cannot snatch the club of Hercules** means
that it is impossible to steal the power and ability of a great
man.

A gift which causes pain and trouble is often called a **shirt of Nessus.**

III. In Other Connections

The Hercules Beetle

The name "Hercules" has been given to a powerful beetle to signify its chief characteristic—physical strength.

Fig. 115. The Hercules beetle

The Hydra in Science

The hydra with which Hercules fought has been commemorated in scientific terminology.   A certain poisonous sea-snake has been called a "hydra," and, more interesting still, certain fresh-water polyps which have the power of renewing themselves by division (that is, any part which is cut off from the rest becomes a complete creature) have the same name.   Moreover, this hydra has six or seven arms with which it stings its prey and carries food to its mouth, thus resembling still more the many-headed monster of antiquity.

A Possible Origin of a Scientific Term

The Ca na'ry Islands just off the African coast are perhaps connected by legend with the story of Atlas.   Since the Greeks spoke of the garden of the Hesperides with its golden apples lying "somewhere in the West," and since the islands just mentioned are famous for oranges and other "golden" fruit, it is barely possible that the Greeks had these in mind when they made up the story about the "apples of gold."   Scientists, at any rate, knew of this theory when they coined the term "hesperidium" to denote that kind of fleshy fruit with many partitions in it of which oranges are a type.

Everyone Has an "Atlas" in His Body

Just at the back of the neck, where the skull is fastened to the spine, is a bone called "atlas," which supports the head.

Why the Atlantic Ocean Was So Named

Atlas was supposed to have lived in the regions around what is now known as the Straits of Gi bral'tar (although the Greeks knew the rocks at either side of the strait as the "Pillars of Hercules," and said that the hero himself had set them up in the course of his adventure with Geryon). The waters adjacent to this strait and especially those to the west came to be thought of as "the waters of Atlas," hence the name "Atlantic."

The Atlas Mountains

As one approaches the Straits of Gibraltar and enters the Med i ter ra'ne an Sea, he sees a mountain range in northern Africa called "Atlas." According to one version of the story, the giant Atlas was changed to stone by the sight of Me du'sa's head, and appeared as a mountain ever after. But there is another explanation which is indicated under the heading of "Optional" on page 227.

A South American River

Of course the Amazons, powerful women who fought like men in battle, are well known from their connection with the story of Hercules. It is a curious fact that one of the largest rivers in the world, the Amazon in South America, is named from these women. So is a genus of birds which haunt it, and a beautiful green stone found near it. This came about from the fact that the Spaniards who first discovered the river reported that they had seen huge female warriors along its banks.

Among the Stars

Both Hercules and the Hydra are prominent among the constellations.

QUESTIONS FOR REVIEW

1. Why was Hercules so many times exposed to danger, and why did he not try to avoid it?

2. What physical feat did he perform when he was only ten months old?

3. Mention as many of the "Twelve Labors" of Hercules as you can, and tell why they were assigned to him.

4. Relate the hero's adventure with the Hydra.

5. What mantle did he wear as evidence of one of his victories, and what peculiar quality did it possess?

6. What method did Hercules use for cleaning the Augean stables?

7. Tell the story of how Hercules brought the cattle of Geryon to King Eurystheus.

8. How did he obtain the golden apples of the Hesperides?

9. On what occasion was the hero victorious in a contest with Death?

10. What caused the death of Hercules? What part did Jupiter play in the last rites?

11. Whence did the Atlantic Ocean receive its name? The Amazon River?

12. Explain the terms *an Augean task, a modern Antaeus, hydra-headed, Atlantean shoulders.*

13. What was the Greek name of Hercules?

QUESTIONS FOR CONSIDERATION

1. What does the Latin phrase *ex pede Herculem* mean? This appears now and then in books and periodicals and is usually explained in the back of any large dictionary.

2. What is the book in the library which contains maps of the world called?

3. Some people think that the parallel bars in the sign for our dollar, which came to us from Spain and which was equal in value to eight Spanish coins, represented originally the "pillars" of Hercules, that is, the rock now known as Gibraltar and the corresponding one on the coast of Africa. The line curved about them is explained as the figure eight. Do you know any better explanation?

OPTIONAL

FOR THOSE WHO HAVE TIME FOR FURTHER STUDY

A. ADDITIONAL READING

I. In Textbooks Dealing with Classical Mythology

1. Hercules, a youth, meets Pleasure and Duty — his "choice," Gay., p. 216.
2. A contest with Acheloüs for the hand of Dejanira, Gay., pp. 203-204 (sec. 146); B., 177-179.
3. Why Atlas was changed into a mountain, Gay., p. 211 (sec. 153); B., 117-118.
4. Why Hercules was often called "Alcides," Gay., p. 216.
5. How Hercules was honored after death by Jupiter, B., 149.

For other references see pages xxviii ff., under the heading of subjects mentioned in this chapter.

II. In Books in General

1. "The Three Golden Apples" in *The Wonder Book* by Nathaniel Hawthorne, pp. 73-91 (Everyman's Library).
2. "The Pygmies" in *Tanglewood Tales* by Nathaniel Hawthorne, pp. 175-193 (Everyman's Library). This story is concerned with Antaeus.
3. *Life and Death of Jason* by William Morris, ll. 234-249 in Book III (Everyman's Library), contains a striking picture of Hercules. The loss of Hylas is related in IV, 360-657. (See page 233.)
4. "The Golden Apples," part of a poem called *The Earthly Paradise*, by William Morris.
5. Translation of the *Odyssey* by Butcher and Lang: Even the ghosts in Hades fear Hercules, XI, pp. 190-191.

6. Translation of Ovid's *Metamorphoses* (Loeb Classical Library, G. P. Putnam's Sons); Hercules fights with Acheloüs, a rival for the hand of Dejanira, IX, pp. 3–9; a dramatic account of the death of Hercules, IX, pp. 15–23.

7. Poems listed below, the titles of which are starred.

B. FURTHER STUDY OF LITERARY ALLUSION

If you are interested in seeing more at length how good writers make use of the myths, look up the following references:

Amazons: Cable's *Dr. Sevier*, p. 197 (Scribners); Locke's *Septimus*, p. 19 (John Lane); Byron's *Childe Harold*, Canto I, 57. **Atlas:** Macaulay's *Prophecy of Capys*, xxxi, 285–286. **Dejanira:** *Count of Monte Cristo*, Vol. I, p. 312 (A. L. Burt). **Hercules:** Holmes's *Autocrat of the Breakfast Table*, p. 110 (Everyman's Library); Thackeray's *The Newcomes*, Vol. I, p. 287 (Everyman's Library); Shakespeare's *Hamlet*, Act I, Sc. 2, l. 153. **Gates of Hercules:** Joaquin Miller's *Columbus*, 2 (Poems). **Hesperides:** Milton's *Comus*, ll. 393–395, also 981–983; Shakespeare's *Pericles*, Act I, Sc. 1, ll. 27–29.

C. PROJECTS FOR INDIVIDUAL OR GROUP WORK

To be selected from the list of projects on pages xx–xxvi, in case the subject matter of this chapter lends itself readily to any one of them.

POEMS FOR REFERENCE

BROWNING, ROBERT	Balaustion's Adventure (certain passages)
CALVERLEY, G. S.	Translation from Theocritus, Idyll XXIV, The Infant Hercules (*Complete Works;* George Bell and Sons, London)
EURIPIDES	Translation of Alcestis (Loeb Classical Library; G. P. Putnam's Sons, N. Y.)
GUITERMAN, ARTHUR	* Hercules & Co. (*Balladmaker's Pack;* Harper and Brothers, N. Y.)
LOWELL, JAMES RUSSELL	* The Shepherd of King Admetus

MONTGOMERY, ROSELLE MERCIER	His Wife, to Atlas (*Ulysses Returns and Other Poems;* Brentano's, N. Y.)
MORRIS, LEWIS	Deianira (*Epic of Hades;* Kegan Paul, Trench, Trübner and Company, London)
MORRIS, WILLIAM	The Golden Apples; *also* The Love of Alcestis (*The Earthly Paradise,* Longmans, Green and Company. N. Y.)
ROGERS, SAMUEL	The Torso of Hercules
TENNYSON, ALFRED	The Hesperides

Capitoline Museum, Rome

Fig. 116. Hercules

Fig. 117. Margaret Anglin as Medea

JASON AND THE ARGONAUTS

THERE is a story that a certain stepmother in Cor'inth, wife of a king, tried to persuade her husband to sacrifice one of his children,

What was the Golden Fleece? a boy named Phrix'us, to Jupiter. But the god interfered and sent a ram with golden fleece to carry off both the boy and his sister Hel'le. Helle lost her hold and fell into the sea, but Phrixus kept on his way until he reached Col'chis on the east shore of the Eux'ine Sea (now called the Black Sea). There he sacrificed the ram to Mars and hung up its fleece of gold on a tree guarded by a sleepless dragon.

Such a treasure as the Fleece would naturally be greatly desired, and many a ship sailed to Colchis in a vain attempt to carry off so rich a prize. And while it was a well-known fact that no one returned alive from this hazardous enterprise, there were still persons so adventurous in spirit that they welcomed the opportunity to have a part in this dangerous undertaking. Therefore when a hero named Ja'son found it necessary to set off on the quest, he had no difficulty in discovering companions for the voyage.

The circumstances connected with Jason's departure in search of the Fleece are these: He was the son of King Ae'son in

Why Jason sailed to Colchis Thes'sa ly, and when very young was sent away to be educated. Upon his return he found that Pe'li as, his uncle, was ruling in his father's place. The usurper did not wish to give up the throne, and so he bargained thus with his nephew: Jason was to sail to Colchis and bring back the Golden Fleece, and in return for this treasure, Pelias was to hand over the kingdom to his nephew. In making such a pact the king doubtless thought that Jason would never return from his perilous journey.

Jason at once set about preparing for the adventure. A very stout ship was built, which was called "Ar'go" from the name of its builder. All possible pains

Preparations for the voyage

were taken to make it seaworthy and to equip it well for encountering the dangers of the sea. Minerva herself helped in its construction by placing in its prow a beam from an oak tree, which, strange to say, could speak and utter prophecies.

British Museum, London

Fig. 118. The building of the Argo

Then Jason gathered around him the most valiant heroes of Greece, most of them sons or grandsons of the gods, among whom were Her'cu les, Cas'tor and Pol'lux, and Pe'leus, whose son A chil'les was then but an infant. Or'pheus also went along to cheer the men with his lyre.

This musician was especially inspiring on the homeward voyage (for this proved to be both long and dangerous), and in moments of discouragement he would sing:

> A little more, a little more,
>   O carriers of the Golden Fleece!
> A little labor with the oar,
>   Before we reach the land of Greece.[1]

Whereupon the sailors would redouble their efforts and feel new strength for encountering difficulties.

---

[1] *Life and Death of Jason* by William Morris, XIV, 137–140 (Everyman's Library).

The Ar'go nauts, for so the sailors (Latin, *nautae*) of the "Argo" were called, met with many adventures on the way, two of which are related in the following paragraphs.

At one of the stopping places Hercules went into the forest accompanied by a very handsome youth named Hy'las. As the **Hylas is lost** latter was drinking from a spring, the nymphs, struck by his beauty, fell in love with him and drew him down into the waters. At least Hercules believed that this fate must have befallen the young man, for although he hunted for a long time, he could not find him.

Just at the entrance to the Euxine Sea were the Sym pleg'a des, or clashing rocks, which occasioned another exciting incident in **The clashing** the journey of the Argonauts. Curiously enough, **rocks** these rocks had a habit of crashing together whenever anything, even a bird, tried to pass between them. The clever Jason met this danger by sending through the passage a dove, which escaped with the loss of only its tail feathers. Then, while the rocks were rebounding, the "Argo" slipped between them.

As soon as Jason landed at Colchis he went at once to King Ae e'tes to ask for the Fleece. He was told that he might have **King Aeëtes** it if between dawn and sunset he could harness **makes** some brazen-hoofed bulls and with them plow the **conditions** field of Mars. After this he must also sow the dragon's teeth which Minerva had given him. Undaunted by these seemingly impossible tasks, Jason, having no alternative, accepted the conditions.

But the hero was very fortunate in having almost immediately excited a friendly interest in the king's daughter Me de'a, other-**Medea helps** wise his success would have been doubtful. This **Jason** maiden, being very well versed in charms and magic, was able to be of great assistance. She gave the hero an ointment with which to rub his body before he encountered the bulls, so powerful in its effect that Jason had little difficulty in harnessing the animals to the plow and completing the task assigned. He was equally successful in planting the dragon's teeth and in escaping the danger that confronted him when a crop of armed men sprang up from them; for he remembered Medea's directions to throw a stone into their midst, as Cad'mus had done at Thebes. This caused the warriors to turn against one another, and so in a short time all of them were killed.

Although Jason had carried out the imposed conditions, Aeëtes even then was slow to point out the tree upon which the Golden Fleece was hanging. Again Medea came to the aid of the hero. Not only did she tell him where to find the tree, but she also gave him a liquid to pour over the eyes of the dragon which guarded it. As soon as the monster's eyes had closed in sleep, Jason seized the prize which he had come so far to obtain.

Jason was of course unwilling to leave Colchis without Medea, who had been so good a friend, and Medea wished very much to **The lovers escape** accompany him in his journey back to Greece, for she had loved the hero from the first. But they both saw that while no attempt might be made to interfere with the sailing of the "Argo," even though it bore the Golden Fleece, the king would not stand quietly by while Jason carried off a princess in the person of his own daughter.

As usual, Medea's quick wit did not fail her. Knowing that escape depended upon delaying her father's pursuit, she resorted to the only device that seemed to promise success, horrible though it was. Her young brother, Ab syr'tus, was cut into pieces and the fragments flung into the sea as the "Argo" sailed away. She knew that her father would not leave the pieces floating in the water, for to the Greeks an unburied body meant that the spirit would be doomed to wander eternally. The horrified father therefore stopped to gather up the remains and give them proper

Fig. 119. The dragon, charmed by music, is slain by Jason

burial, thus affording Jason sufficient time to outdistance the ships which Aeëtes sent in pursuit. In this way the lovers escaped and in due time reached Greece.

For many years Jason and Medea lived happily together in Corinth.

Sichel © *H. K. T.; Gramstorff Brothers*

Fig. 120. Medea meditates the murder of her children

A wrong avenged But in the course of time Jason tired of her, even after several children had been born to them, and he proposed to take another wife. So fierce was Medea's anger at this insult that she slew her own children, so that they might not live to bring comfort to Jason and perpetuate his race. Moreover, she caused her rival to die in great agony by means of a beautiful robe which she sent to her under the guise of friendliness, but which she had steeped in poison. Then, mounting her chariot drawn by dragons, she flew away to Athens. Here she married Ae'geus, the father of the great hero, The'seus.

IN THE WORLD OF TODAY

I. IN LITERARY ALLUSION

The winds that once the "Argo" bore
Have died by Neptune's ruined shrines,
And her hull is the drift of the deep-sea floor,
Though shaped of Pe'li on's tallest pines.

You may seek her crew on every isle
Fair in the foam of Ae ge'an seas,
But out of their rest, no charm can wile
Jason and Orpheus and Hercules.

EDNA DEAN PROCTOR, *Heroes*

II. IN A WORD

Persons who undertake a long journey involving much hardship, with a view to gain of some sort or other, are called **Argonauts.** The name is particularly applicable to those American pioneers who in 1849 and 1850 made their difficult way across the country to the gold fields of the West.

III. IN OTHER CONNECTIONS

The Order of the Golden Fleece

In Spanish countries and in Austria men are still decorated for unusual achievement with the Order of the Golden Fleece. The custom dates back to the fifteenth century. The badge given by this order bears these Latin words: *Pretium laboris non vile*, meaning "No cheap reward for toil." This is an excellent motto for everyone who cares about doing something that is really worth while, regardless of the effort it may cost.

Several theories have been advanced to account for the name of this order, but it is commonly supposed that it goes back for its origin to the story of the Argonauts.

Medea as a Theme for Opera and Drama

Thirty-one operas have been based upon the story of Medea and Jason, and no Greek play is more often seen on the stage than the tragedy written by Eu rip'i des, called *Medea*. She has become the type of a proud, angry, and outraged wife whose revenge is swift and terrible.

The Greek Name for the Dardanelles

The ancient name for what is now the Dar da nelles' was "Hel'-les pont" (*pontus* means "sea"), so called because Helle is said to have fallen into these waters when, together with her brother, she was trying to escape on the ram's back.

The Constellation Called "Gemini" (Twins)[1]

The Greeks honored two of Jason's companions, Castor and Pollux, by naming the constellation known as "Gem'i ni" after them. The Romans held them in high regard because they thought that it was by their divine assistance that the battle of Lake Re gil'lus had been won, and in commemoration of their timely aid a temple was erected to them in the Roman Forum. The story says that after assisting the Romans on the battlefield Castor and Pollux rode into the Forum and watered their horses.

These lines from Macaulay's *Lays of Ancient Rome* describe the incident :

> Then burst from that great concourse
>   A shout that shook the towers,
> And some ran north, and some ran south,
>   Crying, " The day is ours!"
> But on rode these strange horsemen,
>   With slow and lordly pace;
> And none who saw their bearing
>   Durst ask their name or race.
> On rode they to the Forum,
>   While laurel-boughs and flowers,
> From house-tops and from windows,
>   Fell on their crests in showers.
> When they drew nigh to Vesta,
>   They vaulted down amain,
> And washed their horses in the well
>   That springs by Vesta's fane.

[1] See Star Map, Fig. 24.

And straight again they mounted,
   And rode to Vesta's door;
Then, like a blast, away they passed,
   And no man saw them more.

      "Battle of Lake Regillus," XXXIX, 733–752

St. Elmo's Fire

The strange phosphorescent light sometimes seen on the ends of masts was associated in ancient times with Castor and Pollux, who, by this manifestation, were thought to show their protecting power over mariners. It is now called "St. Elmo's fire," and is looked upon by sailors as a sign of good luck.

A Symbol for Close Friendship between Men

Castor and Pollux were half brothers, for while Le'da was the mother of both of them, Castor had Tyn da're us, king of Sparta, for his father, and Pollux was known as the son of Jupiter. Their devotion to each other was so great that when Castor, a mortal, was killed, Pollux, though immortal, insisted upon taking the former's place in Hades every other day. In this way each of the brothers spent half of his time on earth and half in the Lower World.

Castor was a patron of horse-trainers and Pollux presided over the art of boxing.

QUESTIONS FOR REVIEW

1. Where and what was the Golden Fleece?

2. What were the circumstances connected with Jason's quest for the Golden Fleece?

3. What was the name of Jason's ship? Describe its construction. Who built it?

4. What were the men called who sailed on this expedition? Name five of the heroes.

5. What exciting adventure did they experience when they reached the Symplegades?

6. Upon what conditions only was Jason permitted to obtain the Golden Fleece?

7. Who helped him and in what way?

8. Relate at length the difficulties he encountered in securing the Golden Fleece.

9. Describe the elopement of Jason and Medea. Did they "live happily ever after"?

10. What names from this story are used in modern times, and in what connection?

QUESTIONS FOR SOMEONE WITH INITIATIVE

1. What is the name of one of San Francisco's leading papers, suggested by the story of Jason's adventure in search of the Golden Fleece?

2. The Greeks and Romans were accustomed to use in their oaths the names of certain gods and heroes. For example, they often said, "By Hercules." Having learned that two famous heroes were called "gemini," can you suggest a possible origin for a harmless oath which most schoolboys have used at some time or other?

OPTIONAL

FOR THOSE WHO HAVE TIME FOR FURTHER STUDY

A. ADDITIONAL READING

I. In Textbooks Dealing with Classical Mythology

1. Medea by her magic powers restores Jason's father to youth, and by the same means destroys his wicked uncle, Gay., pp. 233–235; B., 134–136.

2. Circumstances of Castor's death, Gay., p. 243.

For other references see the Appendix, pages xxviii ff., under the headings of subjects mentioned in this chapter.

II. In Books in General

1. " The Golden Fleece " in *Tanglewood Tales* by Nathaniel Hawthorne, pp. 227–310 (Everyman's Library).

2. * *Life and Death of Jason* by William Morris (Everyman's Library, (E. P. Dutton and Company). Jason's early education, I, 103–184; 223–266; Juno carries Jason over a stream, I, 285–343; Story of Phrixus and Helle, II, 344–785; Jason resolves to undertake the search for the Fleece, II, 786–910; The Argonauts assemble, III; * * The ship " Argo " departs, IV, 41–96; The Palace of Aeëtes, VI, 459–504; Jason sees Medea, VII, 1–116; Medea prepares to help, VII, 117–427; An account of how Jason tamed the bulls, plowed the field, and sowed the dragon's teeth, VIII; ** Jason and Medea steal the Fleece, IX, 39–230 · The return voyage, X–XV; Death of Jason, XVII, 1323–1328.

3. Story of the Argonautic expedition as related in Ovid's *Metamorphoses*, VII, pp. 343–353 (Loeb Classical Library, G. P. Putnam's Sons); An interesting account of the restoration of Aeson to youth, VII, pp. 355–367.

4. Poems listed on page 242, the titles of which are starred.

B. LINES TO BE MEMORIZED

Orpheus hath harped her,
Her prow hath drunk the sea.
Fifty haughty heroes at her golden rowlocks be!
His fingers sweep the singing strings,
Her forefoot white before she flings,
Out from the shore she strains — she swings —
And lifts, oh, gallantly!

Orpheus shall harp for her,
The Talking head speak wise for her,
Lynceus [1] gaze sharp for her
And Tiphys [2] search the skies for her!

May Colchis curse the dawn of day when first she thundered free
And our golden captain, Jason, in glory put to sea!

WILLIAM ROSE BENÉT, *The Argo's Chantey*, ll. 1–13

[1] Lynceus, renowned for his clear vision.   [2] Tiphys, pilot of the "Argo."

C. Further Study of Literary Allusion

If you are interested in seeing more clearly how good writers make use of the Greek myths, look up the following references:

Argo: Milton's *Paradise Lost*, II, 1017; Kingsley's *Westward Ho*, p. 43 (Macmillan). **Argonauts:** Holmes's *Autocrat of the Breakfast Table*, p. 92 (Everyman's Library); Locke's *Tale of Triona*, p. 60 (Dodd, Mead). **Golden Fleece:** Grahame's *The Golden Age*, p. 146 (John Lane). **Hylas:** Milton's *Paradise Lost*, II, 353. **Jason:** Shakespeare's *Merchant of Venice*, Act III, Sc. 2, 242. **Medea:** Shakespeare's *Merchant of Venice*, Act V, Sc. I, 12–13.

D. Projects for Individual and Group Work

To be selected from the list of projects on pages xx–xxvi, in case the subject matter of this chapter lends itself readily to any one of them.

POEMS FOR REFERENCE

Benét, William Rose	* The Argo's Chantey *and* * The Centaur's Farewell (*Merchants of Cathay;* Yale University Press)
Carman, Bliss	* Hylas (*Pipes of Pan;* L. C. Page and Company Boston)
Cawein, Madison	* Argonauts (*Poems;* The Macmillan Company, N. Y.)
Euripides	Medea, Translation (Everyman's Library; E. P. Dutton and Company, N.Y.; also Loeb Classical Library, G. P. Putnam's Sons, N. Y.)
Macaulay, Thomas B.	* Battle of Lake Regillus (*Lays of Ancient Rome*)
Morris, William	** Life and Death of Jason (Everyman's Library)

ORPHEUS

Or'phe us inherited musical ability both from his father, Apollo, god of music, and from his mother, the muse Cal li'o pe. That
A great musician
the son of such parents should be a great musician did not seem at all strange to the Greeks. But when they saw the stones in the field moving in accord with the notes of his lyre and noticed that the wild animals of the forest forgot their savage nature and gathered around the player, they were greatly amazed.

Lord Leighton   © H. K. T.; Gramstorff Brothers

Fig. 121. Orpheus bids Eurydice farewell

The fame of Orpheus spread over all the world, and even today he is not forgotten, as the illustrations in this chapter show.

Orpheus dearly loved his wife and when she died he was over-
The story of Eurydice
come with grief. So deeply did he long for her that he resolved to brave the dangers of a descent to the Lower World in an effort to recover her, although he knew well that the grim god who presided over these realms would not easily be induced to let Eu ryd'i ce return to earth. His heart sank as he found himself at last a suppliant before Pluto's throne. He began his plea, touching the strings of his lyre from time to time as an accompaniment to his words. But as he continued to bring forth

Fig. 122. The music of Orpheus attracts the wild creatures of the forest

divine harmonies from the instrument, putting his very soul into the music, the expression upon the king's face softened and his eyes filled with tears. He granted Orpheus' prayer, although upon condition. "Eurydice may return with you," he said, "but should you look back upon her during the journey you will lose her forever."

Orpheus did his best to live up to these cruel terms, and the light of the earth was very near before he allowed himself even to think of looking backward. Then the fear that she might be in some danger or that she was really not behind him at all overcame him. He turned, and so broke the compact. He never saw his wife again.

After Eurydice returned to the Lower World, Orpheus avoided all companionship. He sought out lonely regions where he might wander about undisturbed by men and mourn his great loss in solitude.

One day the Bac chan'tes chanced upon him as he sat upon the **The death of** mountain side, playing softly upon his lyre. Indig- **Orpheus** nant at him because he refused to join in their wild orgies, these savage women determined to kill him. But when they threw a shower of stones at him, they saw to their amazement that their missiles fell harmlessly to the ground. This they perceived was due to the influence of Orpheus' music. The wild shouts which they at once raised deadened the sound of the notes and so left Orpheus helpless. So great was the rage of the Bacchantes that they actually tore him limb from limb and threw his head and his lyre into the He'brus River.

But even in death the musical power of Orpheus did not depart. Legend says that the lyre continued to play softly as it floated down the stream, and that the notes it gave forth strangely resembled in sound the syllables of Eurydice's name.

The Muses had always deeply loved Orpheus, and it was

through their care that the fragments of his body were carefully gathered and buried at the foot of Mt. Par nas'sus. The monument in Figure 123, designed by the sculptor for his own grave, is concerned with this story.

Edward Berge   *Courtesy of Lorraine Park Cemetery, Baltimore*

Fig. 123. A Muse and the head of Orpheus

IN THE WORLD OF TODAY

I. IN OTHER CONNECTIONS

Or bid the soul of Orpheus sing
Such notes as warbled to the string
Drew iron tears down Pluto's cheek,
And made Hell grant what love did seek.

MILTON, *Il Penseroso*, 105–108

National Museum, Naples

Fig. 124. Orpheus, Eurydice, and Mercury

Orpheus has broken his contract with Pluto; Mercury
waits to take Eurydice back to the Lower World.

> I am Eurydice,
> That for one moment was so near the day,
> When Orpheus backward looked and all was night.
>
> STEPHEN PHILLIPS, *Ulysses*, Act II, Sc. 2

II. IN A WORD

Orpheum is a common name for a music hall or opera house.

III. IN MISCELLANEOUS WAYS

In Music

The story of Orpheus has been a favorite theme for musical
works. Twenty-seven operas bear either his name or that of

Eurydice. The best known are those by von Gluck and Of'fenbach.

Orpheus is also a favorite name for musical clubs and for choirs.

In Art and Decorative Design

Orpheus and his symbol, the lyre, are very common decorative designs for indicating the idea of music. For example, the monument to Francis Scott Key at Fort Henry, New York, bears a frieze in which Orpheus is shown playing upon a five-stringed lyre.

From the Raguenet drawings

Fig. 125. This decoration on a theater in France is self-explanatory for anyone who remembers that the lyre is symbolic of music and the drama.

A Name for a Book

During the last two years, the publishing firm of E. P. Dutton and Company has been bringing out a series of books known as "The World of Tomorrow," the titles of which with few exceptions have been chosen from the Greek myths. One of the latest volumes is entitled *Orpheus, or the Music of the Future.* Look up some of the other titles.

QUESTIONS FOR REVIEW

1. Who were Orpheus' parents?

2. What story is told to illustrate the effect of Orpheus' music upon animals and even inanimate objects?

3. What was the name of the wife of Orpheus? What effort did the hero make to recover her after she died and passed to Pluto's realms? What was the result?

4. Relate the circumstances in connection with the death of Orpheus.

5. What strange tale has come down to us through the myths regarding the musician's lyre as, after the death of its owner, it floated down the stream?

6. How does the name "Orpheus" occasionally appear today?

POEMS FOR REFERENCE

BOURDILLON, FRANCIS W.   * Eurydice (*Home Book of Verse;* Henry Holt and Company, N. Y.)

BROWNING, ROBERT   Eurydice to Orpheus

COATES, FLORENCE E.   Eurydice (*Lyrics of Life;* Houghton Mifflin Company, Boston)

LOWELL, JAMES RUSSELL   * Eurydice

MORRIS, LEWIS   Orpheus; Eurydice (*Epic of Hades;* Kegan Paul, Trench, Trübner and Company, London)

NOYES, ALFRED   Orpheus and Eurydice (*Collected Poems;* Frederick A. Stokes Company, N. Y.)

SAXE, JOHN G.   * Orpheus and Eurydice

SWINBURNE, ALGERNON C.   Eurydice

WHARTON, EDITH   Orpheus

PERSEUS

A CRIS'I US, king of Argos, shut up his daughter Dan'a e in a chamber of bronze, thinking in this way to prevent her marriage

A tale about his birth

to any of her numerous suitors. This cruelty was caused by an oracle to the effect that Acrisius was doomed to perish by the hand of his grandson; by thus secluding his daughter the king hoped to escape such a fate.

Canova (*Vatican, Rome*)   *Photograph by Alinari*

Fig. 126. Head of Perseus

A god, however, interfered, for Jupiter loved Danaë and appeared to her in a shower of gold. Afterward a little son was born, whom the king at once took steps to destroy. Putting both him and the mother into a wooden chest, he set it afloat upon the sea, never dreaming that it could escape destruction from the rough waves. Strangely enough, however, the chest was washed upon the shore of an island, where a king named Pol y dec'tes reigned. A fisherman discovered Danaë and her infant son, Per'seus, and brought them before Polydectes. The king was amazed at the woman's beauty. He saw to it that she was hospitably received at his court, and for many years he continued to show her respect and kindness.

Perseus was approaching manhood when Polydectes proposed a plan which he had long had in mind, namely, to make Danaë his **Perseus is led** queen. He saw at once that the boy did not take **to undertake a** kindly to the idea. "I will get rid of him," thought **hazardous task** the king, "and then I shall have no trouble in accomplishing my purpose." Accordingly he suggested to Perseus that it would be a very fine thing for him to set out on some adventure in the course of which he might perhaps win honor by the accomplishment of a brave deed. "You may even succeed," he said, "in cutting off the Gor'gon's head. It is a task in which many a hero has failed." The boy's imagination was fired by the idea of so bold an undertaking, and he gladly set out to seek the monster.

Knowing, as he did, that the Gorgon called Me du'sa had the power of turning into stone everything upon which she gazed, Polydectes had no doubt that Perseus would never return.

The Gorgons were horrible-looking sisters who lived together in a remote region far in the West. To seek them out without **Perseus** divine guidance would be nothing less than folly. **returns with** Fortunately Mercury and Mi ner'va came to the **the head of** assistance of the hero. "First find the Grae'ae," **Medusa** they said, "and make them tell you where you can find three things: the magic helmet which will make you invisible; the winged sandals by means of which you may mount into the air; and a wallet into which you may put Medusa's head after the monster is slain."

So Perseus went off to find these strange women. At last he came upon them; but the Graeae would grant no favors except upon compulsion, and had the hero not devised a stratagem, he would have failed in his undertaking. He noticed, however, that the creatures had only one eye and one tooth among them, and that they passed these around as they seemed to be needed. He was fortunate enough to get hold of these essentials, and he refused to return them until he had been told where the nymphs lived who kept the helmet, the sandals, and the wallet. Compelled by necessity, the Graeae yielded.

In due time, thanks to the information which he had extorted, Perseus discovered the Gorgons. Among them was Medusa. She was by far the most horrible of all, for her head was covered with writhing serpents and her gaze killed all upon whom it fell. The hero was very glad indeed that Mercury had given him as a parting gift a magic looking-glass (probably a highly polished bronze shield). By holding this up and looking into it instead of at the monster, he succeeded in cutting off her head. This he put into the wallet and at once started home.

While Perseus was on his way to the kingdom of Polydectes **Andromeda is saved** after his adventure with Medusa, he chanced to see upon the shores of Ae thi o'pi a a beautiful girl chained to a rock and surrounded by a crowd of people, most of whom were weeping bitterly. When he made inquiries, he found that the king of the region was about to sacrifice his daughter An drom'e da to a horrible sea-monster, which might at any moment appear.

This strange situation, the hero found, had been brought about from the fact that Cas si o pe'ia, the girl's mother, had offended Neptune by boasting that she was more beautiful than the Ne're-ids. To avenge what seemed to him an insult, Neptune had sent a monster to ravage the land. The unhappy king had been unable to appease it in any way except by offering up his daughter. And so the crowd was awaiting the approach of the beast.

Soon it came in sight, breasting the waves and making straight for Andromeda. Just then Perseus approached, and by the aid of his winged sandals, rose into the air and attacked the monster from above. To kill him in this way was not a matter of great difficulty, and within a short time Andromeda was free and the king relieved from his anxiety.

When Perseus departed, the girl went with him as his wife, and they returned together to the home of Perseus.

Piero di Cosimo (Uffizi Gallery, Florence)   *Photograph by Alinari*

Fig. 127. Perseus rescues Andromeda

When Perseus entered the palace of Polydectes, he found the king surrounded by his court. At the first hostile movement

The fate of King Polydectes
against him the hero took from his wallet the head of Medusa and raised it aloft; instantly the king and his attendants were turned into stone. Thus Perseus was rid of the wicked monarch who had tried to bring about his destruction.

Returning later to Argos, where his grandfather, King Acrisius, lived, Perseus found some games in progress. While taking

A prophecy fulfilled
part in these contests, he happened to throw a quoit which struck his grandfather and put an end to his life, thus fulfilling the oracle.

IN THE WORLD OF TODAY

I. In Literary Allusion

What new Gorgon's head
Have you beheld that you are all turn'd statues?

Fletcher, *Queen of Corinth*, V, 2

And Perseus dreadful with Minerva's shield.

Pope, *Temple of Fame*, 80

II. In a Word

We sometimes call a person a **gorgon,** meaning that her aspect is so stern and forbidding that it almost turns one into stone.

III. In Other Connections

The Scientific Term for Coral

The power which the Gorgon possessed of turning everything to stone is commemorated in the term "gorgonia" which scientists have applied to one kind of coral because of its habit of hardening in the process of its formation.[1]

According to the myths, coral was a plant growing beneath the water, which hardened as soon as it came to the surface and was exposed to the air. This transformation is said to have come about in the following way. After Perseus had killed the monster which threatened Andromeda, he laid the head of Medusa upon the shore, first placing beneath it a carpet of seaweed, so that it might not be injured by the sand. Instantly the plant was changed into stone.

[1] For colored illustrations of gorgonia, see *The National Geographic Magazine*, January, 1927.

The sea-nymphs who were looking on were very much interested, and amused themselves for a long time by gathering twigs and watching them harden as they touched Medusa's head. Later on they sportively threw pieces of the twigs into the water, from which, as seeds, according to a Roman poet, the coral "plant" was produced.

A Sea Creature Named "Medusa"

Scientists have named a small animal that lives in the water "Medusa" because of the fact that it is characterized by trailing threads or tentacles springing from a circular body. A poet has described it for us in the following lines:

> Or fringed Medusa floats like light in light,
> Medusa, with the loveliest of all fays
> Pent in its irised bubble of jellied sheen,
> Trailing long ferns of moonlight shot with green,
>   And crimson rays and white.

ALFRED NOYES, The Rock Pool

Serpents in Libya

According to the myths, the poisonous serpents in the Lib'y an deserts were created from the drops of blood that fell from Medusa's head as Perseus bore it aloft in his flight over the sandy wastes of northern Africa.

Perseus and the Stars

The constellations Perseus, Cassiopeia, and Andromeda recall to our minds the stories related in this chapter. Meteors which radiate from two of them are known as "Per'se ids" and "Androm'e des." (See Fig. 24.)

Fig. 128.   Medu-
sa's head used as a
trade mark

Medusa in the Business World

The makers of a certain kind of cement have gone back to the story of Medusa for the name of their product.

QUESTIONS FOR REVIEW

1. Why did King Acrisius wish to get rid of Perseus?

2. Who sent Perseus to kill the Gorgon, and why?

3. (1) What was the name of the Gorgon that Perseus was sent to kill?

(2) Describe her appearance.

4. Who were the Graeae, and in what way did Perseus receive help from them?

5. How did Perseus succeed in killing the Gorgon?

6. Tell how Perseus saved a beautiful maiden from a horrible fate.

7. How was Polydectes punished for his wickedness?

8. How was the oracle's prophecy in regard to King Acrisius fulfilled?

9. What kind of person is sometimes called a "gorgon"?

10. Explain the formation of coral as given in the myths.

11. What names in this chapter have been given to constellations?

OPTIONAL

FOR THOSE WHO HAVE TIME FOR FURTHER STUDY

A. ADDITIONAL READING

I. In Textbooks Dealing with Classical Mythology

1. Why Atlas was changed into a mountain, B., 117–118.

2. Why Cassiopeia's head is sometimes upside down in the sky, B., 120.

3. Scene in the palace of Cepheus when Perseus turns his foes into stone, B., 120–121

For other references see the Appendix, pages xxviii ff.

II. In Books in General

1. "The Gorgon's Head" in *The Wonder Book* by Nathaniel Hawthorne, pp. 7–28 (Everyman's Library), and similar books.

2. Ovid's account of how Atlas was changed into stone, *Met.* IV, ll. 604–662, pp. 221–225 in the Loeb Classical Library translation; also the tale of how Perseus slew his foes in the palace of Cepheus, V, ll. 1–176, pp. 239–255.

B. FURTHER STUDY OF LITERARY ALLUSION

If you are interested in seeing more clearly how good writers make use of the Greek myths, look up the following references:

Andromeda: Van Dyke's *The Golden Key*, chap. vi (Scribners); Edith Wharton's *Custom of the Country*, p. 84 (Scribners). **Cassiopeia:** Milton's *Il Penseroso*, 19–21. **Danaë** Tennyson's *Becket*, Act I, Sc. 2, 221–222. **Gorgon:** Dickens's *Tale of Two Cities*, pp. 135–147 (Scribners); Byron's *Childe Harold*, Canto I, 55; Milton's *Paradise Lost*, II, 611, 628. **Medusa:** Hugo's *Toilers of the Sea*, p. 294 (Houghton Mifflin). **Perseus:** Churchill's *Mr. Crewe's Career*, p 192 (Macmillan).

C. PROJECTS FOR INDIVIDUAL OR GROUP WORK

To be selected from the list of projects on pages xx–xxvi, in case the subject matter of this chapter lends itself readily to any one of them.

POEMS FOR REFERENCE

MORRIS, WILLIAM	The Doom of King Acrisius (*The Earthly Paradise;* Longmans, Green and Company, N. Y.)
ROCHE, JAMES JEFFREY	Andromeda (*Home Book of Verse;* Henry Holt and Company, N. Y.)
ROSSETTI, DANTE G.	Aspecta Medusa
SAXE, JOHN G.	* Jupiter and Danaë
SIMONIDES	Danaë, translated by J. A. Symonds (part of this is translated in Tatlock's *Greek and Roman Mythology*, p. 202; Century Company, N. Y.)

THESEUS

The'seus, the son of King Ae'geus of Athens, was widely known for his heroic deeds, which in many ways resembled the achieve-

Another Hercules ments of Her'cu les.   Like this hero he is remembered for his amazing strength and valor, of which he gave evidence when he was still but a boy.

Before the child's birth his father went on a journey, leaving behind him his sandals and sword concealed beneath a stone of immense weight.   "When my son is able to lift the stone," he said to his wife, "tell him to take the sandals and the sword and join me in Athens."   Theseus was not more than sixteen when he accomplished this extraordinary feat and joyfully set out to find his father.   He met with many adventures on the way and in each case proved himself a valiant hero.

Travelers along a certain mountain road near the sea were often seized by a giant named Sci'ron, who made them stoop over to

Sciron is hurled into the sea wash his feet.   Then he kicked them over the cliff where they were devoured by an enormous sea-turtle. The hero succeeded in hurling this inhuman creature into the water to meet the same death which he had so often inflicted upon others.

Another monster met a well-deserved death at the hands of Theseus.   Pro crus'tes (the word means "stretcher") was a wicked

Procrustes is slain man who kept an inn at which travelers were accustomed to stop for the night.   He had an iron bed in which they were obliged to sleep and to which he insisted upon

G. F. Watts (Tate Gallery, London)

Fig. 129. The Minotaur

fitting them.   To do this, he had to cut off their legs if they happened to be too long, or, on the other hand, to stretch them out if they chanced to be too short.   Theseus put an end to this cruel practice by killing Procrustes.

But it was after Theseus reached Athens that he performed the exploit for which he is best known, namely, the slaying of the Min'o taur on the island of Crete.

King Mi'nos ruled in Crete and became so famous for his justice and wisdom that after his death he was made one of the judges in the Lower World.

But his grandson, named Minos also, did not inherit the fine qualities of his ancestor, for when king he did not hesitate to try **What was the** to cheat Neptune.   This is the story.   He begged **Minotaur?**   from the sea-god a beautiful white bull, saying that he wished to offer it up as a sacrifice to the gods; but when he got possession of it, he put it among his own herds.   Of course Neptune could not brook such an insult as this.   He therefore inspired the king's wife with love for the bull so that she left her husband in order to become the companion of this animal. The result of their union was a strange and horrible creature, half-man and half-bull, which came to be known as the Minotaur.

In order to have some safe place in which to confine this monster, the king had the Lab'y rinth constructed.   This was an inclosure **The Labyrinth** with many winding galleries or passages, so intricate in their nature that no one who entered could ever find his way out.   Indeed, not even the builder himself, a man named Daed'a lus, who was once confined here with his son Ic'a-rus, could retrace his steps to the entrance.   Only the fact that he was a person of unusual resource and an artisan of such extraordinary skill that he was known throughout the entire Greek world, enabled him to save his own life and that of his son.

The plan which Daedalus devised was most unusual.   He made

wings which he fastened with wax to his own body and to that of
The strange
escape of
Daedalus and
Icarus
Icarus, and as there was no roof to the inclosure, both father and son by rising into the air succeeded in escaping from the maze. Legend says that Daedalus was fortunate enough to make his way by means of his wings to the island of Sicily, but that the fate of Icarus was not so happy. Unfortunately, in spite of the father's warning, the boy flew so high that the heat of the sun melted the wax by which his wings were fastened, and he fell headlong into the sea.

Since only by such superhuman efforts as Daedalus put forth
Why Theseus
came to Crete
could one hope to escape from the Labyrinth, King Minos very properly considered it a very safe place in which to keep prisoners. It was in these winding passages, therefore, that he was accustomed to confine the seven young men and the seven young women whom the

Fig. 130. Daedalus fashioning wings by means of which he and Icarus hope to escape from King Minos

Athe'ni ans were forced by reason of a defeat in war to send to him each year as tribute. Their fate was a most dreadful one, as it was only a question of time until they were devoured by the Minotaur, who was shut up with them in the Labyrinth.

Theseus resolved to put an end to this state of affairs. Accordingly, he boarded a ship and set sail for Crete.

The hero would have met the usual fate probably had not the king's daughter, Ari ad'ne, been touched with pity. She presented him with a sword and also gave him a skein of thread or

a ball of cord, telling him to unwind this as he went along so
that when the time came for him to retrace his steps he might
Saved by have something to guide him in his search for the
Ariadne entrance. This device saved his life, for after putting the Minotaur to death, he had no difficulty in following the
windings of the maze and thus escaping from the Labyrinth.

Vatican, Rome

Fig. 131. Ariadne sleeps

Filled with gratitude, Theseus took Ariadne with him; but
when they reached the island of Nax′os he deserted her, and only
the kindliness of Bac′chus, who passed that way, preserved her
life.

Within the last twenty years scholars have become deeply interested in the excavations which have been made at Crete, and

especially in those which have brought to light the ruins of a splendid palace belonging to King Minos. It used to be thought

Did King Minos really live? that there was no foundation in fact for the legends that have come down to us in classical mythology about the king and his Labyrinth. But there are now reasons for thinking that a rich and powerful monarch by this name actually lived, although it is exceedingly difficult to separate legend and historical fact. Some scholars regard the name "Minos" just as they do "Pha'raoh," that is, as a title of royalty. But at any rate Minos was a "real" person to the Greeks who coined the myths, and he is so regarded by the story-teller of today.

The civilization of which Crete was the center is called the "Ae ge'an" or the "Mi no'an," and it may be that the city of Troy was one of its later outposts.

After Theseus became king of Athens he continued to enter upon hazardous undertakings and to perform deeds of valor. He is said, for example, to have carried off An ti'o pe, queen of the Amazons, and to have defended his city most bravely when the queen's people came to attack it. But his astounding adventure in the Lower World is of greater interest.

Theseus had an intimate friend named Pi rith'o us, who was bold enough to desire a divinity for his wife. He therefore con-

A vain attempt to abduct the queen of the Lower World ceived the idea of descending to the Lower World and seizing Pluto's queen, Pro ser'pi na. Theseus was persuaded to join his friend in this daring enterprise. But, as might have been expected, they failed in their attempt. The myths say that the heroes were confined in the Lower World, and that it was only through the efforts of Hercules when he came down in search of Cer'ber us that Theseus was freed.

The Greeks always thought of Theseus as one of their national

heroes and honored him in Athens by erecting a splendid temple
called the "The se'um." However, the structure

Honored by a temple in Athens

that passes today under this name is probably not the
one that the Greeks built for Theseus — it is now
supposed to be a temple to Vulcan (the Hephaesteum) —
although it may mark the spot of an earlier shrine dedicated to
this hero.

IN THE WORLD OF TODAY

I. IN LITERARY ALLUSION

Mother Earth, are the heroes dead?
  Do they thrill the soul of the years no more?
Are the gleaming snows and the poppies red
  All that is left of the brave of yore?
Are there none to fight as Theseus fought,
  Far in the young world's misty dawn?
Or to teach as gray-haired Nestor taught?
  Mother Earth, are the heroes gone?

EDNA DEAN PROCTOR, Heroes

He who died
For soaring too audacious near the sun
Where that same treacherous wax began to run.

KEATS, Endymion, IV, 441–443

II. IN WORDS AND EXPRESSIONS

Our word **labyrinth** doubtless takes its meaning from the maze
of King Minos.

The term **I ca'ri an** still stands for some misfortune attendant
upon a bold undertaking. For example, a man who fails in some
rather daring political venture may speak of it as having an
Icarian ending.

A **pro crus'te an system** is one that makes everyone or everything conform to the same scheme or outline. In other words, there is one pattern or type and everyone must be made to fit it regardless of individual differences. School systems, for example, are often described as " beds of Procrustes," because they seem to insist that all pupils shall be subjected to the same training.

Someone once called Napoleon "the imperial **Minotaur,**" meaning that just as the Minotaur of the Cretan Labyrinth devoured Athens' finest young men, so Napoleon sacrificed French youth in the wars which he waged to satisfy his own ambition.

To have the **thread of Ariadne** indicates that one has a clew by which he may unravel a mystery or escape from some danger.

III. In Other Connections

Why a Certain Sea Is Called Aegean

When Theseus sailed from Athens to kill the Minotaur, he told his father, Aegeus, that he would hoist white sails if he should be successful, in place of the black ones with which he started out. But he forgot to make the change. The father, therefore, thinking that his son was dead, in his grief threw himself into the sea. This incident is the legendary explanation for the name "Aegean" by which the waters between Greece and Asia Minor are still called.

Icarus and Aviation

The development of the science of aviation, especially on its tragic side, has often recalled the story of Icarus. The poem that follows is only one of many that appeared during the World War when the papers were filled with accounts of disasters to fliers on the various fronts.

REMEMBRANCE

"An aeroplane has been brought down in the Aegean Sea." (*Dispatch*)

Wounded, the steel-ribbed bird dipped to the sea,
Its vast wings twisted, struggling with the air
That would not bear it up — and heavily
Struck the still water, sleeping idly where
The gold-arched noon had lulled it into dream.
So there was foaming tumult and the fret
Of waves on heated steel — then silver steam,
That hung like fallen cloud, where they had met.
And that small, striving thing that fought away,
Free of the wreckage, did he, dying, hear
The waters murmuring of another day,
A noon, now long ago, yet strangely near;
The waters telling drowsily of one
Who with his wings of wax dared woo the sun?

HORTENSE FLEXNER

QUESTIONS FOR REVIEW

1. What similarity was there between Theseus and Hercules?
2. Upon what condition was Theseus permitted to join his father in Athens?
3. How did Theseus rid the country of the giant Sciron?
4. How were travelers treated at Procrustes' inn, and how was this evil practice ended?
5. What was the Minotaur and where did it live?
6. How did Daedalus and Icarus escape from the Labyrinth, and what befell Icarus?
7. What was Theseus' purpose in going to Crete?
8. How was Theseus saved by the king's daughter?
9. What facts have been brought to light by recent excavations in Crete?

THESEUS

267

10. How did Theseus assist a friend in an attempt to seize a bride by force, and what was the result of their efforts?

11. In what way was Theseus honored by the Greeks?

12. Why is a certain sea called "Aegean"?

13. Why has Napoleon been called "the imperial Minotaur"?

14. What is a "procrustean" system?

15. What is meant by "the thread of Ariadne"?

OPTIONAL

FOR THOSE WHO HAVE TIME FOR FURTHER STUDY

A. ADDITIONAL READING

I. In Textbooks Dealing with Classical Mythology

1. An adventure with a savage, Gay., p. 251; B., 151.
2. An escape from death by poison, Gay., p. 252.
3. How a lover's gift preserved the memory of Ariadne, Gay., p. 258; B., 165.
4. Details about Theseus' friend, Pirithoüs, Gay., p. 258-259.
5. Talus, the terrible monster who patrolled the island of Crete for King Minos, meets his death at Medea's hands, Gay., pp. 242-243.
6. The death of King Minos, Gay., p. 247.
7. How a maiden's love for King Minos betrayed her father and her city, B., 98-101.
8. Story of Theseus' cruelty toward his son, B., 154.
9. Why the scientific name of "perdix" was applied to the partridge, a story about Daedalus, Gay., p. 248.

For other references see pages xxviii ff., in the Appendix.

II. In Books in General

1. "The Minotaur" in *Tanglewood Tales*, by Nathaniel Hawthorne, pp. 149-174 (Everyman's Library).
2. Plutarch's *Lives*, "Theseus," 6-12; adventures in Crete, 15-19 (Loeb Classical Library, G. P. Putnam's Sons, or any translation).

3. Passages in Ovid's *Metamorphoses*, translated in the Loeb Classical Library.   Examples :
   (1) An account of the Minotaur, VIII, pp. 417–419 (Latin lines, 152–182).
   (2) Daedalus and Icarus, VIII, pp. 419–425 (Latin lines, 183–259).
4. The civilization of Crete in the time of King Minos, from which the Greeks borrowed largely, Breasted's *Ancient Times: A History of the Early World*, chap. viii, pp. 225 ff. (Ginn and Company) ; also, by the same author, *The Conquest of Civilization*, pp. 241–267 (Harper and Brothers).
5. Poems listed below, the titles of which are marked with a star.

B. Lines to Be Memorized

Behind him there came
The winner of a great and dreadful name,
Theseus, the slayer of the fearful beast
Who soon in winding halls should make his feast
On youths and maidens.
                WILLIAM MORRIS, *Life and Death of Jason*, III, 99–103.

NOTE : A reference to Theseus when as a young man he offered himself to Jason as a member of the Argonautic expedition.

C. Further Study of Literary Allusion

If you are interested in seeing more clearly how good writers make use of the Greek myths, look up the following references :

Daedalus: Dumas's *Count of Monte Cristo*, Vol. I, p. 221 (A. L. Burt).
Icarus: Florence E. Coates's *The Unconquered Air*, II.   **Theseus:** William Morris' *Life and Death of Jason*, III, 100–103 ; Churchill's *Mr. Crewe's Career*, p. 247 (Macmillan).

D. Projects for Individual and Group Work

To be selected from the list of projects on pages xx–xxvi, in case the subject matter of this chapter lends itself readily to any one of them.

POEMS FOR REFERENCE

BENÉT, STEPHEN VINCENT   * The Winged Man (*Modern American Poetry;*
                    Anthology by Louis Untermeyer; Harcourt, Brace and Company, N. Y.)

BURR, AMELIA JOSEPHINE	*Icarus (*The Roadside Fire;* George H. Doran and Company, N. Y.)
CHAUCER, GEOFFREY	Ariadne (*Legends of Good Women*)
HEWLETT, MAURICE	Ariadne Forsaken
JACKSON, HELEN HUNT	Ariadne's Farewell (*Poems;* Little, Brown and Company, Boston)
MONTGOMERY, ROSELLE MERCIER	*Daedalus (Braithwaite's *Anthology of American Verse,* 1925; B. J. Brimmer Company, Boston)
SAXE, JOHN G.	*Icarus, or The Peril of Borrowed Plumes
TROWBRIDGE, JOHN G.	*Darius Green and His Flying Machine

Fig. 132. A Greek temple at Segesta in Sicily,
sixth century B.C.

THE TROJAN WAR

HOMERIC RETROSPECT

I saw blind Homer by the oceanside:
He dreamed of furrowing ships and voyaged men
That left the hearth where peace and love abide
To plunge the embattled shock of life again. . . .
Peril that burns the soul clean, watches kept
With unseen gods, till heroes they had grown,
Becoming part of distant seas they swept
And every fronting action they had known.

Glad with the motion of the world's affairs,
They tautened sail for wind, they rode the tide;
Wonder went with them; living joy was theirs;
Song was their good bedfellow for a bride,
And beauty, that blind, passionate child of God,
Walking ahead, their ways to brightness trod!

HARRY KEMP, *The Sea and the Dunes
and Other Poems*

THE TROJAN WAR

PE'LEUS, the descendant of one of the proudest families of all Greece and a grandson of Jupiter himself, was to marry The'tis, the loveliest by far of all the sea-nymphs. No wonder, then, that the preparation for the wedding in his ancestral palace in Thessaly should have been extraordinarily magnificent. The list of invitations for the banquet was very long, for of course all the princes in that part of Greece would naturally be present. Moreover, it was whispered about that the gods themselves would be guests on this occasion. And the rumor proved true. They came down from their home on Mt. O lym'pus and took their places on the splendid banquet couches just as the mortals did who had come to honor Peleus and his bride. Only one had failed to be invited and that was E'ris, the goddess of Discord. Greatly

A startling incident at a wedding feast

Vatican, Rome

Fig. 133. Paris

angered by this insult, she resolved to take revenge. Right into the midst of the guests she threw a golden apple marked with the words, "For the fairest." At once there was great consternation. Who was the "fairest"? "Don't ask me to decide," said

Jupiter. "Take the apple to Paris, King Priam's son, who tends his sheep upon the slopes of Mt. Ida."

And so three goddesses, Juno, Minerva, and Venus, suddenly appeared before the young Trojan prince and asked for his judg-**The judgment of Paris** ment. "You shall have power and riches if you award the prize to me," said Juno. "And I," said Minerva, "can give you the honor and glory that come to the successful warrior." Then Venus spoke: "My gift will make you far happier, Paris, than those which have been promised to you. I will give you as a wife Helen, the most beautiful woman in the world."

When Paris learned that she meant no other than Helen, wife of Men e la'us of Sparta, whom suitors from all over the world had sought, he immediately awarded the apple to Venus.

When Menelaüs, prince at Sparta, heard that a guest of highest rank at Troy was on his way to his palace, he at once made prep-**Immediate cause of the Trojan War** arations to receive him with all honor. His wife Helen also busied herself to see that nothing should be left undone that might contribute to the stranger's comfort. So when Paris arrived he was not only met with all the courtesy that high-born Greeks were accustomed to show to visitors, but, as the days went on, he found himself treated quite as an old friend. Under such circumstances it seems strange that he could so far forget honor as to take advantage of the absence of Menelaüs to induce Helen to leave Sparta and to accompany him to Troy. But that is what he did. Of course the Greeks could not let so infamous a deed go unavenged. They at once set about recovering Helen and punishing the Trojans, whose prince had so shamefully violated the laws of hospitality. The long ten-year struggle that followed is known as the Trojan War.

Almost all the leading young men of Greece had at one time or another been suitors for Helen's hand. Her father, Tyn da're us,[1]

---

[1] Some myths say that Jupiter was Helen's father.

had been foresighted enough to make use of their devotion as
a safeguard against future peril for his daughter, by asking

**The Greek
warriors
assemble**

them all to promise that, if danger ever threatened
Helen, they would at once go to her assistance.
This oath they all gladly took.   So now, when the
call to arms was sent out, the
heroes assembled, among them
Ag a mem'non of Mycenae,
Ajax, Di'o mede, and of course
Menelaüs. However, two of
the princes did not appear,
U lys'ses and A chil'les. The
reasons for it and the ways in
which they were finally won
over to the war are told in
the following paragraphs.

While Ulysses was every
inch a warrior and greatly

**A trick that
failed**

loved adventure,
he was just now
very happy and contented in
his home on the island of
Ith'a ca. He deeply loved his

von Deutsch   © H. K. T.; Gramstorff Brothers

Fig. 134. Paris carries Helen away

wife, Pe nel'o pe, and a small son named Te lem'a chus was very
dear to his heart. Why leave them and this peaceful life in
order to take part in a troublesome war?

One day Ulysses saw Pal a me'des, one of the Greek leaders,
approaching the house. Being very quick-witted, he at once
guessed that the visitor had been sent to urge him to join the
expedition to Troy. Only one thing could save him and that was
a trick. Pretending to be mad, he yoked an ass and an ox to the
plow and began sowing a field with salt. But the ambassador was

not easily fooled. He took the infant Te lem'a chus and placed him in a furrow in front of the plow, smiling to himself as he saw the driver skilfully turn the plow aside in order to save the baby's life. Ulysses knew at once that his trick had been found out, and in a very few minutes Palamedes had gained his promise to enlist in the war.

No sooner had Ulysses decided to join the Greeks than he became one of the most enthusiastic supporters of the enterprise. His first thought was to find Achilles. He had heard that the hero's mother, Thetis, because of a prophecy to the effect that Achilles would die at Troy, had sent her son, disguised as a girl, to serve at the court of a princess on the island of Scy'ros. Ulysses, therefore, had first of all to devise a plan for making Achilles disclose his identity.

Battoni   © H. K. T.; Gramstorff Brothers

Fig. 135. Achilles at the court of Lycomedes

One day the maidens of the princess were told that a peddler

Through the cunning of Ulysses, Achilles is brought into the war with a huge bag upon his back was asking for admittance, saying that he had silks and jewels to sell and many other things which young women like. The old man seemed quite harmless and so the door-keeper let him come in. The princess and her attendants were delighted with the feminine adornments which the peddler displayed. Achilles, however, passed them all by with scarcely a glance and seized upon a sword which he found in the bottom of the pack. His eyes sparkled as he held it up, and the very movement of his arm betrayed the warrior. Ulysses at once put off his disguise and told Achilles the reason for his coming. It was not long before the hero determined to disregard his mother's wishes and throw in his lot with the rest of the Greeks.

In due course of time the fleet of about twelve hundred ships assembled at Au'lis on the eastern coast of Greece. Agamemnon, the brother of Menelaüs and, as the Greeks thought, the one best fitted to conduct the war, was in command.

The time set for starting came, but, very strangely, there was no wind to fill the sails. For many days the calm continued. At **The fleet delayed; a miracle sends it on its way** last through a priest named Cal'chas the Greeks found out the explanation. Agamemnon while hunting had killed a stag sacred to Di a'na, and the goddess was showing her anger by thus withholding the winds. The question of how to placate the divine wrath was long delayed. "There is but one way," said Calchas. "Agamemnon's own daughter, Iph i ge ni'a, must be offered as a sacrifice upon Diana's altar."

For a long time the Greek leader could not persuade himself to so horrible a step. But considerations of patriotism finally prevailed, and the maiden was led to the altar. Just at the critical moment, however, the goddess was moved to pity. The girl was borne away in a cloud to a distant place inhabited by the Tau'ri-ans, where she became a priestess in one of Diana's temples.

At once the wind arose, and under full sail the ships of the Greeks put to sea.

As the Greeks approached the stretch of coast at the entrance to the strait which we know as the Dar da nelles', they saw a plain **First glimpse of Troy** stretching down to the sea and at some distance back a rocky hill upon whose summit they could dimly make out the walls of a city. This they knew to be Troy, the capital of a great and powerful empire in this section of Asia

Giovacchino Agricola (Doria Palace, Rome)   *Photograph by Alinari*

Fig. 136. Diana saves Iphigenia

Minor. Some of the warriors were curious to know more about the Trojans, who they really were, who built the city, and who was the reigning king. Agamemnon could answer some of the questions, but it was the aged Nes'tor, friend and counselor of a former generation of the Greeks and much respected by the leaders of the present day, who told them most about the city and the race of men who lived there.

"The Trojans," he said, "have descended from Dar'da nus, who was a grandson of Jupiter, and they take their name from a powerful prince named Tros. One of his sons was called I'lus and it was he who built Il'i um, a name which the Trojans sometimes use in place of Troy. The son who followed him, La om'e don, constructed the huge walls which you now see. The ruler of the city today is his son Pri'am, an old man much loved by his subjects and possessed of all those virtues which befit a king. Hec'u ba is his wife and queen, mother of nineteen children. The great Hec'tor is one of these sons, and those who have met him say that he is no mean foe and that only such of us as Achilles or Diomede are a match for him. Moreover, they mention one Sar pe'don in the same breath with our Ajax, saying that both are giants in strength and as brave as they are strong. The name of Ae ne'as also has come to my ears, who, although not one of Priam's sons, is said to be a wonderful warrior."

The Greeks very soon discovered that they could not capture Troy by assault, because of the strength of the walls and the valor of the soldiers who manned them. The best they could do was to keep the Trojans within the city and to raid the surrounding country. Year after year went by until nine had passed, and apparently the Greeks were no nearer victory than they had been when they first came. It is always difficult to keep up the morale of an army under such circumstances, and Agamemnon found it true in this case. Many of the men

The siege of Troy begins

were discontented. They wanted to go back to Greece and abandon the whole enterprise. And there might have been a mutiny then and there had not Ulysses and Diomede caught the man who was loudest in his complaints and drowned him.

John Singer Sargent   © *Museum of Fine Arts, Boston*

Fig. 137. Chiron

Achilles, as well as other Greek heroes, was educated by the centaur Chiron. The picture shows how the boy is being trained to shoot.

Suddenly the Greek soldiers fell desperately ill with a strange disease which seemed to yield to no remedy. Day by day the **Apollo sends** number of dead increased. At last Achilles insisted **a plague** upon an assembly to try to discover the reason for the pestilence. It was found that Agamemnon had deeply offended Apollo by refusing to return to her father (one of Apollo's priests) a maiden named Chry se′is, whom he had captured in one of his raids and brought back with him to the camp.   Moreover, the haughty and arrogant manner in which he had treated the venerable man had greatly heightened his offense in the eyes of the god. The plague had been sent as a punishment for this impiety.

Every argument was brought to bear upon Agamemnon to induce him to give up Chryseïs and so end the plague.   For a long time he stubbornly refused to submit to such dicta-

Agamemnon and Achilles quarrel

tion.   But he finally yielded to necessity.   Chryseïs was sent back to her father.   "She may go," he said, "for I cannot see my men perish.   But in her place I shall have Bri se′is, Achilles' captive handmaiden.   She shall wait upon me in my tent."   At these words Achilles' eyes blazed with anger. Not only had he become fond of Briseïs, but his proud spirit resented such an interference with his princely rights.   A violent quarrel followed, which proved disastrous for the Greeks.   For Achilles, although forced to give up Briseïs, refused to take any further part in the war.   Nor could the persuasions of his friends or the threats of Agamemnon induce him to change his mind.

At this point in the war someone was wise enough to propose a duel between Helen's two husbands, Paris and Menelaüs, and to

A duel proposed

suggest that the outcome should determine whether Greeks or Trojans had won the war.   This simple solution would have saved much bloodshed for both sides.   But so determined were the gods to have their particular side win (A the′na, Juno, and Neptune favoring the Greeks, and Venus, Mars, and Apollo siding with the Trojans) that they could not forbear interfering and thus prevented so fair a settlement.   For example, when Paris was getting the worst of the fight, Venus carried him away, and it was Athena who inspired someone on the Trojan side to wound Menelaüs with an arrow, thus breaking the truce which had been proclaimed.

Diomede, second only to Achilles as a warrior, won great honor by his deeds.   He even succeeded in wounding Venus and Mars,

Diomede wounds two gods

who were present in person upon the battlefield bearing aid to the Trojans.   It was on this occasion that Venus wept with pain and ran back to Olympus, where she found comfort and sympathy in the arms of her mother.   Mars, too, hastened at once to Jupiter's palace to

Thorwaldsen   © *H. K. T.; Gramstorff Brothers*

Fig. 138. Hector, about to start for the field of battle, is bidding his wife and little son farewell. The story says that when he took the child from the arms of its nurse, the infant was frightened by the warrior's helmet with its bristling crest. Hector therefore took it off and threw it to the ground.

complain of the wound which Diomede had inflicted.   But while the father called the family doctor, Pae'on, to look after his son's wounds, Jupiter at the same time rebuked Mars for his love of strife and his quarrelsome spirit.   "You are like your mother, Juno, in this respect," he said.   "Certainly you do not take after me."

As the battle raged upon the plain about Troy, both Greeks and Trojans won glory for themselves by their heroic deeds.   But as Hector, Troy's foremost warrior, surveyed the scene, it

seemed to him that the enemy was gaining ground. He ran
back to the city to enlist the aid of Paris and to urge the women
to pray to the gods. Here he saw his wife,
An drom'a che, who begged him for her sake and
that of their son, As ty'a nax, to stay within the
walls. Her prayer and Hector's reply are given in the following lines from Homer's famous poem called the Il'i ad:

Hector bids farewell to his wife and son

> " Hector, thou
> Art father and dear mother now to me,
> And brother and my youthful spouse besides.
> In pity keep within the fortress here,
> Nor make thy child an orphan nor thy wife
> A widow." . . . .
> Then answered Hector, great in war, "All this
> I bear in mind, dear wife; but I should stand
> Ashamed before the men and long-robed dames
> Of Troy, were I to keep aloof and shun
> The conflict, coward-like."
>
>   Bryant's Translation, Book VI, 551–556, 564–568

And so Hector went back to the contest. The Trojans gathered
around him, and little by little they drove the Greeks back to the
wall which they had built as a defense for their ships. When
night came, despair filled the hearts of the invaders — the tide of
victory seemed to be against them.

The Greeks knew very well what was the matter. They needed
Achilles. But although Agamemnon begged him in person
to forget their quarrel and offered to return
Briseïs, and even though all the Greek leaders
continued to make appeals to his patriotism, the
proud young Greek refused to put aside the memory of his
wrongs.

Achilles is deaf to the appeals of the Greeks

Just as the Trojans were about to burn their enemies' ships — a proceeding which would have meant the destruction of the Greeks — Pa tro′clus, Achilles' best friend, devised a scheme for driving **Patroclus saves the ships but loses his life** the Trojans back. Why not bring terror to the hearts of their foes by making them think that the great Achilles had really reëntered the ranks and was once more at the head of his invincible band known as the Myr′mi dons? Might not he himself, clad in his friend's armor,

Maignan   © *H. K. T.; Gramstorff Brothers*

Fig. 139. Hector leaves for the field of battle

pretend to be Achilles? The idea met with the approval of the Greeks. Moreover, Achilles himself helped in person as his own armor was brought from his tent and fastened upon the body of Patroclus. At last all was ready. As the young man stepped into the war-chariot and was on the point of starting, Achilles whispered a word of warning: "Save the ships, Patroclus, but do not advance to the walls of Troy."

When the Trojans who were engaged in firing the ships saw the chariot approaching and heard the wild battle cries of the Myrmidons, they thought that the godlike Achilles was upon them. Back they fell in confusion, each one trying as best he might to escape the onslaught of the dreaded warrior. The victorious Greeks drove them from the ships and pressed forward in pursuit as they scattered over the plain, Achilles' warning quite forgotten. Suddenly Patroclus found himself separated from his followers and looked up to see Hector confronting him. The huge stone which Patroclus threw missed its aim. The Trojan's lance was swift and sure and in an instant the Greek hero lay dead upon the ground.

While the Greeks could not prevent Hector from getting possession of the armor which Patroclus had been wearing, they **The fight for the body of Patroclus** succeeded after a desperate fight, in which both Ajax and Menelaüs took part on the one side and some of the greatest of the Trojan warriors on the other, in bearing away the body of the hero.

Word was sent ahead that Patroclus was dead, and when the bearers finally reached the camp they heard cries of grief and **The grief of Achilles** lamentation on every side. But nowhere was there such sorrow as in the heart of Achilles, and even his friends forbore at first to seek his tent with words of comfort. But his mother, Thetis, was there, for even in the depths of the sea where her palace was she had felt that her son was suffering and had hastened to him.

The one thought of Achilles was, of course, to avenge the death of his friend. But he could not enter battle without armor and **How Thetis procured new armor for her son** his own suit was now in Hector's possession. "Only wait until tomorrow," begged Thetis, "and I will bring from Vulcan's shop some armor which is far more splendid than anything you have ever seen." The picture below shows Vulcan carrying out the orders of Thetis. (See also Figure 106.)

If the Trojans in the old days had hesitated to stand against Achilles, still less did they care to do it now when the hero's **Achilles reënters the war** onslaught was made more terrible by his burning desire to avenge his friend's death. No wonder, then, that even the bravest of the Trojan warriors fell back as the chariot of Achilles advanced. It is true that

Giulio Romano (Ducal Palace, Mantua)   *Photograph by Alinari*

Fig. 140. Vulcan makes armor for Achilles at the request of Thetis

Aeneas dared to stand against him, but he barely escaped with his life and then only because Neptune spread a cloud about him and so bore him away to the rear. In fact, the whole Trojan army at one time seemed to be in flight toward the city. When Priam, who was watching the battle from the top of the walls, observed this, he had the gates opened, and through them the panic-stricken horde poured into the city.

But when the gates of Troy closed after the last fugitive had passed through, there was one warrior who remained outside; Hector scorned to save himself by such a **The death of Hector** means. He heard his father from the tower above commanding him to enter and saw his mother beckoning to him. But the thought that so many had followed him that day to battle and had died in so doing, made him resist all entreaties.

Almost at once he saw a warrior approaching. Could it be Mars himself? Had this god not been friendly to the Trojans, the hero would have had no doubt that it was the divinity in very person, such was the fierceness of his gaze and such the dazzling radiance of his armor. But he soon saw that it was Achilles. There was but one hope of safety and that was to out-run his foe. Three times the pursued and the pursuer encircled the walls, Apollo giving strength to Hector so that he might not fall from exhaustion. All the time the Trojan was hoping for a chance to make a stand, and when he saw his brother De iph'o bus near him (although Deïphobus was only Athena in disguise), he thought that it had come. With such assistance there was surely hope of success in attacking the Greek. He turned and hurled his spear. But as he reached toward Deïphobus for another weapon, he perceived that his brother was gone. Then he saw it all — some god had planned his death! A moment later he fell, mortally wounded by Achilles.

Death did not seem to Achilles to be sufficient punishment for the man who had killed Patroclus. He therefore fastened the body, from which he had removed the armor, to his chariot and let it trail in the dust as he drove thrice around the walls of the city. No words can picture the grief of King Priam and his queen, Hecuba, as they saw the body of their favorite son thus defiled. And still less can they describe the suffering of Andromache who, summoned to the ramparts by the noise, beheld the dreadful sight below.

The vengeance of Achilles

While Achilles was high-spirited and had a quick temper which he did not always try to control, and while he was capable of such cruelty as had been shown toward Hector, he possessed at the same time many noble qualities of mind and heart. The magnanimous way in which he responded to the appeal of King Priam, who after Hector's death came to beg for his son's body, is an illus-

Generous conduct   tration.   Not only did Achilles grant the old man's prayer, touched by the thought of his own father far away in Greece, but he proclaimed an eleven-day truce so that the funeral ceremonies for the dead hero might be properly performed.

Drawing by Flaxman

Fig. 141. The vengeance of Achilles

Hector's body is dragged behind the car of Achilles; Apollo protects the body from disfigurement.

After the death of Hector, the Am'a zons, famous women war-riors who had been trained to fight like men, came to the relief of

Chivalry on the battlefield   the Trojans.   Pen thes i le'a, the queen, herself led the ranks in a charge against the Greeks.   Legend says that Achilles refrained from striking her down as they met in personal combat until he was forced to do so in self-defense. As she lay dying, the thought of how Hector's body had been mistreated came to her mind and she implored Achilles to spare her such defilement.   The hero raised her in his arms so that she might die more easily, and when the Amazons and Trojans rushed forward to claim the body, he willingly yielded it to them, at the same time praising the beauty and bravery of the queen.

While the Trojans were greatly discouraged by the death of Hector and the loss of so many other brave warriors, they still **Achilles dies** continued to fight although the outlook seemed very dark. But one day the city was thrilled by a piece of news which seemed too good to be true — Achilles was dead! Paris had slain him with an arrow which had chanced to hit his heel, the one vulnerable spot in his body. There was great rejoicing in Troy, for it had long been clear that he was the chief support of the Greeks. Surely now that they had lost him, they would give up the struggle and go home.

For seventeen days the mourning continued in the camp of the Greeks. Then the body was burned and the ashes buried with **Funeral rites** those of Patroclus in a mound near the shore. Splen-**for Achilles** did funeral games were held, in which Thetis offered the armor of her son as a prize to the bravest contestant. Ulysses and Ajax contended for it. When victory fell to the former, Ajax was so filled with humiliation that he killed himself.

Through a man to whom Apollo had given the power of proph-ecy, the Greeks learned that three things were necessary for **A seer speaks** the destruction of Troy: First, Ne op tol'e mus, the son of Achilles, must lend his aid; second, the poisoned arrows of Hercules, now in the possession of a Greek named Phil oc te'tes, must be obtained; and, third, a wooden image of Athena in one of the temples of Troy must be brought to the Greek camp. The first and second requirements were easily met. But to steal the statue of Athena from an enemy's city was a difficult under-taking. However, by disguising themselves, Ulysses and Dio-mede succeeded in entering the gates and in carrying away the Pal la'dium.

After carrying out the directions of the seer as indicated above, the Greeks had reason to think that they were near the end of their long struggle. They were strengthened in this conclu-

sion by the death of Paris, who a few days after the arrival
of Philoctetes had been slain by one of the arrows of Hercules.

**Paris dies;
Troy still
holds out**
But still the gates of Troy remained closed to
them. They devised many plans for taking the
city by surprise, but none of them seemed to afford
any real hope of success. Finally Athena came to their aid by
suggesting the device of the Wooden Horse.

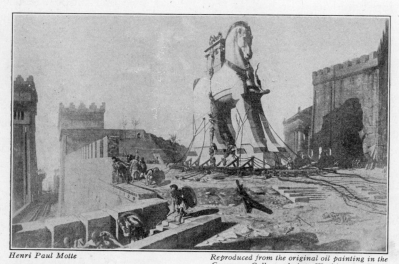

Henri Paul Motte   Reproduced from the original oil painting in the
Corcoran Gallery of Art, Washington, D. C.

Fig. 142. The Greeks leave their hiding place in the body of the Wooden Horse

Suddenly the Greeks seemed to vanish utterly. The plain
was deserted and the ships no longer in sight. Not far from the

**The Wooden
Horse enters
Troy**
walls, however, the Greeks had left a large wooden
structure in the form of a horse, in the hollow body
of which some of their bravest warriors were concealed.
Largely through the lies of a Greek named Sinon, who told them
among other things that Athena's favor could only be won by
offering this huge horse to her as a tribute, the Trojans were per-

suaded to take it into the city, in spite of the fact that in order
to do so they had to break down a part of the walls. Both the
Trojan princess Cas san′dra and La oc′co on, Neptune's priest,

warned them that it was a trick designed to bring ruin upon Troy. To
Cassandra's prophecy they paid not
the slightest heed. They attached
more weight, however, to Laocoön's
words, particularly as they heard the
sound of clanking armor within when
the priest hurled a spear against the
body. They might perhaps have
given up their idea of admitting the
horse had they not seen two enormous
serpents come up out of the sea, and,
making their way straight to the spot
where the priest and his two young
sons were standing, coil their slimy
bodies around the three and crush
them in their powerful embrace.
Surely this could only mean that the
gods were punishing Laocoön for impiety. They therefore threw aside all
precaution and drew the huge Wooden
Horse within the city. Great was the
rejoicing in Troy. The end of their
long labor had come, the enemy had
departed, and Athena's favor was won.

© *Underwood and Underwood*

Fig. 143. Edith Wynne Matthison
as Andromache in Euripides' play
entitled *The Trojan Women*

Tired by the festivities of the day, the Trojans slept soundly.
No one heard Sinon stealthily loosen the bolts in the Horse's side
The city falls or saw how one by one the Greek warriors slipped to
the ground. They did not see the fiery torch which signaled to

the Greeks, whose fleet was in hiding behind the island of Ten′e-
dos, that the city was theirs.   Before the inhabitants were awake,
the guards at the gates were killed and the streets filled with the
enemy.   Such resistance as the Trojans could make, thus taken
unawares, was useless.   A few leaders like Aeneas collected about
the palace of the king, hoping to defend this at least.   But they
could not save even Priam, who was slaughtered before his household shrine, or Hecuba and her daughters, who were dragged
away to become the slaves of the conquerors.   The whole city
was blazing with the conflagration, and soon only ashes remained
of what had once been the proud and splendid city of Troy.

Legend says that the Trojan War was undertaken by the Greeks
for the purpose of bringing Helen back to her home in Sparta.
The account of the war will not therefore be complete without
some statement about Helen's fortunes.

After the death of Paris, Helen had married his brother Deïphobus.   But the poets say that she had always loved Menelaüs

What happened to Helen
and was very glad to return with him to Greece.
They lived happily together for many years and,
while no one excused Paris for the part he played in
their elopement, on the other hand no one except Aeneas seems
to have cherished resentment against Helen, attributing her act
not to human weakness but to the power of Venus, too great a
goddess for a mortal to resist.

Was There a Real City Called Troy?

For a long time historians looked upon the story of the Trojan
War as a myth, and we might have gone on believing so had it not
been for a German named Schliemann, who, when he was a clerk
in a grocery store, heard a sailor reciting the poems of Homer,
and so became interested in these battles between the Greek and
Trojan warriors.   "As soon as I get rich," he said to himself,

"I am going over to Asia Minor to see if there are any remains of Troy." This purpose he never forgot. He applied himself so diligently to business that he finally became wealthy and was able to carry out the plan which he had so long cherished. He set about excavating the hill which legend had connected with the

© *Underwood and Underwood*

Fig. 144. The plain of Troy as seen from the ruins of the city

name of Troy. Other people became interested and, after Schliemann's death, continued the work. The discoveries which were made proved beyond a doubt that there had been a city called Troy, although it was left for later scholars[1] to assert that

---

[1] James H. Breasted in *The Conquest of Civilization* (Harper and Brothers, 1926), p. 254, speaks of "the splendid and cultivated city of Troy," and states on page 272 that "it is now perfectly evident that this Trojan expedition of the Greeks was a historical event." For further confirmation, see Walter Leaf's *Troy: A Study in Homeric Geography*, p. 13 (The Macmillan Company).

the Greek expedition known as the Trojan War was a historical event. The illustrations on pages 291 and 306 show the ruins of the city as they appear in modern times.

How Old Is Troy and When Did the Trojan War Take Place?

As far back as 3000 B.C. (and perhaps even earlier) some traders built a small city in the northwestern part of Asia Minor, which as the years went on became an important and wealthy commercial center. About 1500 B.C. the Trojans were living there, and it was their city, known as the Sixth — for there were nine settlements one above the other, which came to light as the spade cut down through the hill — which the Greeks destroyed during the twelfth century B.C. in what is known as the Trojan War. This diagram shows how long ago it all happened (notice that each of the groups of dots at the bottom represents five hundred years):

3000 B.C. (A town built at Troy)	1500 B.C. (Homer's Troy) 1100 B.C. (The city taken by the Greeks, traditional date, 1184)	B.C. ←┬→ A.D.	1900 A.D. (Today)
----- ----- -----	----- ----- -----	----- ----- -----	----- ----- -----

Who Were the Trojans and What Kind of Civilization Did They Have?

We are not sure who the Trojans were or just what their civilization was like. But we know that from 3000 to 1100 B.C. the ruling race in this part of the world was the Ae ge'an, a highly gifted people whose civilization, starting from Crete, spread over not only the islands of the Aegean Sea but the adjacent coast

as well.   Their nobles lived comfortably, even luxuriously.   One
is surprised to find that their palaces were equipped with a system
of heating and plumbing, and that in other ways they resembled

Photograph by Richard Stillwell

Fig. 145. Gallery of a Homeric palace in Tiryns

wealthy homes of today.   Their cities, moreover, contained theaters, gymnasiums, and many other buildings which we commonly
associate with times much later than those in which the Aegeans

lived.   Since it is altogether likely that after 1500 B.C. the Trojans absorbed much of this civilization (they may indeed have been of the same race), it is safe to say that when the Greek warriors came over from the mainland of what is now Greece, they found much to attract them in this rich city of Troy.   Back of the legend of Helen's beautiful face as the reason for the expedition against this place, is doubtless the idea of conquest for commercial ends.

IN THE WORLD OF TODAY

I. IN LITERARY ALLUSION

THE TROJAN WAR

And Priam's wail is heard no more
    By windy Il'i on's sea-built walls;
Nor great Achilles, stained with gore,
    Shouts, "O ye gods! 'tis Hector falls!"
On Ida's mount is the shining snow,
    But Jove has gone from its brow away;
And red on the plains the poppies grow
    Where Greek and Trojan fought that day.

EDNA DEAN PROCTOR, *Heroes*

HELEN

Was this the face that launched a thousand ships
And burned the topless towers of Ilion?

MARLOWE, *Dr. Faustus*

PARIS

Fronting the dawn he moved; a leopard skin
Drooped from his shoulder, but his sunny hair
Clustered about his temples like a god's.

TENNYSON, *Oenone*, 56-58

Paris is one of the central figures in a well-known poem by Tennyson called "Oe no'ne." In order to understand it, one must be familiar with certain details of the life of Paris.

When Paris was born his parents, Priam and Hecuba, were told that if the infant were allowed to grow up he would bring disaster upon Troy. He was therefore left to die from exposure upon the slopes of Mt. Ida. Here a shepherd found him. For many years the boy lived with his foster father, tending his sheep and sharing in his labors.

One day he met a girl named Oenone, with whom he fell in love, only to desert her a little later when Priam, who had learned that his son was alive, repented of his cruelty and summoned Paris to the Trojan court. The excitement of the life which the young prince led, however, and the popularity he won because of his charming manners, made him forget the country maiden for whom he had once cared.

But when Paris was wounded in the Trojan War and could not get any relief from his pain, he sought Oenone. Remembering how she had been wronged, the girl refused to heal his wound. However, her grief at the death of Paris was so great that she hanged herself, unable to endure the remorse for the unforgiving spirit that she had shown towards her former lover.

II. In Words and Expressions

We often say that a certain person **works like a Trojan** or **fights like a Trojan.** This usage comes from the fact that for ten long years the Trojans withstood the Greeks, enduring all sorts of hardship in their efforts to save their city. Their name has therefore become synonymous with hard work.

"Will England's landships bring victory as the **Trojan Horse** brought victory to the Greeks?" This quotation from a newspaper published in 1918 refers to the use of "tanks" which the

Allies used with great success during the last months of the World War.

"I fear the Greeks even when they bear gifts," said Laocoön when he warned the Trojans not to take the Wooden Horse into the city, although the Greeks said it was a present which would insure the safety of Troy. This expression is often used today in newspapers and literature in general to describe an offer which, while it seems to bring with it some great advantage, is really full of danger.

An **apple of discord** is an expression often used to indicate a cause for dispute.

A **stentorian voice** is a very loud one. The adjective comes from Sten'tor, the name of the Greek herald in the Trojan War. Any command that he transmitted or any announcement that he made was sure to be heard, no matter how great the noise at the time.

The expression **Achilles' heel** is commonly used to indicate the only sensitive spot

Courtesy of the Metropolitan Museum, New York

Fig. 146. Thetis and Achilles

Thetis tried to make her son Achilles invulnerable by dipping his body into the waters of the Styx. But the infant's heel, by which she held him, was not wet; hence this was the one spot in which a wound could prove fatal.

or the one part where an enemy's attack would be successful. The *Chicago Tribune* once said that we were bound to defend the Philippines from invasion by other countries, and that so long as we felt like incurring such a risk the islands would continue to be our **Achilles' heel.**

After our entrance into the World War, a bitter quarrel arose between two men in authority as to whether our ships should be of wood or of steel; meanwhile all construction was delayed. The *New Republic* spoke of this as follows: "The **Agamemnon-Achilles episode** in our shipbuilding has lasted about as long as the American people will stand it."

The expression **a sulking Achilles** is sometimes applied to a politician who, because he has failed to obtain what he wants, withdraws from the activities of his party. The *Wisconsin Journal* for July 17, 1919, thus alluded to a prominent senator.

We sometimes see the phrase **myrmidons of the law** used to indicate policemen or some armed force hired to carry out its provisions. This is often used in a contemptuous sense and is applied to someone who has been engaged to carry out a deed of violence. The expression goes back to the story of Achilles, for it was the Myrmidons who followed this hero in battle and helped him to win the victory.

There is an interesting story about the way in which the Myrmidons were created. Jupiter once wooed the nymph Aegina. The myths say that Juno in her anger sent a plague which devastated the island named from this maiden, a region where Aeacus, one of Achilles' ancestors, was living at the time. Finding himself alone, Aeacus prayed to Jupiter to give him a people. The god responded by turning a tribe of ants into men. These were called Myrmidons and when Achilles' father, Peleus, migrated to Thessaly, they followed him as his armed band.

To **hector** a person means to find fault with him, to treat him insolently, or to bully him. A **hector,** too, is a blustering, noisy fellow, always bothering someone or other. It seems very strange that this meaning has come down to us from the name of the Trojan hero, who, in classical literature seems to typify all manly qualities.

Concerning this point Dr. John A. Scott in a volume entitled *Homer and His Influence*,[1] pages 79–80, writes: "Hector was not only the devoted warrior, but he was a brother who felt deeply the shame brought upon the family and city by Paris, and, because of the indignation over that shame, he soundly berated him, hence this side of his nature has given the words *to hector* and *hectoring*. Other persons suppose that the words are derived from the Greeks' conception of Hector, who was a constant threat and source of annoyance to them."

To call a woman a **Helen of Troy** is only a way of indicating that she is extraordinarily beautiful.

An unusually good-looking young man is sometimes called a **Paris,** the term recalling King Priam's handsome son.

The **judgment of Paris** is a phrase often used to indicate a difficult choice involving rival claims to beauty.

III. In Other Connections

Achilles in Science

A certain ligament in the heel is known as the "tendon of Achilles." The story related in the preceding pages explains its name.

The Soldier at Gallipoli Remembers Achilles

Dardanus, a son of Jupiter, was the first mortal ancestor of the Trojans, and from him has come the modern name of the strait which the World War has made famous — the Dardanelles. This whole region has again become celebrated for heroic deeds, for it was here that the Gal lip'o li campaign was fought. The following poem was written by a soldier who took part in it and who afterwards died in France:

[1] Longmans, Green and Company.

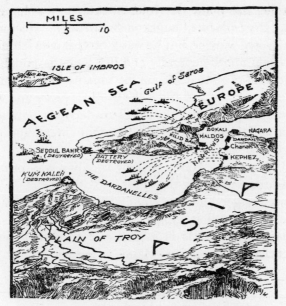

Fig. 147. A war map

A modern map of the region around Troy and the Dardanelles, drawn during the World War. The cross marks the site of Gallipoli, which the Allies tried to occupy although bombarded by fire from the Turkish forts.

LINES WRITTEN IN GALLIPOLI

I saw a man this morning
    Who did not wish to die.
I ask and cannot answer
    If otherwise wish I.

Fair broke the day this morning
    Against the Dardanelles.
The breeze blew soft, the morn's cheeks
    Were cold as cold sea shells.

But other shells were waiting
  Across the Aegean Sea,
Shrapnel and high explosive,
  Shells and hells for me.

Oh, hell of ships and cities,
  Hell of men like me,
Fatal second Helen,
  Why must I follow thee?

Achilles came to Troyland,
  And I to Cher'son ese;
He turned from wrath to battle,
  And I from three days' peace.

Was it so hard, Achilles,
  So very hard to die?
Thou knowest and I know not,
  So much the happier I.

I will go back this morning
  From Imbros over the sea.
Stand in the trench, Achilles,
  Flame-capped, and shout for me!

PATRICK SHAW-STEWART, *The Chicago Tribune*

The Ideal Warrior

Hector survives in the memory of the world as a type of the ideal warrior, a man who was not only brave and skilful on the battlefield but a good son, a loyal friend, a faithful husband, and a devoted father. Like Aeneas he is looked upon as the embodiment of patriotism.

The Pattern of a Wife and Mother

Andromache continues to be regarded as the type of a devoted wife of a warrior husband, and of a loving mother whose son perished by the fortunes of war.

A Charming Woman Immortalized

Helen remains and will always remain in the memory of the world as a symbol for woman's beauty and charm. The titles of the poems on page 305 show that even after many centuries Helen is a favorite theme for poets.

Salvatore Albano   *Courtesy of the Metropolitan Museum, New York*

Fig. 148. Hector, Andromache, and Astyanax

QUESTIONS FOR REVIEW

1. What divinity failed to be invited to the wedding of Peleus and Thetis? What form did her resentment take, and what was the effect upon the guests?

2. What is meant by "the judgment of Paris"?

3. What was the immediate cause of the Trojan War?

4. What circumstance made it possible to unite the leading young men of Greece in an expedition against Troy?

5. How were Ulysses and Achilles led to join the movement?

6. What incident delayed the departure of the fleet?

7. How were the enemy engaged during the first nine years of the war?

8. Relate the reason for the quarrel between Agamemnon and Achilles. What effect did this disagreement have upon the war?

9. What gods favored the Greeks and which ones took the side of the Trojans?

10. What Greek warrior wounded two gods?

11. What was the name of Hector's wife? Of his son? How did Hector reply to his wife's appeal to stay within the walls?

12. Who was Patroclus, and under what circumstances did he meet his death?

13. What effect did the death of Patroclus have upon Achilles?

14. Tell the story of Hector's death and describe the scene that followed.

15. What two incidents show that Achilles was possessed of generous instincts?

16. Who caused the death of Achilles?

17. What fate befell Paris?

18. By what stratagem did the Greeks finally succeed in entering Troy?

19. Tell the story of Troy's last night.

20. What happened to Helen after the war?

21. How do we know that there was a city named Troy?

22. How long ago was Troy destroyed?

23. Who were the Trojans? Discuss their civilization.

Fig. 146. The seal of the Centaur Book Shop

24. A bookshop in Philadelphia is called the "Centaur." What is your theory as to the way in which the centaurs became connected with books and learning?

OPTIONAL

FOR THOSE WHO HAVE TIME FOR FURTHER STUDY

A. ADDITIONAL READING

I. In Textbooks Dealing with Classical Mythology

See references in the Appendix, pages xxviii ff.

II. In Books in General

1. Passages from the *Iliad*, translation by Lang, Leaf, and Myers.
   (1) Helen and the Trojan elders watch the battle from the towers of Troy, III, pp. 54–56.

(2) Hector's farewell to his family, VI, pp. 124–125.

(3) Death of Patroclus, XVI, pp. 336–341.

(4) Achilles grieves for his friend, XVIII, pp. 368–370.

(5) * Achilles slays Hector, XXII, pp. 439–449.

(6) How the body of Hector was ransomed, XXIV, pp. 478–499.

2. Passages from Book II of Vergil's *Aeneid*, translated by John Conington (Scott, Foresman and Company; numbers refer to lines in the translation):

(1) How the Trojans were led to take the horse into the city, 15–274.

(2) Dramatic incidents in the taking of Troy: Street scenes, 328–478; Capture of the king's palace, 479–555; The death of Priam, 556–613.

3. *Helen*, a novel by Edward Lucas White (George H. Doran and Company).

4. Books dealing with Troy and the Aegean civilization:

(1) Breasted's *Ancient Times: A History of the Early World*, pp. 239, 244–247 (Ginn and Company); also by the same author, *The Conquest of Civilization*, pp. 241–267 (for Troy especially, see pp. 260–263); chap. ix, "The Coming of the Greeks," and chap. x, "Civilization in the Age of the Kings" (Harper Brothers, 1926).

(2) Baikie's *Sea Kings of Crete*, chap. iii (A. and C. Black, London).

(3) Tolman and Scoggin's *Mycenaean Troy*, pp. 87–110 (American Book Company).

B. Memorize One or More of These Quotations

TROY

The sacred soil of Ilion is rent
With shaft and pit; foiled waters wander slow
Through plains where Simois [1] and Scamander [1] went
To war with gods and heroes long ago.

ANDREW LANG, *Homeric Unity*, 1–4

[1] Rivers near Troy. The god of the latter stream is said to have fought with Achilles.

ACHILLES

For who can match Achilles? He who can,
Must yet be more than hero, more than man.

HOMER, *Iliad*, XXIII, 933–934, Pope's Translation

HELEN

No wonder such celestial charms
For nine long years have set the world in arms;
What winning graces! what majestic mien!
She moves a goddess, and she looks a queen.

HOMER, *Iliad*, III, 105–106, Pope's Translation

C. FURTHER STUDY OF LITERARY ALLUSION

If you are interested in seeing more clearly how good writers make use of the myths, look up the following references:

Achilles: William McFee's *An Ocean Tramp*, p. 38 (Doubleday, Page). **Briseïs:** Thackeray's *The Newcomes*, p. 263 (Everyman's Library). **Chiron:** Kingsley's *Westward Ho*, p. 51. **Hector:** Milton's *Paradise Lost*, IX, 15–16. **Hecuba:** Edith Wharton's *Custom of the Country*, p. 372 (Scribners). **Helen:** R. W. Gilder's *A Warrior of Troy;* Landor's *Verse;* Oscar Wilde's *Serenade*, p. 92–93. **Iphigenia:** Tennyson's *Dream of Fair Women*, 85–94, 105–110. **Oenone:** Tennyson's *Dream of Fair Women*, 14–15. **Sinon and fall of Troy:** Shakespeare's *Titus Andronicus*, Act V, Sc. 3, 80–87. **Troy:** Milton's *Il Penseroso*, 100.

D. PROJECTS FOR INDIVIDUAL OR GROUP WORK

To be selected from the list of projects on pages xx–xxvi, in case the subject matter of this chapter lends itself readily to any one of them.

POEMS FOR REFERENCE

ARNOLD, MATTHEW   Empedocles on Aetna (certain lines in which
                              Chiron, the centaur, speaks to the young
                              Achilles; quoted in Gayley's *Classic
                              Myths*, p. 274).

BENÉT, STEPHEN VINCENT	* Song of the City of Troy (*Heavens and Earth;* Henry Holt and Company, N. Y.)
BROWNING, ROBERT	The Agamemnon of Aeschylus (parts)
BYRON, LORD	On a Bust of Helen
ERSKINE, JOHN	* Paris, Helen's Lover; *also* * Penthesileia (*Collected Poems;* Duffield and Company, N. Y.)
EURIPIDES	Translations in verse entitled: Hecuba, Daughters of Troy, Andromache, Iphigenia in Aulis, Iphigenia in Tau:ica, by A. S. Way in the Loeb Classical Library (G. P. Putnam's Sons, N. Y.); also a translation by Gilbert Murray called * The Trojan Women (George Allen and Company, London)
GIBSON, WILFRED WILSON	* Noel Dark (Casualties; *Atlantic Monthly,* June, 1919)
HOMER	Verse translation of the *Iliad* by Alexander Pope, the Earl of Derby, Will'am Cullen Bryant, William Cowper, and others.
KEMP, HARRY	* Paris to Helen; Reunion; * Helen's Handmaid; Helen Brought Home (*The Sea and the Dunes;* Brentano's, N. Y.)
LANDOR, WALTER SAVAGE	Iphigenia and Agamemnon; Menelaüs and Helen, Espousals of Polyxena
LANG, ANDREW	* Shade of Helen; Helen of Troy (*Poems;* Longmans, Green and Company, N. Y.)
MASTERS, EDGAR LEE	Helen of Troy (*Songs and Satires;* The Macmillan Company, N. Y.)
MILLER, F. J.	* The Fall of Troy (University of Chicago Press)
MORRIS, LEWIS	Helen; Laocoön (*Epic of Hades;* Kegan Paul, Trench, Trübner and Company, London)
MORRIS, WILLIAM	* Death of Paris (*The Earthly Paradise;* Longmans, Green and Company, N. Y.)
NOYES, ALFRED	Mount Ida (*Collected Poems,* Vol. II; Frederick A. Stokes Company, N. Y.)

ROSSETTI, DANTE G.	Cassandra
TEASDALE, SARA	* Helen of Troy (*Helen of Troy;* The Macmillan Company, N. Y.)
TENNYSON, ALFRED	Achilles over the Trench; * Oenone
WILDE, OSCAR	The New Helen (*Poems;* Brentano's, N. Y.)
WORDSWORTH, WILLIAM	Laodamia

Fig. 150.   The walls of Troy's Sixth City

THE ADVENTURES
OF
ULYSSES

Yet he

When all the other captains had won home,
Was whirled about the wilderness of foam;
For the wind and wave have driven him evermore
Mocked by the green of some receding shore;
Yet over wind and wave he had his will,
Blistered and buffeted, unbaffled still.
Ever the snare was set, ever in vain;
The Lotos Island and the Siren strain;
Through Scylla and Charybdis hath he run,
Sleeplessly plunging to the setting sun.
Who hath so suffered, or so far hath sailed,
So much encountered, and so little quailed?

From the Prologue to *Ulysses* by STEPHEN PHILLIPS.
Reprinted by permission of The Macmillan Company, publishers.

ULYSSES
(O dys'seus)

AFTER the destruction of Troy, the one thought in the minds of the Greek warriors was to return to their homes as quickly as possible. So, having loaded their ships with the spoils of Troy, they at once set sail for Greece. Because they had plundered temples and had committed other acts of violence hateful to the gods in the course of their last night at Troy, their homeward voyage was beset with difficulties and dangers. So many were the disasters, in fact, that only a few of the Greeks succeeded in arriving at their homes. Among the latter were Ag a mem'non, Men e la'us, Di'o mede, Nes'tor, Ne op tol'e mus, and Ulys'ses. The present chapter is concerned with the adventures of the last mentioned warrior, who after ten long years of wandering upon sea and land came at last to the shores of his native Ith'a ca.

The twelve ships of Ulysses met with no disaster until they were rounding the southern end of Greece and were well on their **Driven from their course** homeward way. But there they were overtaken by a violent storm and driven far from their course. Reaching land, the Greeks beached their ships and eagerly disembarked, happy in the prospect of rest from the discomforts of their long and stormy voyage.

The Greeks found the inhabitants of the place very kind and hospitable. Particularly did they enjoy the food which was offered them — a plant called the lotos, so delicious in flavor that they could not leave it alone. Ulysses, however, soon observed that this food not only produced forgetfulness of the past, but robbed those who partook of it of any desire for activity. A feeling of deep content with the dreamy life they were leading seemed to take possession of the sailors. So difficult was it to overcome this feeling that Ulysses was compelled literally to drag his men to the ships, where he tied them fast until they recovered from the effects of this strange food.

The Lotos-eaters

The next stopping place was an island inhabited by a race of men of gigantic size called the Cy clo'pes, whose appearance, unsightly enough in any case, was rendered much more forbidding by the fact that in place of two eyes they had only one, enormous in size and set right in the middle of the forehead. This peculiarity made them seem more like monsters than men. They were really the children of Neptune, but Ulysses did not know this. In fact, he was in total ignorance of the place and its inhabitants when one day he anchored eleven of his ships near by, and in the other ship approached the shore to ask for hospitality.

An encounter with the monster Polyphemus

When Ulysses and his companions landed, they walked about for some time without finding a trace of human habitation. But finally discovering a huge cave in which were jars filled with milk, they knew that some one lived on the island. While they were wondering who the inhabitants were, the entrance of the cave was darkened by an enormous figure which proved to be that of Pol-y phe'mus. Driving before him a flock of sheep and goats, the monster entered the cave and closed the opening with a huge rock. Then he milked the ewes and the she-goats and made a kind of cheese which he put into wicker baskets. Next he stirred up the fire on the hearth.

As the flames lighted up the cave, he perceived the Greeks and cried out in a terrible voice: "Whence come ye, strangers, and why?" "Greeks we are," replied Ulysses, "returning from Troy, and, worn out by our sufferings upon the sea, we have landed to ask for rest and refreshment in the name of Jupiter." "Little do I care for Jupiter," was the reply. "The Cyclopes know not him nor any law." At this he seized two of the trembling sailors and, tearing them limb from limb, devoured them raw. Then he lay down and slept until morning. For his breakfast he

Drawing by Flaxman

Fig. 151. Ulysses presents Polyphemus with wine

again devoured two men, after which he departed to pasture his sheep on the mountains, not forgetting, however, to block the entrance as before.

All the time Ulysses was thinking hard, trying to devise a scheme for saving his companions and himself from the almost certain death that awaited them. Finally he proposed a plan to be put into operation that very night.

When Polyphemus returned at evening, he dined again in the same horrible manner. Then Ulysses came forward, and with courteous words offered the monster a drink of the wine which had been brought up from the ships. The Cy′clops greatly enjoyed it and drank again and again. "Tell me your name, stranger," cried Polyphemus, "so that I may give you a stranger's gift in return for yours, for this wine is as delicious as the nectar which the gods drink." Luckily, as it turned out afterwards, Ulysses was quick-witted enough to answer, "My father and mother and all my companions call me No′man. This is my name." To this the Cyclops replied, "I shall reward you, Noman, as I promised. Not until all your friends have been devoured shall I eat you. You shall be the last."

Giulio Romano (Palace near Mantua)   Photograph by Alinari

Fig. 152. Polyphemus in love

Although so unsightly to look upon, Polyphemus saw no reason why a maiden named Galatea should not accept him as her lover. He besieged her with attentions. When he saw they were all in vain, he hurled a huge rock upon the girl's sweetheart (you can see them sitting together) and so killed his rival. But legend says that Galatea continued to shun the Cyclops.

Then, drunken with the wine, to which he had not been accustomed, Polyphemus fell into a deep slumber. As the monster lay stretched out upon the floor of the cave, Ulysses and his men brought out a long pole, sharpened and burning at the end, which they had spent the day in preparing. The point of this they plunged into the eye of the Cyclops and turned it round and round.

With a yell of pain and rage Polyphemus sprang to his feet. All about the cave he stumbled, reaching out blindly in an effort to find the Greeks, who, however, were always quick enough to elude his grasp. Then he sat down at the door. So loud were his cries that the Cyclopes outside heard them and came to the cave to see what was the matter. " Who is hurting you, Polyphemus? " they asked. "No man is hurting me," was the answer. "Then, if no man is troubling you," they said, "it must be that you are afflicted by the gods. You cannot escape the sickness which they send. Pray to your father Neptune." Then they went away.

But the troubles of Ulysses were not over. How was he to get out of the cave? No human hands could move the bowlder at the entrance. So again he was forced to strategy. When morning came, Polyphemus rolled the rock away and sat at the door of the cave, reaching out over the backs of the sheep as they came crowding out, to see that Ulysses and his men were not among them. He did not notice particularly the fact that the sheep came out in groups of three, and therefore did not discover that under the one in the middle of each group a Greek was tied. Nor did he detect Ulysses clinging to the wool beneath a large ram, even though he felt its back and wondered why the animal came last instead of leading the flock as usual. He could not realize that Ulysses, after helping to fasten his men under the bodies of the sheep, had stayed behind until they were all in safety, and then had himself escaped in the manner related.

The Greeks reached their ships unharmed in spite of the pursuit of Polyphemus, whose rage was increased a hundred fold by the discovery that the men had escaped from the cave. But it was only by good luck that Ulysses' overwhelming desire to taunt the blinded Cyclops did not destroy them, for as he was sailing away he called out exultantly, "If anyone asks who has blinded

Polyphemus, tell him it was Ulysses, the destroyer of cities, he who fought at Troy." Thereupon the Cyclops was able to locate the position of the ship and to hurl at it the huge rocks which even today remain along the coast of Sicily as evidences of the monster's wrath.

As a result of this adventure in the land of the Cyclopes, the

Fig. 153. Legend says that these are the rocks on the coast of Sicily which Polyphemus threw after Ulysses and his companions as they sailed away.

anger of Neptune was aroused, and to it were due many of the disasters upon the sea which later befell Ulysses.

The reception which the Greeks met on the occasion of their next landing, which was at the islands of Ae′o lus, was quite differ-
The gift of ent in character from that just described. The king,
King Aeolus who was the god of the winds, extended to them every courtesy and, when they departed, presented Ulysses with a wonderful gift, a leather bag fastened with a silver cord and con-

taining all the winds except that which the hero would need in
sailing to Ithaca. Had matters gone as Aeolus expected, the
troubles of Ulysses would soon have been over. In fact, Ithaca
was actually in sight when the disaster happened that wrecked
all Ulysses' plans. Once while the hero lay asleep, the men, who
had been told never to open the bag, grew suspicious of their
leader. Did it contain treasure, they wondered, which Ulysses
was keeping for himself and in which they were to have no share?
The temptation to satisfy their curiosity proved too strong to
resist and the bag was opened. Instantly all the winds were set
free. The ship was seized in their blasts and driven far from
Ithaca. Soon Ulysses found himself once more at the land of
Aeolus. But the king would have nothing more to do with him,
and so in despair the hero continued his voyage.

The Laes try go'nes, with whom the Greeks next came in contact, seem to have been cannibals. They not only destroyed
An encounter eleven of Ulysses' ships but killed all of the sailors.
with cannibals Only one boat with its crew escaped, and in this ship
Ulysses succeeded in reaching land once more.

The island at which the Greeks now arrived was heavily
wooded, and it was therefore impossible to discover whether or
not it was inhabited without sending out a scouting party. This
Ulysses decided to do.

As time went on and the men whom he had sent to explore did
not return, Ulysses began to be worried. Finally their leader
The   came back and told a very strange story. The party
enchantments had made their way through the forest and had come
of Circe   upon an opening, the sight of which filled them with
astonishment. Before their eyes was a beautiful palace. Following Ulysses' example, the leader decided not to risk the lives
of all by entering the palace in a body lest, if they met with
death, no one would be left to bear the news to the ship. Accord-

ingly Eu ryl'o chus, the leader, remained outside. As the hours went by and he saw no one come out of the palace, he had thought it best to acquaint Ulysses with the strange facts.

Ulysses knew that some disaster must have happened to the men and determined to find out for himself what had befallen them. On the way he met a young man (really Mercury in disguise), who told him that a wonderfully beautiful woman named

Rivière   © H. K. T.; Gramstorff Brothers

Fig. 154. Circe

These animals are really people who through Circe's magic have lost their human form.

Cir'ce lived in the palace, and that it was her custom to entertain strangers lavishly. "But," he said, "while she is serving them with wine, she pours into it some magic drops whereby, at the touch of her wand, the guests are changed into swine. This herb," continued the young man, "will protect you from Circe's spell." Thereupon he gave Ulysses a plant called "moly."

No sooner had Ulysses entered the house than Circe came forward to greet him with words of kindliest welcome. He drank the wine she offered, but as she raised the wand to transform him

into an animal, the usual result failed to follow.   Instead, she
was seized and threatened with instant death if she did not
release the Greeks from her spell.   Circe knew at once that some
god was aiding this stranger, and therefore complied with Ulysses'
demand.   Moreover, she sent for the men who were still in the
ship and entertained Ulysses and his whole company very royally
for an entire year.

When Ulysses finally insisted upon leaving the island, Circe
gave him the advantage of her strange prophetic power by telling
him that before he could hope to see his home in Ithaca he must
descend to the Lower World to consult the seer Ti re′si as.   She
also gave him very clear directions about how to find the
entrance, and what to do after he arrived.

When Ulysses found himself in the Lower World he first sacrificed some sheep ; then he dug a trench into which he poured their
Ulysses visits blood as libations to the dead.   Immediately a
Hades　　　throng of spirits came to drink, because only after a
taste of blood could they speak to mortals.   Ulysses pushed them
all back from the trench except Tiresias, with whom he held a
long conversation.   Among other things affecting the hero's
future, Tiresias told him that on no account must he let injury
be done to the cattle of the sun-god on the island of Tri na′cri a
(Sicily).   Ulysses resolved to remember this warning, whatever
else he forgot, so earnestly did the old man caution him.

Ulysses then let the other spirits approach, among them his
mother.   She told him all about his family — how La er′tes, his
aged father, was sorrowing, and how she herself had died of grief
at the loss of her warrior son.   The hero rejoiced to hear that his
son, Te lem′a chus, was well, and that his wife, Pe nel′o pe, had
remained faithful and still looked forward to her husband's
return.

A chil′les, still a great prince even here among the shades, came forward also. He begged Ulysses to tell him what he knew of Pe'leus. "How fares my aged father," he asked, "and has Ne op tol'e mus proved himself a worthy son of Achilles?" Ulysses was glad to tell him of the many heroic deeds which the young man had performed at Troy. "Some of our heroes grew pale with fright as they entered the Wooden Horse," he said, "and a few of them wept, but the color of your son's face, Achilles, did not change nor were there any tears upon his cheeks."

Ulysses also saw Tan'ta lus, Ix i'on, and Sis'y phus, and therefore must have entered Tartarus, where these sinners were suffering punishment, a region usually closed to mortal visitors. But it seems not to have been forbidden territory to this dauntless man.

This visit to the Lower World made Ulysses even more eager to reach Ithaca, and accordingly, after one day at Circe's island, he set sail in another attempt to finish his long voyage.

Not long after Ulysses had left Circe's land, the ships came in sight of the shores where the Sirens lived. These were beautiful **The song of** women whose song bewitched all who heard it. **the Sirens** Many a sailor, lured by its sweetness, had jumped overboard, only to perish pitiably in the sea or, if he succeeded in reaching land, to meet death at the hands of the Sirens.

Had not Ulysses been warned by Circe of this danger, doubtless both he and his men would have perished then and there. But as the ship approached the spot, Ulysses ordered his men to tie him tightly to the mast and under no circumstances to set him free until the vessel had passed far beyond the land. The ears of the sailors he filled with wax, so that they might be deaf to all sounds.

Ulysses' precaution proved to be wise, for no sooner did he hear the wondrous notes of the Sirens than he made frantic gestures to the crew to untie the cords. But, following his instructions, they did nothing of the sort, and only when the Sirens were lost to sight did they release him.

Between Italy and the island of Sicily there is a strait which legend associates with the monsters Scyl'la and Cha ryb'dis, who **Scylla and** lived in caves on either side of the narrow stretch of **Charybdis** water and preyed upon vessels as they passed. Scylla was a most dreadful creature to look upon. Her body

Drawing by Flaxman

Fig. 155. Scylla

The monster has just seized some of the companions of Ulysses.

from the waist up was that of a woman, but she had twelve feet and six long necks, and as many heads, each one, as Homer says, " with three rows of teeth set thick and close with black death." On the other side lived Charybdis, who three times each day sucked in the water of the sea and three times belched it forth, in this way wrecking any ship that chanced to be passing.

Ulysses escaped the danger from Charybdis as he went through the strait, but he had to look on while Scylla, extending her six heads, seized as many sailors in her cruel grasp and drew them up squirming and calling out in agony to Ulysses to save them. But although the hero had many times rescued them from death through his valor or his cunning, he was powerless in this case to give them any aid.

When his ship reached the island where the cattle of Helios were pastured, Ulysses remembered the warning of Tiresias. He **The sun-god's cattle** resolved to spend only one night on land and then to depart as quickly as possible. But favorable winds failed him, and for a month he was detained upon the island. Little by little his store of provisions gave out and the men became desperate with hunger. One day, while Ulysses had gone off by himself to pray to the gods for help, they yielded to temptation and killed some of the sacred cattle.

As soon as the hero, returning to his companions, smelled the odor of roasted flesh, he foresaw that the god's anger would bring disaster upon him. And this proved to be true. Helios begged Jupiter to punish this injury to his herd. In answer to his complaint, a violent storm wrecked the ship of Ulysses, drowning all his men but leaving the hero clinging to the mast in the midst of the angry billows.

Ulysses was fortunate enough to be carried to the shores of a land ruled over by a nymph named Ca lyp'so. Here Ulysses **Calypso detains Ulysses** lived a most luxurious life for eight years. Nothing that ministered to his comfort seemed to be lacking, and in Calypso he found an interesting and intelligent companion. To be sure, she was more than human, otherwise she could not have kept the hero so long from his purpose of returning to Ithaca. Her powerful charm was broken only when Jupiter at Minerva's suggestion sent Mercury to tell the nymph that the time had come for her guest to depart. Obedient to this command, she helped Ulysses build a raft, gave him food and other supplies, and sent him on his way with counsel and friendly wishes.

For eighteen days Ulysses sailed, before the relentless Neptune discovered him and sent a storm which broke up the raft. Ulysses was now at the mercy of the sea, with not even a stick of timber to which to cling. For two days and two nights he swam, greatly helped by Minerva, who made the waters smooth in front of him and kept the wind at his back to help him on his way. At last land appeared and, more dead than alive, Ulysses was washed upon the shore.

The hospitality of King Alcinoüs

One sunny day Nau sic′a a, the daughter of King Al cin′o us of the island of Phae a′ci a, loaded a mule cart with the family laundry and, together with her companions, drove down to the shore to wash the clothes. Soon the garments were spread out to dry upon the hot sands. Then the maidens unpacked the lunch which Nausicaä's mother had put in the cart and, after they had eaten it, they began to play ball. In the midst of their fun, they were startled to see a strange man appear, who, as he had no clothes, was holding before him branches which he had broken from the bushes. Nausicaä, however, being a princess, did not lose her self-possession, although she, too, was a little frightened. She listened to Ulysses' explanation of his presence and, in reply to his request for help, said, " The poor and the stranger are from Jupiter." Then she gave him some clothes from the supply on the beach and food

Vatican, Rome   *Photograph by Alinari*

Fig. 156. Minerva (Athena)

to bring back his strength. Afterwards she told him that her father's palace was not far away and gave him directions for reaching it.

King Alcinoüs, being a god-fearing man and just and kind in all of his dealings, received Ulysses hospitably. A feast was prepared in his honor, and so much was the host attracted by the stranger's charm that he proposed to him that he marry Nausicaä and become heir to his vast wealth. But when the hero, while expressing gratitude for so generous an offer, said that he could not linger at Phaeacia but must continue his journey to Ithaca, the king, far from being offended, said, " We detain no man against his will and you shall be taken wherever you desire to go." Thus Ulysses awoke one day to find himself actually on his native shores, the Phae a'cians having taken him there as he slept, for he was still very tired from his long struggle with the sea.

For some years after Ulysses left for the war, matters had gone well with Penelope and her young son, Telemachus. But when after sixteen years her husband had not yet returned, **How Penelope fared during her husband's absence** many suitors began to press their claims for Penelope's hand. Not only was she a beautiful woman whom any man might wish to have as a wife, but she possessed wide lands, many flocks and herds, and large numbers of men and women servants. And so there was great rivalry among the princes in this part of the country and much speculation among people in general as to who would take Ulysses' place. But Penelope refused to listen to any offer of marriage, firm in her faith that her husband would one day return.

When the war was over and other leaders arrived at their homes and still Ulysses did not come, it seemed probable that the hero was dead. However, Penelope's faith in the ultimate return of her husband did not waver. But she found it increas-

ingly difficult to withstand the arrogance of her suitors. Knowing that Telemachus was too young to protect his mother, and

The suitors deceived by a trick

Ulysses' father, Laërtes, too aged to guard her, they
almost took possession of her palace, drinking her
wine, consuming her food, and ordering her servants
about as though they were indeed the masters. Finally Penelope
was forced to promise that when she had finished a certain garment which she was making for Laërtes, she would choose one of
the suitors for her husband. But though she worked for many
weeks and months, the garment was still unfinished. No one
but Penelope's faithful women attendants knew that, in order to
put off the decision as long as possible, she undid at night all that
she had woven in the daytime. But of course Penelope could
not hope to continue to deceive her suitors in this fashion forever.

About this time Telemachus, who was nearing twenty years
of age, resolved to go to Sparta to see if Nestor or Menelaüs could

Ulysses' son learns that his father is alive

tell him whether his father was dead or alive. Nestor
could not help him, and Menelaüs could give him no
definite information except to say that Pro'te us
once told him that Ulysses was living on Calypso's island. This
was joyous news for Telemachus, who soon started home to tell
his mother what he had heard. Just before he reached Ithaca,
Ulysses had arrived and, disguised by Minerva as an aged beggar,
was staying in the hut of the swineherd Eu mae'us.

As soon as Telemachus came, Ulysses threw off his disguise.
Both father and son were overcome with emotion as they found

A plan devised

themselves actually face to face in the hut of Eu-
mæus. They at once set about devising a plan for
ridding the house of the haughty suitors, as a preliminary step
to the announcement of Ulysses' return. When all the details
were arranged, Ulysses once more assumed his disguise and entered the palace as an old and ragged beggar, asking only to sit

by the hearth in quiet and to receive bits of food left from the feasts.

So well had Minerva disguised Ulysses that even those who had known him in the old days failed to recognize him. But

The hero's dog and an old nurse remember their master

his dog Ar'gus was not deceived. He knew his master at once. So great, however, was the shock of seeing him again that the aged animal died at Ulysses' feet. And Eu ry cle'a, an old woman who had cared for him as a child, observing a certain scar on his leg as she bathed his feet, cried out with joy, knowing that it was her beloved master who was before her. But Ulysses told her to be quiet and to tell no one of her discovery.

One evening as the throng of suitors, together with Telemachus and others of the household, were sitting about the court, Penel-

The suitors are slain

ope suddenly appeared with the bow of Ulysses and, to the astonishment of all, announced that she would choose as her husband that man who could bend the bow and shoot through the holes in twelve axes' heads set up as a target. All the suitors sprang to their feet in great excitement, each one boasting loudly of his skill, and each eager to display it. One after another made the trial, but among them all not one could even bend the bow.

Then the ragged old man who for days had been sitting quietly in a corner, the butt of the suitors' jokes and an object for occasional mistreatment, came forward. A shout of laughter greeted him as he took the bow from Penelope's hand. Amid the jeers of the crowd he stretched the tough wood and with precision sent an arrow through the twelve holes. At once his disguise fell from him and the powerful master of the house stood revealed. Before the suitors could make a move to escape, Ulysses turned his bow upon them and killed many. Some looked to the walls for the weapons which usually hung there, but, as Telemachus had removed them all, they found themselves helpless. They rushed to the doors only to find them barred and escape in that direction cut off. So they perished miserably, meeting the death they so well deserved.

Penelope was filled with joy to have her lover and husband with her once again, and legend says that they enjoyed many years of prosperity in their home at Ithaca.

IN THE WORLD OF TODAY

I. In Literary Allusion

Fate hath decreed that Ulysses should abide
More toils and fiercer than all men beside.

Stephen Phillips, Ulysses, Prologue, p. 20

A little Cyclops with one eye
Staring to threaten and defy.

William Wordsworth, The Daisy

This is the ship of pearl, which poets feign,
    Sails the unshadowed main,
    The venturesome bark that flings
On the sweet summer wind its purpled wings
In gulfs enchanted where the Siren sings,
    And coral reefs lie bare,
Where the cold sea-maids rise to sun their streaming hair.

Oliver Wendell Holmes, The Chambered Nautilus

                    Who knows not Circe,
The daughter of the Sun, whose charmèd cup
Whoever tasted lost his upright shape,
And downward fell into a groveling swine?

Milton, Comus, 50–53

II. In Words and Expressions

An **odyssey** is a tale of adventure. Not long ago an aviator took part in an exciting race across the continent. His diary was described in newspaper headlines as " A Vivid Odyssey."

Lotos-eaters is an expression very commonly used to describe persons who lead an untroubled life, are averse to any effort, and are without ambition.

Walls which are built of such huge blocks that only a people as powerful in physical strength as the Cyclopes could have made them, are called **cy clo pe′an**. Many examples of such structures are found among the ruins of Greece and Italy.

Men′tor was a friend and counselor of Ulysses and his son. It is customary today to speak of an adviser (especially if he is a friend also) as a **mentor**.

A person who is very skilful in strategy is sometimes called a **Ulysses,** in allusion to this hero's striking characteristic, i.e., the ability to invent a means of escape from impending danger.

Aeolus was the god of the winds, and music caused by the breezes is called **ae o′li an**. The word is so used in the following passage :

> The breezes blow the fountain's glass
> And wake aeolian melodies.
>
> Thomas Bailey Aldrich, *Pampinea*

Scylla and **Charybdis** still symbolize two dangers between which one must choose, just as passing ships had to decide which side of the strait was safer, that where Charybdis lived or the one where Scylla had her cave.

A **feast of Alcinoüs** is a splendid banquet. This descriptive phrase recalls details of Ulysses' visit at the palace of the Phaeacian king.

A fascinating woman is often called a **Circe** or a **Siren**.

The expression **he cannot bend Ulysses' bow** is sometimes applied to a person who is trying in vain to imitate one who is much his superior in ability.

III. In Other Connections

How Aeolus Appears in Physical Geography

Dust carried by the winds from one region to another forms "aeolian" deposits. Certain plains are called by this name.

How the Aeolian Harp Gets Its Name

Because the music of the Aeolian harp is dependent upon the breezes that sweep across its strings, the instrument has been called from the name of Aeolus, the god of the winds. A poet mentions it thus:

> Like that wild harp whose magic tone
> Is wakened by the winds alone.
>
> Scott, *Lay of the Last Minstrel*, Canto I, xxxi

A Sea Creature Named Cyclops

Since the Cyclopes were monsters with but one eye, and that in the middle of their foreheads, the term "cyclops" has been applied to a certain fresh-water creature with but one eye in the front of its head.

Fig. 157. The Polyphemus Moth

Why a Moth Is Called Polyphemus

Surely nothing could be less like the huge, ungainly creature called Polyphemus than a moth. But just because it has a large spot resembling an eye on each back wing, it has been given this name.

Origin of the Name for the Whistle Known as the " Siren "

This harsh-sounding whistle frequently used as a fire signal or to sound a warning of some kind probably goes back for its name to the story of the beautiful maidens whose song, irresistible in its charm, lured men to destruction. But see the explanation given in the Oxford Dictionary.

A Strange Tale about a Small Island

As one enters the port of Corfu, a large island off the western coast of Greece, which is connected by legend with the land of the Phaeacians, he sees Mouse Island, a tiny piece of land, which according to the myths was once the ship which conveyed Ulysses to Ithaca.   Neptune in his anger at the escape of Ulysses is said to have wrought this transformation.

Penelope as a Symbol for the Faithful Wife

Penelope has become the type for the wife who never forgets her absent husband and still awaits his return, even though all probabilities point to his death.

QUESTIONS FOR REVIEW

1. What famous books have been written in Greek about the adventures of Ulysses and the Greeks, and by what author?
2. (1) Where was Ulysses' home?
   (2) What was the name of his wife? Of his son? Of his father?
3. What was the cause of the Trojan War?
4. What circumstances led to Ulysses' extended wanderings?
5. (1) How long did it take Ulysses to journey from Troy to Ithaca?
   (2) How large was his fleet when he set out?
   (3) Trace his journey on the map, making a list of all the places he visited.

6. How were Ulysses' men affected by a certain delicious food, and what did Ulysses do about it?

7. (1) Who were the Cyclopes?

    (2) Describe their appearance.

    (3) Relate in detail the encounter with Polyphemus and the escape.

8. To what were many of the disasters due which later befell Ulysses?

9. How did a present which Ulysses received from King Aeolus prove disastrous?

10. In what way did Ulysses lose all but one of his ships with their crews?

11. (1) What fate befell Ulysses' men at the hands of a beautiful enchantress?

    (2) How did Ulysses master this situation?

12. Describe Ulysses' visit to Hades.

13. How did Ulysses' quick wit save him from the song of the Sirens?

14. Describe Scylla and Charybdis and relate the dangers encountered in passing by them.

15. How did yielding to hunger lead to the death of Ulysses' remaining men?

16. How did the nymph Calypso aid Ulysses in continuing his journey?

17. What help did Ulysses receive from a princess who was playing ball?

18. How did Ulysses secure ships for the remainder of his journey?

19. How did Ulysses' wife fare during his long absence?

20. In what way did Penelope show that she, as well as her husband, could get out of a difficult situation?

21. Describe the meeting between Telemachus and his father; between Ulysses and both his faithful dog and his aged nurse.

22. How was Penelope relieved of her importunate suitors and restored to her happy husband?

23. What kind of person may be called a "Ulysses"?

24. For what is Penelope a symbol?

25. How does Aeolus figure in the realm of music today?

26. Explain the expressions: *a feast of Alcinoüs, he cannot bend Ulysses' bow, lotos-eaters.*

27. Keeping in mind the fact that the rocks and whirlpools between Sicily and Italy are dangerous for ships, what theory have you to propose as a possible explanation for the curious myth about Scylla and Charybdis?

28. Why should a magazine devoted to art, literature, history, science, and travel be called "The Mentor"?

OPTIONAL

FOR THOSE WHO HAVE TIME FOR FURTHER STUDY

A. ADDITIONAL READING

I. In Textbooks Dealing with Classical Mythology

See references in the Appendix, pages xxviii ff., under headings which are concerned with subjects mentioned in this chapter.

II. In Books in General

1. Passages from the *Odyssey*, translated by Butcher and Lang:

    (1) * The Lotos-Eaters, IX, pp. 136–137.
    (2) * Encounter with Polyphemus, IX, pp. 137–152.
    (3) The gift of King Aeolus, X, pp. 153–155.
    (4) Circe, X, pp. 157–171.
    (5) Ulysses' descent to the Lower World, XI, pp. 172–191.
    (6) * The Sirens, XII, pp. 193, 197–198.
    (7) * Scylla and Charybdis, XII, pp. 194–196, 199–200.
    (8) Cattle of the sun-god, XII, pp. 200–204.
    (9) Calypso allows Ulysses to depart, V, pp. 81–84.
    (10) Ulysses meets the princess Nausicaä, VI, pp. 92–102.
    (11) King Alcinoüs helps Ulysses, VII, pp. 105–114.
    (12) The hero returns to Ithaca, rids Penelope of her troublesome suitors, and takes possession of his estate, XIV–XXIII.

2. Passages from the translation of the *Aeneid* by John Conington (lines refer to the translation in the Scott, Foresman edition) :
   (1) Scylla and Charybdis described, III, 470–483.
   (2) An account of Polyphemus, III, 678–754.
3. Galatea scorns Polyphemus, her lover, translation of Ovid, *Met.*, XIII, pp. 281–291 (Loeb Classical Library, G. P. Putnam's Sons).
4. The Sirens, *Life and Death of Jason*, by William Morris, XIV, 1–429 (Everyman's Library).
5. " Circe's Palace " by Nathaniel Hawthorne in *Tanglewood Tales*, pp. 221–247 (Everyman's Library).
6. Poems listed on page 330, the titles of which are starred.

B. Lines to Be Memorized

He who planned
To take the towered city of Troy-land ;
A mighty spearsman, and a seaman wise ;
A hunter, and at need a lord of lies,
With woven wiles he stole the Trojan town
Which ten years' battle could not batter down.

STEPHEN PHILLIPS, *Ulysses*, Prologue, p. 12

C. Further Study of Literary Allusion

If you are interested in seeing more clearly how good writers make use of the Greek myths, look up the following references :

Charybdis and Scylla: Roosevelt's *The Strenuous Life*, p. 45 (Century) ; Conan Doyle's *Memoirs of Sherlock Holmes*, p. 157 (A. L. Burt). **Charybdis:** Cable's *Dr. Sevier*, p. 338 (Scribners) ; Milton's *Comus*, 259 ; *Paradise Lost*, II, 1019–1020. **Calypso:** Byron's *Childe Harold*, Canto II, 29. **Circe:** Keats's *Endymion*, p. 228 (Everyman's Library). **Cyclops:** Alcott's *Little Women*, p. 81 (Little, Brown) ; Maeterlinck's *Life of the Bee*, p. 48 (Dodd, Mead). **Lotos-eaters:** Scott's *Quentin Durward*, p. 30 (Henry Holt). **Scylla:** Milton's *Paradise Lost*, II, 650–655 ; *Comus*, 257–258. **Ulysses:** Kipling's *Private Learoyd's Story;* Holmes's *Autocrat of the Breakfast Table*, p. 207 (Everyman's Library).

D. Projects for Individual or Group Work

To be selected from the list of projects on pages xx–xxvi, in case the subject matter of this chapter lends itself readily to any one of them.

POEMS FOR REFERENCE

AUSLANDER, JOSEPH	Ulysses in Autumn (*The Cyclops' Eye;* Harper and Brothers, N. Y.)
BRIDGES, ROBERT	Return of Ulysses (*Poetical Works;* Oxford University Press, Oxford and N. Y.)
BROWNING, ELIZABETH BARRETT	The Cyclops
BURR, AMELIA JOSEPHINE	* Ulysses in Ithaca (*Life and Living;* George H. Doran and Company, N. Y.)
DOBSON, AUSTIN	The Prayer of the Swine to Circe
HOMER	Translations in verse of the *Odyssey* by Bryant, Way, Mackail, and Murray
LANG, ANDREW	* Isle of Circe Revisited; * The Odyssey; * The Sirens; * In Ithaca (*Poems;* Longmans, Green and Company, N. Y.)
LOWELL, JAMES RUSSELL	* The Sirens
MONTGOMERY, ROSELLE MERCIER	* Ulysses Returns (*Ulysses Returns and Other Poems;* Brentano's, N. Y.)
PHILLIPS, STEPHEN	* Ulysses
ROSSETTI, DANTE G.	For "The Wine of Circe"
SAXE, JOHN G.	* Polyphemus; *also* * Spell of Circe
STEDMAN, EDMUND C.	Penelope (*Poetical Works;* Houghton Mifflin Company, Boston)
TENNYSON, ALFRED	* Ulysses; *also* * The Lotos-Eaters
THOMAS, EDITH M.	* Moly (*Home Book of Verse;* Henry Holt and Company, N. Y.)

THE WANDERINGS
OF
AENEAS

Fig. 158. Scene in the Forum at Rome

It is with the small beginnings of this mighty city that the legends
in the pages that follow are concerned.

AENEAS

On Troy's last night the sleep of Ae ne'as was broken by a dream. The dead Hector, all bloody with his wounds, seemed to stand beside the bed, exhorting him to save himself and the

Aeneas escapes from burning Troy
sacred objects of Troy from an enemy already in possession of the city. Aeneas rushed from the house to find Hector's statement, that doom had overtaken the Trojans, all too true. The streets were filled with exultant Greeks. After heroic but vain attempts to repulse the foe, the hero, aided by the small band of warriors who gathered around him, hastened home to try to save his family. Taking upon his shoulders his aged father, An chi'ses, in whose arms he placed the household gods, he seized the hand of his young son, As ca'ni us, and, telling his wife, Cre u'sa, to follow him, hurried by side streets to the gate of the city. Not until he was outside and had joined a small group of other Trojans who had managed to escape the swords of the Greeks, did he observe that Creusa was missing. In his anxiety, he retraced his steps, but though he sought her everywhere and cried her name aloud again and again, he could not find her. He ceased his efforts only when her ghost appeared, telling him that she had perished.

For a year the small band of survivors lived between Mt. Ida and the sea, during which time they built twenty ships and pre-

The Trojan refugees set sail
pared themselves in other ways for a long voyage. Just where they were going they did not know, but they had great faith in the protecting care of the gods and knew that they could rely upon the courage and wisdom of

Aeneas.   So it was with confidence that they finally set sail from the shores of Troy.

After stopping a few days at Thrace, the Trojans reached the small island of Delos, sacred to Apollo and the seat of one of his oracles.   Upon consulting the priestess, Aeneas learned

A message from Apollo

that the Trojans must seek a home in the country from which their race first sprang.   This place, they thought, was the island of Crete, for one of their traditions seemed to indicate that their earliest ancestor had come from there.   Very happy in the thought that their journey was to be a short one (for Crete is not far from Delos), they embarked for the land which they had been led to believe would be their lasting home.

No sooner had the Trojans landed in Crete and started to build a city

The Penates speak; Crete is abandoned

than a dreadful pestilence broke out.   Aeneas felt sure that the gods would not have sent this had they wanted the Trojans to stay.   The following incident strengthened this conviction.   He awoke one night to see in the bright moonlight which was pouring through the window the figures of the Pe na'tes (a name for the household gods) standing by his bedside.   They spoke to

*Villa Borghese, Rome   Photograph by
                                         Alinari*

Fig. 159.   **Aeneas carries his
father from the flames of Troy**

him and said, " Crete is not the cradle of your race. It is a land called Hes pe'ri a (land to the West) where you shall finally build your city." He did not know where Hesperia was, but he hoped that by continuing to heed the divine revelations he might finally discover the land.

A violent storm drove the ships to the islands known as the Stroph'a des just off the western coast of Greece. Here the Tro-

An encounter with the Harpies

jans encountered the Harpies (the name means " seizers "). These were very strange creatures. They seemed to be half-human in that the upper parts of their bodies were like those of women. But their wings and claw-like feet made them seem like huge birds. Perhaps if the Trojans had not been driven by hunger to kill some of the cattle on the island, the Harpies would not have troubled them. But these bird-like women were so angry at this deed of violence that they gathered in great flocks, and when the Trojans had spread out food upon the grass and were preparing to eat, they swooped down with hideous shrieks, sometimes carrying the food away — for they were always desperately hungry — and on other occasions covering it with filth so that it was uneatable.

The Trojans devised all kinds of schemes for destroying the Harpies, but, since their feathers were like metal, no weapon produced any effect. The only way to escape the attacks was to leave the island, and this they hastened to do. But for a long time after they left, the shrill voice of one of the Harpies who was gifted with prophetic power rang in their ears : " You shall reach the land you seek, but, before you build the walls of your city, hunger will force you to devour even your tables."

After leaving the Strophades, the Trojans sailed north along the coast of Greece, passing Ulysses' home at Ithaca and the island where the Phae a'cians lived. Finding a suitable harbor on the coast of E pi'rus, Aeneas landed and went up to the town which he saw in the distance. To his great astonishment he found that the city was modeled after that of Troy. But he A visit with old friends was still more surprised to learn that Hel'e nus, one of Priam's sons, was the ruler, and that An drom'-a che, Hector's widow, was the king's wife. Both had been carried there as captives after the fall of Troy, by Achilles' son, Neoptolemus. And when he went to distant parts to marry a maiden called Her mi'o ne, Helenus came into possession of the city, and soon after took Andromache as his wife.

Helenus and Andromache were greatly delighted to see Trojan faces again after their long exile in a strange land, and showed the utmost kindness to their guests. Before the Trojans left, Helenus, who, like his sister Cas san'dra, had prophetic power, gave Aeneas directions as to his future course. Among other things he told him of certain dangers that he must avoid, the Greek cities, for example, on the coast of southern Italy, and Scyl'la and and Cha ryb'dis. " Better sail around the island of Sicily," he said, " no matter how long it takes, rather than look upon these dreadful monsters." Aeneas remembered the warning and was therefore able to save his men from the horrible death that some of Ulysses' sailors had met as their ships sailed by Scylla's cave.

The Trojans rounded the island of Sicily and landed on the western coast. Here they were hospitably received by King A great grief comes to Aeneas in the death of his father A ces'tes. Not only did he entertain them royally but he helped to equip their ships for continuing the journey to Italy, the " Hesperia " which the wanderers had so long been seeking. But the pleasure of Aeneas was overshadowed by the death of his father, Anchises, who, though an old man and frail, had bravely endured all of the hardships of the voyage and had been his son's best friend and counselor in every crisis of his affairs.

The Trojans were well on their way to Italy when they were

overtaken by a violent storm which scattered their ships in every direction. So black was the sky and so high were the waves —

A storm scatters the ships

they seemed, in fact, to touch the very sky — that Aeneas gave up all hope of safety, but by reason of Nep′tune's assistance all of the vessels except one finally came together on the shores of northern Africa.

This disaster on the sea had been brought about by Juno's determination to prevent the Trojans from settling in Italy and founding there a kingdom which the Fates said would rule the world for many years. She hated this race too much to allow this thing to happen if she could prevent it. So she had gone to King Ae′o lus, god of the winds, whose home was said to be on an island northeast of Sicily, and had bribed him to unbar the cavern in which the storm winds were confined. No sooner were the barriers withdrawn than the blasts rushed forth, just like eager warriors to battle, and in an instant there was confusion and wild uproar upon the sea.

As Aeneas and his faithful friend, A cha′tes, were exploring the woods back of the shore upon which they had landed, they met a

Aeneas' mother guides him to Carthage

young woman in the dress of a huntress, carrying a bow and a quiver of arrows. They were astounded to see any woman in these wild regions, but especially one who was so beautiful. She was really Venus, Aeneas' mother, in disguise, but only after she had told them how they might make their way to the city of Car′thage near by did she assume the form of a divinity, and then only for an instant. But Aeneas recognized her and, full of confidence now that he knew he was under her care, followed the path to the city. Of course he did not know that, in order to keep them safe from any interference on the way, Venus had enveloped both him and Achates in a cloud which made them quite invisible to men.

A beautiful woman named Di′do was the queen of Carthage.

Some years before she had fled from a very cruel brother in
Phoe ni'ci a (a region on the coast of Syria), and with a few

**The early
days of
Carthage**

devoted followers had set up a kingdom in Africa.
Here she laid the foundations of a splendid city —
fast nearing completion when the Trojans landed
— and was ruling her people justly and wisely.

Pietro Cortona

Fig. 160. Venus meets Aeneas and Achates in the forest

Aeneas and Achates found Dido in a temple where she was
holding court. As the cloud about them disappeared, the queen

**A gracious
reception**

saw two strange men before her, one of them strikingly handsome and with the bearing of a prince.
When she learned that it was the Trojan warrior, Aeneas — second only in fame to the great Hector — who was seeking hospitality, Dido at once gave orders that all courtesy be shown to
him and his companions.

For many months, attracted by the charm of the queen, with
whom he had contracted a secret marriage, Aeneas lingered at
Aeneas, filled Carthage, seeming to forget entirely his duty to
with sadness, his people and the task that awaited him in Italy.
leaves
Carthage   And it was only when a sharp command came
from Jupiter, conveyed to him by Mercury, that Aeneas left

From an old print

**Fig. 161. Mercury has come from Olympus to warn Aeneas that he must leave
Carthage**

Carthage and once more set sail for Italy. His heart was filled
with sadness as he departed, for he really loved Dido. His grief
would have been still greater if he could have known that the
flames which he saw rising from the palace as he looked backward
to the city from the deck of his ship were those of the queen's
funeral pyre. For, unable to bear the separation from Aeneas,
Dido had killed herself upon hearing that the Trojans had left
Carthage.

After meeting with several misfortunes, among which was the loss of his faithful pilot, Pal i nu′rus, whom the god of sleep overcame as he stood by his helm on Aeneas' ship, the Trojans at last reached the country which they had long been seeking.

Domenichino (Capitoline Museum, Rome)   *Photograph by Alinari*

Fig. 162. The Cumaean Sibyl

As soon as they landed on the Italian shore, Aeneas sought out the cave of the Cu mae′an Sib′yl, a prophetess who, inspired by Apollo, could foresee the future and all that was to happen to men. Her home was in a vast cavern deep in the earth. Here she sat and read the fates of those who came to consult her. But her visitors seldom obtained much satisfaction, because the wind which blew into the cave as the door was opened threw into confusion the

Aeneas gains the help of the Sibyl at Cumae

leaves upon which the Sibyl had written her prophecies and which she had arranged in order on the floor of the cave. But Aeneas could not be content with such a procedure. So earnestly did he beg her to tell him what fate awaited the Trojans and just how he might visit his father in the Lower World in order to talk over with him plans for establishing the Trojan race in Italy, that the priestess finally consented to speak and, what was even more important, agreed to be his guide through the dark realms beneath the earth.

After securing at the Sibyl's suggestion a golden

The journey to the Lower World begun branch from a tree hidden in a dense forest, as a gift for Pro ser'pi na, and after performing sacrifices in due order, Aeneas followed the priestess as she entered upon the dark path which led downward into the depths of the earth from the shores of Lake A ver'nus.

From an old print

Fig. 163. Aeneas realizes that his sword is useless against ghosts

The hero was frightened as the descent grew steeper and the blackness increased. He knew that only gods and, in rare cases, great heroes who for some reason or other were under divine protection, ever returned safely from the Lower World. And as he saw ghosts beginning to appear, particularly such monsters as Scylla, the Chi mae'ra, and the hundred-handed giant called Bri'a reus, he drew his sword after the habit of a warrior, but put it back in its sheath when his companion reminded him that these creatures were only shadowy images and not really bodies at all.

Presently they came to the dark waters of the Ach'e ron. Cha'ron's boat was already full when the Sibyl asked for passage **Crossing the** for Aeneas and herself; but after the ferryman's **river** objections to transporting a mortal — a crime for which he had been severely punished on several occasions — were overcome, he unceremoniously dislodged the ghosts and made room for the new passengers. The boat almost sank under the weight of Aeneas, for it was a very frail skiff and was designed to carry only ghostly forms. But Charon brought it safely to the opposite bank.

At sight of Aeneas, Cerberus, the three-headed watchdog who guarded the entrance to Hades, growled savagely and his back **Cerberus is** bristled with anger. But as the hero threw him a **pacified** cake steeped in honey and drugs, which the foresight of the Sibyl had provided, all his fierceness vanished. He at once became quiet and allowed Aeneas and his companion to pass.

In spite of the gloom of the place, Aeneas was able to distinguish ghostly forms here and there as he passed along. "These," said **The journey** the Sibyl, "are those who died in infancy, and just **continued** beyond you see those who, though innocent of crime, were put to death upon false testimony. And near them are the shades of others who killed themselves for love." Aeneas was startled to distinguish Dido's form in this group and tried to approach her. But she turned away from him as if in anger, so that the hero could only suppose that she could not have forgiven him for seeming to desert her at Carthage.

A crowd of warriors next attracted his attention. As soon as they saw him, some ran away in fear, especially the Greeks who remembered him as one of their fiercest foes at Troy, while others, his fellow Trojans, came crowding around him, full of joy at seeing one of their own race and anxious to learn the outcome of the war. He would have liked to linger there, but the Sibyl hurried him away.

Lofty walls now appeared in the distance and the flames of the fiery river of Phleg'e thon surrounding them. " Yonder is Tar'ta rus," explained the Sibyl, " a place of torture for the wicked. It is the blows of whips and the cries of pain that you hear." Aeneas noted in passing that the gate was guarded by hideous figures whom he recognized as the Furies, and that in their hands were writhing serpents with which they fiercely lashed those who passed through the entrance.

Leaving the fearful place of torment behind them, the Sibyl showed him next the glorious landscape of the E ly'sian Fields.

Aeneas speaks with his father in Elysium Here were the children of the gods and the founders of the Trojan race, and many others who for various reasons had deserved a life of bliss. Among the latter, Aeneas found Anchises. At the moment he was engaged in reviewing in a green valley the vast number of souls who, having drunk of the stream of Le'the, were ready to be born again into the Upper World, this time to become descendants of Aeneas and to be known as Romans.

Anchises unfolded to his son the glorious destiny of Rome as leader of the world and told him of the many dangers and hardships that must accompany the establishment of the race in Italy. Much wise counsel he added before Aeneas left him to return to the light of earth.

The Trojans stayed for a time in a region near the Tiber River, ruled by King La ti'nus, whose daughter La vin'i a married

The Trojans establish themselves in Italy Aeneas and gave her name to the first town built by the Trojans. But because the princess had long been sought in marriage by Tur'nus, one of the powerful Latin chieftains in the neighborhood, Aeneas found

Boucher (Louvre, Paris)   *Photograph by Alinari*

Fig. 164. During the Trojan War Venus asks Vulcan to make armor for Aeneas

himself engaged in a long and bitter war which was ended only by the death of his Latin rival.

As the years went by, I u'lus, Aeneas' son, founded Al'ba Lon'ga, and it was his descendants who afterwards built the city known as Rome. But long before this Aeneas had died, although there is no story to mark the passing of so great a hero. Legend merely says that he was last seen on the banks of an insignificant stream near Lavinium.

Just as the story of the return of Ulysses from the Trojan War was related by Homer in a poem in Greek called "The Od'ys sey," **Two famous poems — the Odyssey and the Aeneid** so the fortunes that befell Aeneas as he was conducting the small band of Trojans who survived the destruction of their city to their new home in Italy, is told by Ver'gil in a Latin poem called "The Ae ne'id."

Both of these poems are famous and are ranked among the finest of the world's literature.

IN THE WORLD OF TODAY

I. IN LITERARY ALLUSION

Ay, as Aeneas, our great ancestor,
Did from the flames of Troy upon his shoulder
The old Anchises bear, so from the waves of Tiber
Did I the tired Caesar.

> SHAKESPEARE, *Julius Caesar*, Act I, Sc. 2, 112–115

Oh, think how to his latest day,
When death, just hovering, claimed his prey,
With Pal'i nure's" unaltered mood,
Firm at his dangerous post he stood!
Each call for needful rest repelled,
With dying hand the rudder held;
Till, in his fall, with fateful sway,
The steerage of the realm gave way!

> SIR WALTER SCOTT, *Marmion*, Introduction to Canto I

Sir Walter Scott makes use of the story about the devotion of Palinurus to his duty (clinging to the helm of Aeneas' ship until overcome by the god of sleep) in thus celebrating the faithfulness of Sir William Pitt, an English statesman, who, to the day of his death, tried to steer the destinies of his country.

II. IN WORDS AND EXPRESSIONS

That the name of the lovely and unfortunate Car tha gin'i an queen should survive in the somewhat degrading expression **to cut up didoes** is one of the curious pranks to which etymology sometimes lends itself. The expression as we use it means " to play tricks, to make mischief, or to ' cut up ' in the sense of playing some prank or other." This perhaps comes from the story that when Dido was bargaining for land upon which to build her city, and was told that she could have as much as could be covered by an ox's hide, she cut this hide into strips so that it might enclose a very considerable amount of ground.

The faithful devotion of Achates for Aeneas has become crystallized in the well-known expression, a **fidus Achates,** applied to a loyal friend. Here is an illustration from *Harper's Magazine* of such usage: "'What's he doing here?' 'Hatching mischief with a political friend of his — a **fidus Achates** who lives near here,' said the chaplain."

We apply the term **harpy** to a grasping person who is repulsive in his greediness.

To give a sop to Cerberus means to present some one who is likely to cause trouble with a gift in order to keep him quiet.

III. IN MISCELLANEOUS WAYS

As a Symbol for Roman Ideals

The poem called the Aeneid was written with the purpose of setting before the Romans of the time of Au gus'tus the ideals of life and conduct which had at one time prevailed in the Roman state and made it truly great. The author tried to embody in the character of his hero, Aeneas, certain qualities which characterized the Romans at their best, namely, physical courage, skill as a warrior, ability to lead men in difficult undertakings, love for one's family and friends, unselfishness, and, particularly, devotion to the gods, and patriotism in the highest sense. The modern world has come to associate these ideas with the name of Aeneas.

The poet knew too much about life, however, to represent his hero as perfect. Like all human beings, Aeneas sometimes made mistakes.

QUESTIONS FOR REVIEW

1. Relate the incidents in connection with the escape of Aeneas and his family on the night when the Greeks took possession of Troy.

2. What preparations did Aeneas make for saving those Trojans who had survived the disaster to their city?

3. What piece of news did the Trojans learn at Delos? (From this point continue to trace on the map the wanderings of the Trojans until they reached the land of Italy.)

4. Why did Aeneas leave Crete?

5. Describe the strange creatures which the Trojans encountered on the Strophades Islands.

6. What acquaintances did Aeneas find in Epirus, and what help did they give him?

7. What personal misfortune befell Aeneas while the Trojans were in Sicily?

8. How did it happen that the ships of Aeneas failed to reach Italy when they were well on their way to this land?

9. What divine guide assisted Aeneas and Achates to make their way to Carthage? How was she related to Aeneas?

10. How did the queen of Carthage receive the Trojans?

11. (1) Why did Aeneas linger in Carthage, and what incident led him to depart at last?

(2) How did his leaving affect Queen Dido?

12. What purpose did Aeneas have in seeking Apollo's priestess as soon as he reached Cumae in Italy?

13. Who was his guide in the journey to the Lower World?

14. What was the character of the landscape in these regions beneath the earth? What monsters did Aeneas see as he advanced?

15. How did he cross the river Acheron?

16. How did he succeed in passing Cerberus?

17. What ghostly forms of persons whom he had known in the world above did Aeneas meet?

18. Describe Tartarus.

19. Describe Elysium.   What kind of existence did those who were in this region lead?

20. Where did Aeneas meet his father, Anchises, and what assistance did the latter render?

21. Relate the circumstances that led eventually to the founding of Rome.

22. What is the name of the Latin poem in which the wanderings of Aeneas and his companions are related?

23. What is the meaning of the expression *a fidus Achates*?

24. What is meant by giving *a sop to Cerberus*?

QUESTIONS FOR THE THOUGHTFUL PERSON

1. The phrase, "the descent to Avernus (Hades) is easy," is often quoted.   These words are a part of the Sibyl's reply to Aeneas when he asked her about the journey to the Lower World.   She added that, although it was easy to go down, it was exceedingly hard to climb up. To what situation in life might this famous phrase be applied?   (The author knows a Latin teacher who was accustomed to write these words on the monthly reports of certain pupils.)   •

2. How is the name for the month of July connected with one of the characters mentioned in this chapter?   (Remember that in Latin the letter *j* is generally written as *i*.)

OPTIONAL

FOR THOSE WHO HAVE TIME FOR FURTHER STUDY

A. ADDITIONAL READING

I. In Textbooks Dealing with Classical Mythology

See references on pages xxviii ff. under the headings of characters mentioned in this chapter.

II. In Books in General

1. Passages from Vergil's *Aeneid*, translated by John Conington (Scott, Foresman edition.   Lines mentioned are those of the translation and not the lines of the Latin text).

(1) A murdered man warns Aeneas to continue his journey, III, 17–83.

(2) An account of the Harpies, III, 241–301 ; on this subject see, too, William Morris' *Life and Death of Jason*, V, 153–363 (Everyman's Library).

(3) Incidents of the stay of Aeneas at Carthage : Dido falls in love, IV, 1–102 ; The queen entertains her guests by a hunt, IV, 146–186, and by a banquet, I, 787–855 ; Aeneas tells Dido why he cannot stay at Carthage, IV, 368–401 ; An account of Dido's death, IV, 525–575, 692–773.

(4) The Sibyl at Cumae foretells the fortunes of Aeneas (the account of how she uttered her prophecies is very interesting), III 491–514 ; VI, 44–59, 86–109.

(5) A detailed description of the journey of Aeneas to the Lower World, VI, 261–971. (For an account of the experiences of Ulysses under similar circumstances, see Stephen Phillips' *Ulysses*, Act II, Sc. 2.)

NOTE. Those who wish to gain an adequate idea of the character of Aeneas and the Roman ideals embodied in the *Aeneid*, should read the translation of the first six books of the poem, in case they are not reading the original in the Latin class. Translations in meter which some persons find more attractive than those in prose are mentioned on page 348.

B. MEMORIZE ONE OF THESE QUOTATIONS

Aeneas was our king, than who
The breath of being none e'er drew,
More brave, more pious, or more true.

> VERGIL, *Aeneid*, I, 544–545 (Conington's Verse Translation)

Roman Vergil, thou that singest Ilion's lofty temples robed in fire,
Ilion falling, Rome arising, wars, and filial faith, and Dido's pyre.

> TENNYSON, *To Vergil*

C. FURTHER STUDY OF LITERARY ALLUSION

If you are interested in seeing more clearly how good writers make use of the myths, look up the following references :

Dido: Shakespeare's *Merchant of Venice*, Act V, Sc. 1, 9–12. **Furies:** Milton's *Paradise Lost*, II, 596. **Troy's wandering prince:** Tennyson's *On a Mourner*, vii.

D. Projects for Individual or Group Work

To be selected from the list of projects on pages xx–xxvi, in case the subject matter of this chapter lends itself readily to any one of them.

POEMS FOR REFERENCE

Chaucer, Geoffrey	Legend of Dido in *Legend of Good Women*
Marlowe, Christopher	The Tragedy of Dido
Miller, Frank J.	Dido, the Phoenician Queen (University of Chicago Press)
Tennyson, Alfred	* To Vergil
Vergil	Translations in verse of the *Aeneid*, by John Conington (Longmans, Green and Company), Theodore Chickering Williams (Houghton Mifflin Company), and others

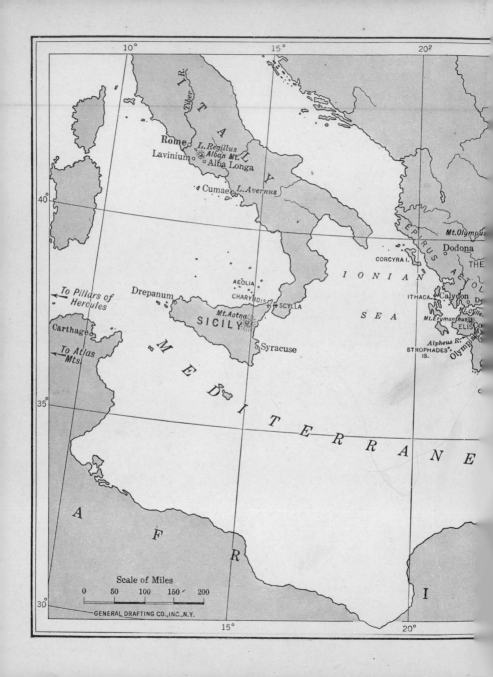

10°   15°   20°

Tiber R.

ITALY

Rome
L. Regillus
Lavinium • *Alban Mt.*
Alba Longa
• Cumae • *L. Avernus*

40°

EPIRUS *Mt. Olympus*

Dodona

CORCYRA I.

IONIAN THE
AEOLIA *AEOL*

AEOLIA
CHARYBDIS
To Pillars of
Hercules
Drepanum

SCYLLA

ITHACA Calydon De

Mt. Cylle
SEA *Mt. Erymanthus* ELIS Co
Mt. Aetna
Carthage • SICILY

To Atlas
Mts.
Syracuse

Alpheus R.
STROPHADES Olymp
IS.

MEDITERRANE

35°

A
F
R
I

Scale of Miles
0   50   100   150   200

30°
GENERAL DRAFTING CO., INC., N.Y.
15°   20°

APPENDIX

A. WHO'S WHO IN CLASSICAL MYTHOLOGY

A

Absyrtus, young son of King Aeëtes, cruelly killed by his sister Medea

Achates, devoted servant and friend of Aeneas

Achilles, perhaps the most famous of the Greek warriors at Troy

Acrisius, father of Danaë and grandfather of Perseus

Actaeon, a young hunter, torn to pieces by his own hounds because by accident he chanced to see Diana bathing in a forest pool

Admetus, a king in Thessaly whom Apollo once served as a shepherd; also husband of Alcestis

Adonis, a handsome youth, dearly loved by Venus

Aeëtes, king of Colchis and keeper of the Golden Fleece

Aegeus, father of Theseus; threw himself into the Aegean Sea in grief at supposed loss of his son

Aeneas, a Trojan prince who after Troy's downfall led his people to Italy and there founded the Roman race

Aeolus, king of the winds

Aesculapius, god of medicine

Aeson, father of Jason

Agamemnon, a Greek prince who led the armed forces of the Greeks in the Trojan War

Ajax, one of the most valiant of the Greek heroes at Troy, renowned for his strength

Alcestis, wife of King Admetus, who died to prolong her husband's life but was restored to the Upper World by Hercules

Alcinoüs, king of the Phaeacians, who entertained Ulysses most graciously

Alcmene, mother of Hercules

Alpheus, god of the river Alpheus and lover of Arethusa

i

Althaea, mother of Meleager, a man who remained alive as long as a certain firebrand was preserved

Amalthea, the goat who nourished the infant Jupiter in Crete

Amazons, warlike women who engaged with men in battle

Amphion, king of Thebes, who was so skilful a musician that when he played upon his lyre as the walls of his city were being built, the stones moved into position of their own accord

Amphitrite, wife of Neptune

Amphitryon, Hercules' father (according to one account)

Amulius, brother of Numitor, grandfather of Romulus and Remus

Anchises, husband of Venus and father of Aeneas

Andromache, wife of Hector

Andromeda, a maiden whom Perseus saved from being sacrificed to a monster

Antaeus, a giant whose strength was renewed every time he touched his mother Earth

Antiope, (1) queen of the Amazons and later the wife of Theseus; (2) a beautiful woman, wooed by Jupiter, and mother of two sons. When cruelly treated by Dirce, wife of the usurping king of Thebes, and condemned to be dragged to death behind a bull, she succeeded in informing the two young shepherds to whom this punishment had been entrusted that she was their mother. They executed their cruel task, but it was Dirce who died instead of Antiope.

Aphrodite, *see* Venus

Apollo, god of the sun and of poetry and music; patron of athletes; source of inspiration for oracles

Arachne, a Lydian princess who challenged Minerva to a contest at the loom

Arcas, son of Callisto, changed into a bear

Ares, *see* Mars

Arethusa, a nymph who through Diana's aid was changed into an underground stream in order to escape a rude suitor

Argo, builder of the ship "Argo"

Argonauts, Jason and his companions, who sailed to Colchis to obtain the Golden Fleece

Argus, (1) Ulysses' faithful hound; (2) the hundred-eyed monster who guarded Io

Ariadne, daughter of King Minos of Crete, who helped Theseus to escape from the Labyrinth

Artemis, *see* Diana

Ascanius, young son of Aeneas

Asclepius, *see* Aesculapius

Astyanax, young son of Hector and Andromache

Atalanta, (1) a princess widely famed for her swiftness in running; (2) a maiden of Arcadia who was the first to wound the boar in the Calydonian Hunt

Athena, *see* Minerva

Atlas, a giant who held the heavens upon his shoulders

Atropos, one of the Three Fates

Augeas, a king in Elis whose stables Hercules cleaned as one of his Twelve Labors

Aurora, goddess of the dawn

B

Bacchantes, women who, filled with religious frenzy, followed in the train of Bacchus and indulged in wild orgies

Bacchus, god who introduced the grape into Greece and became associated with wine

Baucis, an old peasant woman who with her husband, Philemon, extended hospitality to two travelers who chanced to stop at the hut, not knowing that they were gods

Bellerophon, the hero who killed the Chimaera

Beroë, Semele's aged nurse

Boreas, god of the north wind

Briareus, a hundred-handed giant in Tartarus

Briseïs, a captive maiden whom Agamemnon took from Achilles in the Trojan War, thus starting the quarrel which caused Achilles to withdraw from active participation in the conflict

C

Cadmus, founder of Thebes, and grandfather of Perseus

Calchas, a priest and soothsayer among the Greeks

Calliope, Muse of epic poetry and rhetoric

Callisto, a woman loved by Jupiter and changed into a bear

Cassandra, a Trojan princess whose prophecy, though always fulfilled, was never heeded at the time when it was given

Cassiopeia, mother of Andromeda

Castor, son of Leda and King Tyndareus, and brother of Pollux (except that the latter had Jupiter for his father)

Centaurs, creatures half-horse and half-man, but often very intelligent (*see* Chiron)

Cephalus, a young hunter who deserted his wife Procris for Aurora

Cerberus, the three-headed dog who guarded the entrance to Hades

Ceres, goddess of grain and mother of Proserpina

Charon, the grim ferryman who conveyed souls over the river Styx

Charybdis, a monster on the Sicilian side of the strait between Italy and Sicily, who engulfed passing ships in a flood of water

Chimaera, a fire-breathing monster, very curiously formed, slain by Bellerophon

Chiron, a centaur, teacher of Achilles and other famous heroes

Chryseïs, daughter of a priest of Apollo, captured by the Greeks during the Trojan War

Cilix, brother of Cadmus and Europa

Circe, a beautiful enchantress who turned some of Ulysses' followers into swine

Clio, Muse of history

Clotho, one of the Fates who held the distaff and spun the thread of life

Clytemnestra, wife of Agamemnon, who upon her husband's return from the Trojan War murdered him so that she might marry her lover, Aegisthus

Clytie, a maiden changed into a heliotrope because her love for Apollo was not returned

Creusa, faithful wife of Aeneas, who was lost at Troy when the city fell

Croesus, a wealthy king in Asia Minor

Cronus, father of Jupiter

Cumaean Sibyl, a prophetess of Cumae, who preferred eternal old age to Apollo's love, and who acted as guide to Aeneas in his descent to Hades

Cupid, god of love; son of Jupiter and Venus

Cyane, a Sicilian nymph who saw Proserpina's girdle floating on the water of the river Anapus

Cybele, worshiped in Asia Minor as mother of the gods (in Crete she was known as Rhea)

Cyclopes, one-eyed giants whom Ulysses encountered in Sicily

Cycnus, a youth changed by the gods into a swan; friend of Phaëthon

Cynthia, another name for Diana, goddess of the moon

Cyparissus, a young boy who grieved over the accidental killing of his pet stag and was changed by Apollo into a cypress tree

Cytherea, a name applied to Venus

D

Daedalus, a famous artisan who invented wings, by means of which he and his son Icarus escaped from the Labyrinth

Danaë, mother of Perseus

Danaïdes, fifty daughters of King Danaüs

Daphne, a nymph changed into a laurel tree to escape Apollo's amorous advances

Dardanus, progenitor of the Trojans

Deïphobus, one of the Trojan leaders in the Trojan War

Dejanira, wife of Hercules

Demeter, *see* Ceres

Deucalion, a god-fearing man who with his wife, Pyrrha, alone survived a flood

Diana, goddess of the chase and protector of maidens

Dido, queen of Carthage who entertained Aeneas

Diomede, (1) a Greek hero in the Trojan War; (2) a king of Thrace, who fed his horses on human flesh

Dione, a nymph, said to have been the mother of Venus

Dionysus, *see* Bacchus

Dryades, nymphs of the trees

E

Echo, a talkative nymph in love with Narcissus

Enceladus, a giant who, as a punishment for fighting against Jupiter, was buried under Mt. Aetna

Endymion, a young herdsman whom Diana kissed as he lay asleep on the hillside

Eos, *see* Aurora

Ephialtes, a giant who waged war against Jupiter and tried to scale heaven; *see* Otus

Epimetheus, brother of Prometheus

Erato, Muse of love songs

Erebus, the dark realm beneath the Earth

Erinyes, a name for the Furies

Eris, Discord, the goddess who threw the golden apple that brought about the Trojan War

Eros, *see* Cupid

Eumaeus, swineherd of Ulysses

Europa, a maiden carried to Europe by Jupiter

Eurus, the east wind

Euryclea, Ulysses' old nurse

Eurydice, wife of Orpheus

Eurylochus, one of Ulysses' band who escaped Circe's enchantment

Eurystheus, king who exacted twelve labors of Hercules

Euterpe, Muse of lyric poetry

F

Fates, three sister divinities who determined the course of human life

Fauns, rural deities, half-man and half-goat

Faustulus, the shepherd who reared Romulus and Remus

Furies, three avenging spirits, daughters of Acheron

G

Gaea, the earth as a goddess

Galatea, statue of a beautiful woman made by Pygmalion and adored by him; changed by the kindness of Venus into a living person

Ganymede, a Trojan youth who replaced Hebe as cup-bearer of the gods

Genius, household spirit, a man's " guardian angel "

Geryon, a huge monster whose cattle Hercules captured as one of his labors

Gordius, father of Midas; a king who tied the intricate knot cut by Alexander the Great

Gorgons, three monsters which caused beholders to turn into stone

Graces, three beautiful goddesses, daughters of Jupiter, who promoted love and harmony

Graeae, strange old women by whose aid Perseus slew the Gorgon

H

Halcyone, a grieving wife, changed into a kingfisher at her husband's death

Harpies, monsters, half-bird and half-woman

Hebe, Juno's daughter, at one time cup-bearer of the gods

Hecate, goddess of the moon and of the Lower World

Hector, son of Priam and bravest of the Trojan warriors

Hecuba, wife of King Priam

Helen, beautiful daughter of Jupiter and Leda (one account says that a mortal was her father), and wife of Menelaüs, whose abduction caused the Trojan War

Helenus, a Trojan prince having the power of prophecy

Helios, the sun-god whose cattle were killed by Ulysses' men

Helle, a maiden who fell from a ram into the sea

Hephaestus, *see* Vulcan

Hera, *see* Juno

Heracles, *see* Hercules

Hercules, a Greek hero known for his amazing strength, by means of which he accomplished twelve great labors

Hermes, *see* Mercury

Hermione, daughter of Helen, wife of Neoptolemus and later of Orestes

Hero, a maiden beloved by Leander

Hesione, a maiden saved from a monster by Hercules

Hesperides, nymphs who guarded the golden apples in a garden far to the West

Hestia, *see* Vesta

Hippodamia, a princess who became the bride of Pelops after his victory in a chariot race

Hippolyte, queen of the Amazons, whose girdle was obtained by Hercules

Hippomenes, a youth who outdistanced Atalanta in a footrace and won her as his bride

Hyacinthus, a beautiful youth beloved by Apollo, changed at death into a hyacinth

Hyades, nymphs who had aided the infant Bacchus and as a reward were placed by the god in the heavens, where they appear as one of the constellations. Another myth says that they were changed into stars in pity for their grief over a brother's death.

Hydra, a nine-headed monster slain by Hercules

Hygeia, goddess of health

Hylas, a handsome youth who sailed with the Argonauts but disappeared during their expedition

Hymen, god of marriage

Hypnos, god of sleep

I

Icarus, young son of Daedalus, who fell into the sea in his attempt to escape from the Cretan Labyrinth by means of wings

Idas, a mortal lover preferred to Apollo by Marpessa

Ilus, founder of Troy or Ilium

Ino, daughter of Cadmus, who with her child in her arms sprang from a cliff into the sea in order to escape from her husband.   She was changed into a sea-goddess known as Leucothea, and her son became a sea-god under the name Palaemon

Io, a maiden changed into a white heifer

Iolaüs, a friend of Hercules who seared the necks of the Hydra

Iphicles, Hercules' half-brother

Iphigenia, daughter of Agamemnon, saved from sacrifice by Diana

Iris, goddess of the rainbow

Iulus, son of Aeneas, founder of Alba Longa, ancestor of Romulus and Remus

Ixion, a cruel king bound to a wheel in Tartarus

J

Janus, a two-faced deity presiding over entrances

Jason, leader of the Argonauts who obtained the Golden Fleece

Jove, one of Jupiter's names

Juno, wife and sister of Jupiter and queen of goddesses

Jupiter, king of the gods

Jupiter Pluvius, Roman title for Jupiter as god of rain

L

Lachesis, one of the Fates; determined the length of thread of a man's life

Laërtes, father of Ulysses

Laestrygones, cannibals who destroyed Ulysses' ships and men

Laocoön, priest of Apollo at Troy, destroyed with his two sons by serpents

Laodamia, wife of Protesilaüs, the first Greek to be slain at Troy. When her husband died, Laodamia begged the gods to allow him to return even for a brief period.   When he went back to the Lower World, his wife accompanied him.

Laomedon, king of Troy who failed to keep his promise to Neptune

Lares, spirits who kept watch over the welfare of the home

Latinus, Italian father-in-law of Aeneas

Latona, mother of Apollo and Diana

Lavinia, Italian wife of Aeneas

Leander, a youth drowned while swimming the Hellespont to see Hero

Leto, *see* Latona

Lotos-eaters, people whose food caused forgetfulness of the past

Lucifer, herald of approach of day; morning-star

Luna, goddess of the moon (Diana)

M

Maenads, nymphs, attendants of Bacchus

Maia, mother of Mercury

Marpessa, a maiden who rejected Apollo's suit for that of a mortal lover

Mars, god of war

Marsyas, a youth who was defeated in a musical contest with Apollo

Medea, a princess who helped Jason to win the Golden Fleece and later became his wife

Medusa, one of the Gorgons, whose snaky locks turned the beholder to stone

Meleager, a prince who took a leading part in the Calydonian Hunt and perished through his mother's anger

Melpomene, Muse of tragedy

Memnon, son of Aurora, slain by Achilles in the Trojan War

Menelaüs, king of Sparta and husband of Helen

Mercury, messenger of the gods

Midas, a king who had ass's ears and whose touch for a while turned objects to gold

Minerva, goddess of wisdom, patron divinity of Athens (Athena)

Minos, (1) king of Crete and later a judge in the Lower World; (2) king of Crete who built the famous Labyrinth

Minotaur, a monster in the Cretan Labyrinth, slain by Theseus

Mnemosyne, goddess of memory, mother of the Muses

Morpheus, son of Somnus, god of sleep

Myrmidons, soldiers of Achilles in the Trojan War

Myrtilus, a charioteer who loosened a bolt in Oenomaüs' chariot wheel, causing the latter's death

N

Naiades, nymphs who dwelt in streams

Narcissus, a vain youth who pined away and became the narcissus flower

Nausicaä, daughter of King Alcinoüs, who aided Ulysses

Nemesis, goddess of retributive justice

Neoptolemus, brave son of Achilles; surname of Pyrrhus

Neptune, ruler of the waters

Nereids, fifty daughters of Nereus, resembling mermaids

Nereus, father of fifty daughters dwelling in a cave beneath the sea

Nessus, a centaur who indirectly caused the death of Hercules

Nestor, an aged Greek warrior and counselor

Niobe, a Theban queen whose fourteen children were slain by the arrows of Apollo and Diana

Notus, the south wind

Numitor, grandfather of Romulus and Remus

Nymphs, beautiful maidens, inferior divinities of nature

O

Odysseus, *see* Ulysses

Oedipus, son of the king of Thebes who when an infant was left on the mountain side to die. Rescued by a herdsman, he grew up at the court of the king of Corinth. By chance he killed his own father in the neighborhood of Thebes, although he was quite ignorant of the relationship. He was fortunate enough to escape death at the entrance of the city by answering correctly certain questions put to him by a huge creature known as the Sphinx. Later he was made king and became the husband of the Theban queen, all unknowing of the fact that he was her own son. His fate when he found out the truth was tragic.

Oenomaüs, a king who through treachery lost his life in a chariot race with Pelops

Oenone, a maiden once loved by Paris, but deserted by him for Helen

Omphale, queen of Lydia whom Hercules once served as a slave

Ops, wife of Saturn, Roman goddess of sowing and the harvest

Orcus, a god of death

Oreades, nymphs who dwelt in the mountains

Orestes, son of Agamemnon, who killed his mother, Clytemnestra, as a punishment for her share in the murder of his father. In consequence of this unnatural deed, he was long pursued by the Furies.

Orion, a young hunter, companion of Diana, changed into a constellation

Orpheus, a musician whose skill was such that he charmed not only men and gods but animals and objects in nature as well

Otus, a giant who waged war against Jupiter and tried to scale heaven by piling Mt. Ossa on Olympus and Mt. Pelion on Ossa

P

Palamedes, a Greek who proved that Ulysses was sane and induced him to take part in the Trojan War

Palinurus, Aeneas' pilot, who fell overboard as the Trojans were approaching Italy

Pallas, a name for Athena, who destroyed the giant Pallas

Pan, god of the country

Pandora, a maiden whose curiosity caused her to open a box, from which many troubles and ills escaped

Parcae, the Fates, in whose hands were the destinies of gods and men

Paris, a Trojan prince, abductor of Helen

Patroclus, a famous Greek hero and a devoted friend of Achilles, killed by Hector in the Trojan War

Pegasus, winged steed of the Muses, ridden by Bellerophon in his combat with the Chimaera

Peleus, father of Achilles

Pelias, Jason's uncle, who usurped a throne and suggested to his nephew the quest for the Golden Fleece

Pelops, a son of Tantalus, a father cruel enough to serve the roasted flesh of Pelops at a banquet of the gods. But when the fact became known, Pelops was restored to life, although his body was not as that of other men. For the part which had been consumed (a shoulder) was replaced by ivory. This was the young man who defeated Oenamaüs in a chariot race and won Hippodamia for his wife.

Penates, household spirits who looked after the storehouse and the interests of the family in general

Penelope, faithful wife of Ulysses

Penthesilea, queen of the Amazons, prominent in the Trojan War

Persephone, *see* Proserpina

Perseus, son of Jupiter and Danaë, who slew the Gorgon and saved Andromeda from a monster

Phaëthon, Apollo's son, who recklessly attempted to drive the sun-chariot

Philemon, an aged peasant who with his wife Baucis entertained two gods

Philoctetes, one of the Argonauts and possessor of Hercules' invincible arrows

Philomela and Procne, daughters of an Athenian king, who were cruelly treated by a prince named Tereus. As he was about to kill them, the prince was changed into a hawk while Philomela became a nightingale and Procne a swallow.

Phrixus, boy who hung the Golden Fleece on a tree at Colchis

Pierides, a name applied to the Muses

Pierus, a king whose nine daughters were changed into magpies

Pirithoüs, Theseus' friend, who tried to abduct Proserpina from the Lower World

Pleiades, the seven daughters of Atlas, placed in the sky because of their good qualities or because of their grief at the heavy task imposed upon their father. One myth says that Jupiter helped the sisters to avoid the unpleasant attentions of Orion by changing them into doves, whereupon they flew at once to the sky, where they still appear as a constellation.

Pluto, ruler of Lower World (Hades)

Pollux, twin brother of Castor, but with Jupiter for his father instead of a mortal; famous as a boxer

Polydectes, a wicked king who was turned to stone when Perseus showed him Medusa's head

Polydeuces, *see* Pollux

Polyphemus, a one-eyed Cyclops, blinded by Ulysses

Polyxena, daughter of Priam, offered as a sacrifice during the funeral rites of Achilles

Pomona, Roman goddess of fruit trees and gardens

Poseidon, *see* Neptune

Priam, last king of Troy

Procris, deserted by her husband, Cephalus, and killed by a magic javelin

Procrustes, a wicked innkeeper who mutilated travelers and was killed by Theseus

Prometheus, a Titan chained to the Caucasus Mountains by Jupiter as punishment for presenting men with the gift of fire

Proserpina, daughter of Ceres and wife of Pluto

Protesilaüs, a Greek, husband of Laodamia

Proteus, a sea-god who assumed many different shapes and was gifted with the power of prophecy

Psyche, sweetheart of Cupid and later his wife

Pygmalion, a sculptor who made a statue of a beautiful woman, which he dearly loved, and which later became alive

Pyramus, Thisbe's lover, who met a tragic death

Pyrrha, wife of Deucalion, who with him survived the flood which destroyed mankind

Pythia, priestess at Delphi, through whose lips Apollo spoke

R

Remus, son of Rhea Silvia and Mars, and twin brother of Romulus

Rhadamanthus, son of Jupiter and a judge in the Lower World

Rhea, great mother of the gods

Rhea Silvia, mother of Romulus and Remus

Romulus, legendary founder of Rome

S

Sarpedon, an ally of the Trojans who fought bravely at Troy

Saturn, Italic god identified by the Romans with Jupiter's father, the Greek god Cronus

Satyrs, shaggy woodland creatures, attendants of Bacchus

Sciron, a giant who kicked travelers over a cliff into the sea

Scylla, a rock on the Italian coast opposite Sicily; a six-headed monster who seized sailors as the ships were passing through the straits

Selene, goddess of the moon (Luna)

Semele, a Theban princess, mother of Dionysus, who was destroyed by the thunderbolt of her lover, Jupiter

Silenus, foster father of Bacchus and chief among the satyrs

Sinon, a Greek youth who through guile induced the Trojans to take the Wooden Horse into Troy

Sirens, sea-nymphs whose beautiful songs lured sailors to destruction

Sisyphus, a deceitful king who tried to cheat even Death, and was punished in Tartarus by being obliged to roll continually an enormous stone to the top of a hill

T

Tantalus, father of Niobe, punished in Hades by sight of food just beyond his reach

Telemachus, Ulysses' son

Terpsichore, Muse of dancing

Thalia, Muse of comedy

Theseus, hero who slew the Minotaur

Thetis, a beautiful nymph, mother of Achilles

Thisbe, a Babylonian maiden who eloped with Pyramus and met a tragic fate

Tiresias, a seer in the Lower World who gave Ulysses helpful advice

Titans, deities of enormous strength, children of Heaven and Earth (Uranus and Gaea)

Tithonus, Aurora's husband, a mortal, changed by the goddess into a grasshopper

Tityus, a giant who was punished in Hades by having his liver devoured by a vulture

Triton, Neptune's son, who saw to the execution of his father's commands

Tritons, sea divinities who sported with the Nereids

Tros, grandson of Dardanus, father of Ilus and Ganymede

Turnus, suitor of Lavinia

Tyndareus, a Spartan king, husband of Leda and father of Clytemnestra (wife of Agamemnon) and Castor; also known as father of Helen

Typhoeus, a giant with one hundred serpent heads, defeated by Jupiter and confined in Tartarus. It was his fiery breath, so the Greeks thought, which poured forth from volcanoes. He is often identified with Typhon, the personification of the whirlwind or " typhoon."

U

Ulysses, one of the most famous of the Greek heroes, whose adventures in connection with the Trojan War are related in Homer's poem called the Odyssey

Urania, Muse of astronomy

Uranus, son and husband of Gaea, the Earth, father of the Titans, the Cyclopes, and the giants

V

Venus, goddess of beauty and mother of god of love

Vesta, goddess of the hearth

Vestals, virgins who kept the sacred fire at Rome ever burning and guarded objects considered necessary to the safety of the Roman state

Vulcan, god of fire and patron divinity of workmen

Z

Zephyrus, the west wind

Zeus, *see* Jupiter

B. A SUMMARY OF EXPRESSIONS THE MEANINGS OF WHICH ARE DEPENDENT UPON A KNOWLEDGE OF CLASSICAL MYTHOLOGY

1. **An Achilles heel,** a vulnerable spot
2. **An Achilles-Agamemnon episode,** a quarrel between two persons whereby progress in an important enterprise is delayed
3. **An Achilles,** an eminent hero
4. **A sulking Achilles,** a person who withdraws from participation in an important undertaking because of some personal grievance
5. **He cannot bend Ulysses' bow,** he is not equal to the task
6. **An Odyssey,** a tale of wild adventure
7. **A case of the Greeks bearing gifts,** a fatal gift which is presented under friendly guise
8. **A Sinon,** a skilful liar
9. **A Ulysses,** one who is clever in devising schemes
10. **A Cassandra utterance,** words which foretell evil and are not heeded
11. **To fight (or work) like a Trojan,** to fight with amazing boldness (or work with unusual energy)
12. **To hector a person,** to annoy
13. **When Greek meets Greek,** two well-matched contestants
14. **A Helen,** a woman of surpassing beauty and charm
15. **A Ganymede,** a handsome youth
16. **A Hebe,** a maiden as beautiful as Hebe, the cup-bearer for the gods
17. **To cut up didoes,** to play tricks
18. **An apple of discord,** a cause for dispute
19. **A Penelope,** a wife who remains faithful to her husband in spite of his long absence; also one who displays the traditional virtues of the house-wife
20. **A fidus Achates,** a faithful friend
21. **A herculean task,** one that only Hercules could presumably accomplish
22. **An Augean task,** an enormous and seemingly impossible undertaking
23. **A Lerna of ills,** a great many troubles

xvii

24. **Hydra-headed evils (or difficulties),** evils that continue to grow while one is in the act of suppressing them

25. **One cannot snatch the club from Hercules,** it is impossible to steal the power and ability of a great man

26. **The shirt of Nessus,** a harmful gift

27. **Between Scylla and Charybdis,** a choice between two difficulties

28. **A lotos-eater,** one who passes his life in idleness and dreamy ease

29. **A Siren,** a beautiful woman who lures one to destruction

30. **A Circe,** a beautiful woman whose charms are too strong to be resisted

31. **To look to one's laurels,** to take care lest one's position of eminence be lost

32. **Winning laurels,** acquiring fame through some worthy achievement

33. **To work the oracle,** to influence some powerful agency in one's favor

34. **Delphic words,** words which are mysterious and hard to interpret

35. **Apollo serving Admetus,** a highly gifted person forced by necessity to undertake menial work

36. **A paean,** a song of thanksgiving for deliverance from danger

37. **An Apollo,** an exceedingly handsome man

38. **An Adonis,** an exceedingly handsome man

39. **He is Midas-eared,** he is a man without judgment

40. **The Midas-touch,** the power of making money

41. **A Pactolian flood,** a flood of gold

42. **A task of Sisyphus,** one that is never completed

43. **The punishment of Tantalus,** seeing one's desires near fulfillment and yet never really attaining them

44. **A Procrustean system,** a system which insists that everyone shall conform to the same scheme

45. **Sowing dragon's teeth,** proceeding in such a way that troubles are sure to follow from the act

46. **A Pandora's box,** surprises, usually unpleasant although not always so

47. **Mounting Pegasus,** attempting to compose poetry or deliver an eloquent oration

48. **To drink from the fountain of Hippocrene,** to draw inspiration for some literary work (as one might drink from the Muses' fountain on Mt. Helicon)

49. **Halcyon days,** calm and peaceful, untroubled by any care

50. **The waters of Lethe,** an experience that brings forgetfulness of care

51. **Bellerophontic letters,** letters which carry instructions fatal to the bearer although the fact is unknown to him
52. **An Amazon,** a woman of great physical strength
53. **Janus-faced facts,** facts which can be interpreted in two ways
54. **A terpsichorean feat,** unusual skill in dancing
55. **Under the aegis of,** having the authority of some powerful person or institution back of an action or individual
56. **A harpy,** an exceedingly greedy person who stops at nothing in order to gain wealth
57. **A chimerical scheme,** a plan that is purely fanciful and outside the range of probability
58. **A protean artist,** one who can assume various rôles successfully
59. **Extending the olive branch,** an offer of peace
60. **A bacchanalian revel,** a wild orgy
61. **A Triton among minnows,** one who far outshines his competitors
62. **A Cadmean victory,** a victory which is as disastrous as a defeat
63. **A Cerberus,** a forbidding person whom one cannot easily pass
64. **A sop to Cerberus,** a gift to quiet some one who may be about to cause trouble
65. **An Icarian adventure,** a daring adventure which ends fatally
66. **The thread of Ariadne,** a clue that unravels a mystery or leads one out of difficulties
67. **Argonauts,** men who set forth on some adventure involving great risks, usually with the idea of ultimate gain in mind
68. **An Avernus,** hell
69. **An Elysium,** heaven
70. **Promethean fire,** a gift of value to the world, won through great personal suffering
71. **An Argus-eyed person,** one who can see a great deal
72. **A Narcissus,** one who is very fond of gazing at himself
73. **A Titanic effort,** an effort recalling the strength of the Titans
74. **Olympian anger,** such wrath as the king of the gods might show
75. **On the knees of the gods,** the outcome rests with powers stronger than those possessed by men
76. **To feed on ambrosia and nectar,** to have delicious food and drink
77. **Endymion sleep,** perpetual sleep in place of death
78. **A feast of Alcinoüs,** a splendid repast

C. SUGGESTIONS FOR CONNECTING THE STUDY OF MYTHOLOGY WITH THE CITY IN WHICH ONE LIVES

SOME QUESTIONS FOR THOSE WHO LIVE IN NEW YORK

1. What is the figure in Morningside Park, just inside the entrance at One Hundred and Fourteenth Street? Can you see why the artist chose this character from classical mythology as his subject?
2. Where in Central Park may one see Neptune and his steeds?
3. Why should the figure of the god of medicine (with his serpent) appear upon a building on Fifth Avenue, just south of One Hundred and Third Street?

Courtesy of the New York Central Railway

Fig. 165. This decorative group appears above the entrance to the Grand Central Station in New York City.

4. Why should a statue of Mercury have been selected to adorn the rotunda of the International Mercantile Marine Building at No. 1 Broadway? What god other than Mercury is represented over the entrance?

5. Do you see any reason for the central figure in the architectural group over the entrance to the Grand Central Station?

6. How does your knowledge of classical mythology help to explain certain decorations on the ceilings of the Grand Central Station?

From the Raguenet drawings

Fig. 166. The cornucopia or horn of plenty shown in the picture is very common as a decorative design. According to one account, it represents the horn of Amalthea, the kindly goat which nourished the infant Jupiter. It has always been used as a symbol for abundance and prosperity.

7. What figure from classical mythology looks down upon you from the decorations just above the stage at the Strand Theater on Broadway? In what other places have you seen the same architectural device?

8. What Greek god appears conspicuously in the ceiling decorations of the Grand Lobby of the Paramount Theater at West Forty-third Street?

9. Before you step into the elevator of the Public Library, note the design in the iron work just above the door. Does this have any connection with the idea of an elevator?

10. Why has a prominent New York club chosen the name " Lotos "?

11. What is the head above the entrance to the Harlem Evening School? The Metropolitan Museum?

12. Upon what buildings have you seen the " horn of plenty "? (Example: northwest corner of Park Avenue and East Fiftieth Street.)

13. Why should centaurs appear in the wall painting in the Capitol Theater on Broadway?

14. Where have you seen small winged figures (perhaps reminders of Cupid) used as decorations? (Example: Fifth Avenue, south of Eighty-first Street, east side of street.)

15. Have you noticed the lyre of Apollo or Orpheus anywhere in the city? (Example: Steinway Building, West Fifty-seventh Street, north side, east of Seventh Avenue.)

16. Have you found the names of these musicians used in connection with any buildings? If so, tell where.

17. Have you observed the laurel wreath anywhere about the city as a decorative design? If so, where?

18. In walking through the rooms of the Metropolitan Museum which are set apart for Greek and Roman art, what statues have you seen which recall the Greek myths, or what paintings in other rooms have reminded you of classical mythology?

19. Why should incidents in the voyage of Aeneas from Troy to Italy have been chosen as a suitable design for the decoration of the Cunard Steamship Company Building at 25 Broadway? (See the floor in one of the rooms.)

20. What butterflies in the case in the Museum of Natural History on West Seventy-seventh Street and Central Park West are named for characters in the Greek myths? Notice particularly the ones called " Dryad," " Pieris," " Junonia," " Io," " Wood Satyr," and " Grass Nymphs." If possible, make colored drawings of them.

Some Questions for Those Who Live in Philadelphia

1. In what theater does the figure of Pan form a prominent part of the decorative scheme?

2. Where, in City Hall, do you find a representation of Venus, and what does she symbolize?

3. What Muse is represented by the bronze figure on the Lea monument in Laurel Hill Cemetery?

4. Why should Mercury's staff be used as a decoration for a certain tomb at Laurel Hill? What is its meaning as it appears on the walls of the West Philadelphia Railway Station?

5. Is the head over the Quaker City National Bank on Seventeenth and Chestnut Streets used appropriately?

6. Why should the entrance of the Philadelphia Bulletin Building have the head of Mercury above it?

7. What is the curious design in the center of the bronze shield of the Philadelphia Athletic Club?

8. Over the entrance to what theater may one see Orpheus with his lyre?

9. Is there an Apollo theater in the city? Account for the name.

10. In the decorations of City Hall, what symbol does the woman's figure carry to identify her with commerce?

11. The Weightman Building at 1524 Chestnut Street and another structure at the corner of Locust and Fifteenth Streets bear an architectural device connected with the story of the infant Jupiter. What is it?

12. What famous monument in Laurel Hill Cemetery shows the figure of a person once very dear to Diana?

13. Do you see any reminder of Atlas on Twelfth Street, north of Walnut?

14. In what public building do you find Cupids used as decoration?

15. For what does the Orpheus Club stand?

16. Why was the Philomusian Club so named?

17. What reminders are found in Memorial Hall of the following characters from classical mythology: Diana, Achilles, Orpheus, Leander, Minerva, Muses, Ulysses, and Circe?

18. What is the significance of the trident on the Washington Monument in Fairmount Park?

D. PROJECTS WHICH MAY BE WORKED OUT IN CONNECTION WITH VARIOUS CHAPTERS IN THIS BOOK OR WITH THE BOOK AS A WHOLE

1. Watch for all traces of classical mythology in art and decorative designs in the city or town in which you are living and make a list of what you find. For this purpose adapt the questions based upon New York and Philadelphia (pages xx–xxiii) to your local conditions.

2. Make a study of decorative designs based upon the myths as they appear upon the covers of current periodicals received in your public library. The following examples will show you what you may expect

to find occasionally, although these special copies may not be at your command:

> **Apollo.** *Current Opinion*, March, 1914
> **Athena, Mercury, Vulcan.** *Motor Age*, March, 1917
> **Atlas.** *Motor Age*, January 14, 1915
> **Centaur.** *Golden Book*, September, 1926
> **Cupid.** *Saturday Evening Post*, February 16, 1924
> **Mercury.** *Novelty News* (all issues); *Motor Boating*, January, 1918; *Literary Digest*, September 10, 1910; *System*, November, 1907
> **Nymphs.** *Theater Magazine*, February, 1922
> **Pegasus.** *Literary Digest*, October 3, 1908

3. Secure from the dealers whose names are given on page xxvii as many pictures of characters mentioned in this book as you can.

   If you have any skill in drawing or painting, make your own illustrations in the case of certain topics which appeal to you.

4. Discover geographical names which have come down from the myths, for example, the cities of Troy and Ithaca in the state of New York.

5. Discover by reading the translation of the Iliad or Odyssey how Homer characterizes the various heroes and gods. For example, he speaks of Achilles as "fleet of foot"; of Jupiter as "he whose joy is in the thunder"; of Athena as "the bright-eyed goddess," etc. It is interesting to collect and classify epithets for important characters.

From *The Saturday Evening Post*, copyright 1924, by the Curtis Publishing Company

Fig. 167.

6. By the aid of some good star map, such as Stubb's *Improved Planisphere* (C. S. Hammond Company, 30 Church Street, New York) or The Barrett-Servise *Star and Planet Finder* (Leon Barrett Company, 367 Fulton Street, Brooklyn), make a study of the constellations and in particular of those groups of stars which are connected by legend with the stories in this book. The following books will greatly assist you in locating the constellations and in remembering the Greek myths associated with them:

> *Stars and Their Stories*, by Muriel Kinney; D. Appleton and Company, N. Y., 1926

The Book of the Stars for Young People, by William Tyler Olcott; G. P. Putnam's Sons, N. Y.

The Friendly Stars, by Martha Evans Martin; Harper and Brothers, N. Y.

7. Examine the volumes of *The Nature Library*, published by Doubleday, Page and Company, 1920, to discover colored plates which contain many names from classical mythology. Those who are interested in scientific terms will find in any large dictionary, such as the Oxford, Century, etc., names which go back to the myths for their origin.

Fig. 168.
Athena with her owls, as representative of learning

8. If you like music and know something about important musical compositions, watch for themes in your concert programs, which are concerned with Greek myths. Among others you may find a mention of the nymphs, Bacchus, fauns, satyrs, Apollo, the Muses, and Orpheus.

9. Collect allusions to the myths in one or more of the plays of Shakespeare which you chance to be reading.

10. Watch for allusions to the myths in your reading of current periodicals and newspapers as well as in your study of more formal literature. You will find such passages as these:

" One would welcome as a guide through its labyrinth a thread woven by Arachne." — *Harpers Magazine*

" Four years of Herculean effort passed before Venizelos was ready to begin his task of liberating Greece." — *The Century Magazine*

" They content themselves with Cassandra-like predictions of the future." — *Nineteenth Century Magazine*

" It has been a day of delicious lotos-eating." — *The Delineator*

" Butterflies, small Psyches, fluttered in the air about me." — *The Atlantic Monthly*

" The full crop from the dragon's teeth sown during the war did not come to harvest until after the armistice." — *Saturday Evening Post*

" A stygian darkness descended upon them." — *The Cosmopolitan*

" Life (says Charon) comes my way." — *Life*

An editorial entitled " The Clashing Islands." The passage of Jason and the Argonauts through the rocks that rebounded is used as a basis for a discussion of the political situation in the Far East. — *The New York Times*, November 19, 1922

An editorial called " Audible Pictures." Orpheus' power to move those who heard his music is compared with that of the modern musician whose tones are preserved by the radio and similar inventions. — *The New York Times*, August 8, 1926

E. INFORMATION REGARDING PICTURES

For the use of those who wish to collect illustrations for individual or class scrapbooks.

FIRMS FROM WHICH PHOTOGRAPHS AND PRINTS MAY BE SECURED

Alinari, 137A, Corso Umberto, Rome, Italy (Photographs of various sizes)

Anderson, Via Salaria, Rome, Italy (Photographs of various sizes)

Brown Picture Company, Beverly, Mass.   (Prints only)

Chauffourier, Tourist Shop, Piazza di Spagna, 65, Rome, Italy (Photographs on postals)

Congressional Library, Washington, D. C.   Colored prints (postcard size and larger) of wall paintings by Edward F. Simmons, H. O. Walker, and Walter McEwen, including the following subjects: Achilles, Adonis, Bellerophon, Endymion, Ganymede, Hercules, Jason, Minerva, Paris, Perseus, and Theseus.   These cards are sold in sets only.

Cooley, A. S., 631 North New Street, Bethlehem, Pa. (Photographs)

Gramstorff Brothers, 101 Ferry Street, Malden, Mass.   Publishers of the Soule photographs

Museum of Fine Arts, Boston, Mass.   Photographs of the John Singer Sargent wall paintings, most of which deal with subjects taken from the Greek myths

Perry Pictures Company, Malden, Mass.   (Prints only)

Seiler, A. G., 1224 Amsterdam Avenue, New York.   A book dealer who will import photographs from Rome in the case of orders amounting to $5.00 or more

Thompson Picture Company, Syracuse, N. Y.   (Blue prints)

University Prints Company, Newton, Mass.   (Prints only)

Note: Catalogues may be secured in some cases by writing to the dealers. *The Service Bureau for Classical Teachers* at Teachers College, Columbia University, New York, will supply a brief list of pictures dealing with classical mythology, including catalogue numbers.

INDEX

KEY TO PRONUNCIATION

VOWELS

ă as in *hat*
ā as in *late*
ä as in *father*
å as in *sofa*
ȧ as in *senate*

ĕ as in *ten*
ē as in *seed*
ē̆ as in *rather* (in unstressed syllable)

ê as in *event*
ê as in *Athens*

ĭ as in *hit*
ī as in *ride*

ŏ as in *hot*
ō as in *tone*
ô as in *obey*
ŏ̧ as in *soft*

ȯ as in *connect*
ô as in *orb*
ōō as in *food*

ŭ as in *but* (in stressed syllable)
u̇ as in *circus* (in unstressed syllable)
yū as in *use*
yu̇ as in *unite*
û as in *urn, hermit* (in stressed syllable)
oi as in *boy*

CONSONANTS

Consonants are pronounced as in English unless otherwise indicated.
s (voiceless or surd) as *s* in *see*
s (voiced or sonant) as *z* in *buzz*
th (voiceless) as in *think*
j as j, or g in *giant*
g as in *go*

STRESS

When two syllables in a long word are stressed, the principal stress is represented by ″, the slighter stress by ′. But if only one syllable in a word is stressed, it is marked by ′.

Numbers in bold face type indicate the more important passages.